Steve Wright: A spy for peace

Steve Wright:
A spy for peace

Edited by Craig S. Brown

www.irenepublishing.com
irene.publishing@gmail.com

Steve Wright: A spy for peace

Edited by Craig S. Brown

Published by Irene Publishing
Sparsnäs 1010, 667891 Ed, Sweden
www.irenepublishing.com
irene.publishing@gmail.com

First edition 2022
ISBN 978-91-88061-55-3 (Paperback)

Layout: J. Johansen
Photographs used with gracious permission from Steve Wright's family.

Contents

Steve Wright: A spy for peace

16th July 1952 – 21st November 2019

Biography[1]

Born in Newcastle, Steve began his academic career at Manchester University, studying a BSc(Hons) in Liberal Studies in Science (1975). The course inspired him to look at the political consequences of innovation, which he followed through with postgraduate study at Lancaster University's Richardson Institute, looking at "New Police Technologies and Sub-State Conflict Control". Alas, the work progressed too well and resulted in the intelligence agency of a foreign

1 This biography draws on two self-written pieces by Steve, with amendments to update institution names, dates and affiliations when necessary.

power, America's NSA, instructing British Police to raid Lancaster University in April 1977. Steve successfully defended his PhD in 1987.

Steve worked as the first Head of Manchester City Council's Police Monitoring Unit (1984-1988), watching the local police force. This was an extremely high-profile initiative which conducted inquiries into the use of riot tactics adopted during the miners' strike for homeland policing. It also worked on the Northern Ireland shoot to kill policy, which culminated in the so called 'Stalker Affair'. He was the Principal Policy Officer for Manchester City Council (1989-1995), working for the Public Transport Association on a range of issues. Subsequently, Steve worked with Manchester City Council's Nuclear Policy Unit, focusing on two key issues: (i) preparing the City Council's response to the UK Government's Planned Programme of Implementation regarding Civil Defence preparations; (ii) writing the first draft of Manchester City Council's Major Peacetime Emergency Plans (1989-1990).

He went on to become Director of the Omega Foundation (1989-2005), with the organisation pioneering field research into military, security and police technologies and leading to some fundamental shifts in national and international policy. The database from this work was used by Oxfam to mount its ongoing campaigns against small arms. The Swiss Small Arms Survey also used the field data to prepare its international database on small arms producers, which is the most extensive anywhere in the world.

The European Commission grant funded the Omega Foundation for over nine years to track the armourers of the torturers, transfer of military security and police technologies, and create a bedrock of knowledge on the supply lines of repression technology. This work also involved field research for Amnesty International, leading to a series of high-profile reports on torture technology. These in turn led to new European regulations banning the export of torture technologies following a special meeting of the Omega Foundation, Amnesty International and the UN Special Rapporteur on Torture. At this meeting, he elaborated on a new generation of technologies used for mass incapacitation and paralysis, especially at borders.

As part of this work, Steve developed a healthy appetite for travel, working across Europe, Latin America, North America, the Middle East, Russia, China, Asia and Australia..

In 1998, Steve authored the European Parliament's widely influential STOA report on the Echelon Global Spy System, which revealed the extent to which all communications are read by Yorkshire's Menwith Hill station, which taps two million calls an hour. It also led to new approaches to explaining to a wider audience in lay terms just what technologies lay on the horizons for maintaining extant inequalities and under development. These included working with local arts and music NGO's such as Futuresonic in the UK, Worldinformation.org in Austria, and TROIA in Germany.

Steve became Chair of the trustees of Privacy International in 2004, as well as being a trustee of the Mines Advisory Group. He remained active in numerous organisations, including the International Committee for Robot Arms Control, the Dialogue Society, the International Peace Research Association and the European Peace Research Association, in addition to the Pugwash Conferences on Science and World Affairs. In the early 1980s when Steve was a research officer at UMIST Students' Union, he had established the UK's first Pugwash group. As the bibliography in this book shows, Steve wrote extensively for various organisations and media outlets, including *The Guardian* and *Le Monde Diplomatique* and *New Scientist.*

In 2003, Steve was awarded a US-based Social Science Research Council Global Security Research Fellowship, aimed at helping NGO workers to move into academia. In the early 2000s, he was a Visiting Professor at Leeds Metropolitan University (later Leeds Beckett University). Alongside colleagues including Edward Abbott-Halpin and Dave Webb, Steve established the university's Praxis Centre for the Study of Information and Technology in Peace, Conflict Resolution and Human Rights in March 2004, becoming Associate Director. In 2009, he became a Reader with its subsequent manifestation, the School of Applied Global Ethics. He helped to establish the school's new undergraduate and postgraduate modules on peace and conflict research, education and resolution. The US "war against terror" and its human rights fallout pre-occupied Steve, with his later work focusing on information warfare, new border control technologies and the emergence of weapons of mass paralysis.

Editor's introduction

I first met Steve Wright in 2012, when he was a Reader in the School of Applied Global Ethics, at Leeds Metropolitan University (now Leeds Beckett). Steve was one of my PhD supervisors at the university, where I was studying the methods of resistance during the 2010/11 Tunisian revolution.

It is probably fair to say that the most open 'face' of Steve, the one he presented most in his teaching and conversations, related to his impressive and inspiring 'spy for peace' activity—revealing the dark secrets of the arms and torture trade and the British state's complicity in this. However, there were many more facets to Steve's research and activities, as he worked across the broad fields of science, peace and security. The main aim of this book is to compile some of this work, offering a reference for some of Steve's original insights.

Steve the PhD supervisor and educator

For most of my PhD, as one of my supervisors Steve had been a somewhat elusive figure—always enthusiastic, responsive and incisive with his comments via email, although more often than not away on some international endeavour. As I reached the final intensely difficult year of the PhD process, Steve seemed to be around a little more, and there were a few welcome opportunities to have some evenings of conversation in Leeds, alongside Eddie Abbott-Halpin, John Willott and Tom Johnson. Steve was very encouraging at this time, assuring me that the immediate post-PhD period would likely prove exhilarating, with various opportunities to be embraced. During the summer of 2019, he also wrote to me that 'I well remember that feeling of release following the completion of my PhD. So savour the many days and weeks to come where you can think of travel, new horizons and even romance, unencumbered by guilt. 2019 will be a year to remember'. Indeed, much of my post-PhD activity I owe to Steve first putting me in contact with Jørgen Johansen and Majken Jul Sørensen—while their writers' retreat had given me the rejuvenation I needed to finish my PhD in the first place.

I also had the immense privilege of covering some of Steve's lectures and seminars when, with great reluctance, his illness made it impossible for him to continue. The weight of knowledge and experience Steve brought to bear off the back of the bare bones of the lecture slides was apparent, which combined with his personal stories made him utterly irreplaceable as a teacher. The students were taking those modules because of him, and they wanted him to be there teaching his modules. Steve's priority was to be there for his students as well. I was only supposed to be accompanying Steve in January while he taught, that was until the very last moment when I turned up in the seminar room, when with an incredibly heavy heart Steve accepted he was too ill.

However, Steve continued to give me assistance with the courses when he could, pointing me to the really crucial messages of his work he wanted to convey. Yet this was in no way overbearing, despite how inextricably linked his personal escapades were with his teaching, the legendary status of his lectures, and how he lived to pass on his knowledge and to nurture inquiring and critical minds. Rather, in that moment of his personal adversity he conveyed to me with enthusiasm that this was an opportunity for me. This I find incredibly poignant to think about. It is testament to Steve's fortitude, magnanimity and his humility, which will remain with me in exemplifying Steve as a great friend and mentor, at a time when I needed some self-confidence and self-belief.

Steve's work in the time of coronavirus

Steve's passing came just as the first news of a novel coronavirus emerged from China (if one happened to look closely enough). Many of us who knew Steve would have welcomed his insights as the global pandemic developed; we likely have our own sense of what he would have made of it, and for those reading this book and coming to Steve's work for the first time, I hope that the texts included here allow you to form your own impression too, without my mediation as the editor. However, I do think there are two interlinked aspects to the present situation that are worth emphasising.

Firstly, the COVID-19 pandemic is a serious public health crisis, afflicting more disproportionately some of the most vulnerable and marginalised people in our societies and across the world. Secondly, there are serious questions around the strengthening of surveillance, as well as curtailment of civil liberties, as part of the state response to the pandemic. Concerns about this second aspect have stimulated some of the opposition to the pandemic control measures; this makes for incredibly complex circumstances, where there is a need for rational and level-headed guarding against excessive government intrusions, while remaining mindful of the health issues. In this regard, Steve's work can help to clarify how academics and activists within the peace movement must give due attention to strategising in these complex circumstances. Our resistance to excessive government control is important while ensuring those marginalised and at greatest risk from the pandemic are not endangered by 'inaction'. And of course, Steve's life work shows how, while COVID-19 offers a further opportunity for governments to increase surveillance and curtailment of fundamental rights, these efforts are hardly new.

The proliferation of drones in warfare

In the first decades of the 21st Century, the trend in using Unmanned Aerial Vehicles (UAVs), or drones, to kill people was dominated by the US-led 'War on Terror'. This application has remained controversial, at least in some quarters, given the concerns over extra-judicial killing and the many civilians killed during their use.[1] The development of UAVs, particularly as autonomous killing machines, was an enduring concern of Steve's, as was their proliferation in use by non-state actors and states alike. Since 2019, armed drones have been adopted with high effectiveness by Turkey and the UAE in Libya,[2] during the 2020 Azerbaijan-Armenia War,[3] in the Tigray War,[4] and by Ukraine during the 2022 Russian invasion, while the latter has also seen prominent weaponisation of civilian drones. Steve's work emphasises why we should be concerned both about the normalisation of lethal UAVs and the increasing acceptability of this trend.

Normalisation of armed drone use has solidified through proliferation among non-state actors,[5] which have weaponised domestic drones and received supplies from state actors.[6] Meanwhile, drones' proliferation in conventional warfare is hardly surprising, although during the 2022 Russian invasion of Ukraine, lethal UAVs seem to have gained a new acceptability among ordinary people. As well as the repurposing of civilian drones for Ukraine's war effort,[7] there has been crowdfunding to purchase military drones for Ukraine,[8] particularly Turkey's

1 https://www.thebureauinvestigates.com/projects/drone-war

2 https://www.aljazeera.com/news/2020/5/28/largest-drone-war-in-the-world-how-airpower-saved-tripoli

3 https://foreignpolicy.com/2021/03/30/army-pentagon-nagorno-karabakh-drones/

4 https://paxforpeace.nl/news/blogs/turkish-drones-join-ethiopias-war-satellite-imagery-confirms

5 https://www.leidensecurityandglobalaffairs.nl/articles/isis-drone-sovereignty

6 https://www.airuniversity.af.edu/Portals/10/ASPJ/journals/Volume-34_Issue-3/F-Chavez_Swed.pdf
https://www.reuters.com/world/middle-east/attack-refinery-riyadh-did-not-affect-petroleum-supplies-spa-2022-03-10/

7 https://www.france24.com/en/live-news/20220401-punishment-from-above-hobby-pilots-build-ukraine-s-drone-fleet

8 https://www.dailysabah.com/business/defense/norway-canada-start-fundraising-to-buy-bayraktar-tb2s-for-ukraine

Bayraktar TB2. Regardless of any virtues of aiding a country's self-defence, this could mark a growing acceptability, at least among European populations, of armed drones' place in warfare. This could partially explain Israel's public acknowledgement in July 2022 of its longstanding use of armed drones.[9] The relatively low cost of armed UAVs heralds an ambivalent role for crowdfunded war. How this might reflect the creeping securitisation of various peoples and aspects of life can be considered in relation to Steve's article included in this book, 'Techno-politics of exclusion', as well as Schönenbach and Arndt's collaborative article with Steve, 'Second Variety'.

***

The additional contributions to this compilation are from individuals who knew Steve and engaged with him over several decades, which I hope provides a sense of the diversity and creativity of his thought. There are many others with memories and insights into Steve as a person, a friend, intellectual and research activist—a spy for peace—and this book is intended only as one departure point among many others for discussing Steve's legacy. When I told Steve about my activities with the Resistance Studies Initiative, his last words to me were: 'wherever folk like yourselves meet, there is hope of better, saner and more sustainable times to come'. I hope this compilation will make the pursuit of such times a little easier, and sustain inspiration, based on the selfless contribution and guidance that Steve himself provided.

Included works

The first section of this book provides some reflections by a number of colleagues and friends on their work with Steve. Brian Martin's 'Encounters with Steve Wright, mostly at a distance', details his collaborations with Steve for over 30 years. Brian has also graciously taken the time to go through his personal communications with Steve, which he has compiled in 'Resistance to repression the Steve Wright way'. Brian quite rightly states these are 'fascinating insights into his efforts against repression technology and thinking about strategy'. They help give a deeper picture of the efforts and risks that Steve took in visiting arms and security fairs. Yet they also show Steve's insights into nonviolent resistance and peace work broadly, including for example the emerging resistance to neoliberalism at the turn of the millennium, commenting on how security force

https://balkaninsight.com/2022/07/15/poles-raise-money-to-buy-bayraktar-drone-for-ukraine/

9 https://www.jpost.com/israel-news/article-712757

brutality during the 2001 Genoa G8 Summit posed a dilemma for resistance strategy (see page 38-39).

Janneke Schönenbach and Olaf Arndt's text recalls their friendship with Steve and his influence on their work, and further insight into Steve's process of extracting information about the arms trade from people deeply embedded in that world. Janneke and Olaf have also included an unpublished draft of a collaborative text they had been writing with Steve.

Dave Webb recounts how Steve was instrumental in establishing the Centre for the Study of Information and Technology for Peace, Conflict Resolution and Human Rights at Leeds Metropolitan University (now Leeds Beckett), alongside some of their academic collaborations.

Hendrik Bullens narrates his friendship with Steve since meeting him in the early 1990s through the European Peace Research Association (EuPRA), and the impression that Steve's work on arms control left on him.

The second section of this book includes works by Steve himself, beginning with a previously unpublished piece from 2005 which has been compiled by Brian Martin, titled 'A Spy for Peace'. This is a fantastic overview of how Steve operated, the rationale and method behind his activities. The short blog post from 2016, 'Going Full Circle', gives some insight into the prominence of the arms industry in Steve's formative years, growing up near the Vickers-Armstrongs factory in Newcastle. Steve and Tessie Humble's work, 'The Techno-Politics of Exclusion', shows how various lethal and sub-lethal technologies that Steve uncovered at arms fairs have been comprised into the securitised response to the environmental crisis and not-unrelated management of migration at the EU's borders. Brian Martin and Steve Wright's text, 'Looming struggles over technology for border control' has been reproduced as an accompaniment here. Written in 2006, the emphasis on the expansion of non-lethal technology is particularly prescient when considering government responses to the Covid-19 pandemic since 2020. While the pandemic threat is genuine, it also poses an opportunity for increased surveillance measures and securitised management of populations. The final part of this 'spy for peace' section is an article by Steve writing under his pseudonym Robin Ballantyne, about 'Japan's Hidden Arms Trade' (2005). It is an indication of the global reach of Steve's research and actions in the interests of peace.

While much of Steve's research output did focus on 'tools of social and political control', it would be reductive to concentrate solely on this work. His book chapter on 'The work of Fethullah Gülen and the role of non-violence in a time of terror' (2005) is a nuanced assessment of the place of nonviolence within Islam, and specifically the Gülen movement that originated in Turkey. A similarly insightful piece is 'The ECHELON Trail: An Illegal Vision'. This essentially returns to what was Steve's first major activity as a 'spy for peace', helping to uncover the US National Security Agency's mass surveillance system ECHELON. However, the article is rather distinctive for an academic paper in being an open and very personal account of Steve's research experiences. An outcome of this research, the European Parliament's STOA report, was authored by Steve and is linked to in the bibliography.

The final paper of Steve's included is 'A systems approach to analysing sub-state conflicts' (2006), which revisited the focus of his PhD thesis examining the conflict in Northern Ireland. Steve resurrected his research in light of post-9/11 events, reflecting on how quantitative systems analysis of insurgency and counter-insurgency could help to avoid conflict 'lock-ins'. He acknowledges that such a quantiative approach to conflict analysis was and remains obscure and possibly too inaccessible to lay readers, although it is impressive in its intricacy, while Steve's caution regarding the ability to collect sufficient raw data to enable objective analysis of conflict dynamics is crucial.

Finally, there is a 1988 article from the *Manchester Evening News*, 'Big brother is watching you', which combined an interview with Steve and extracts from his recently completed PhD, 'New Police Technologies and Sub-State Conflict Control'. This was written while Steve was working as the head of Manchester City Council's police monitoring unit, which was soon to be closed down. While a physical copy of this newspaper might exist somewhere, I have reproduced it here from a photocopy Steve made, as much for the historical record of genuine media interest in technologies of political control and surveillance.

Encounters with Steve Wright, mostly at a distance

by Brian Martin

In February 1981 I read an article titled "New police technologies" and took a page of notes about it. The author's name was Steve Wright. A few years later I wrote to him, beginning a connection that lasted over 30 years.

A bit of background. In 1976 I moved to Canberra and became an active member of the local Friends of the Earth group. Its main issue was uranium mining and nuclear power. Because Australia had no nuclear power plants, one of the main issues in the nuclear debate was the connection between nuclear power and nuclear weapons. Australian uranium, exported to other countries for supposedly peaceful purposes, might end up in nuclear weapons. This focus on nuclear proliferation attuned me to peace issues, and in 1979 I helped set up a peace group, Canberra Peacemakers. My special interest was in social defence, which is nonviolent community resistance to aggression as an alternative to military defence.

I started reading everything I could find about social defence and related issues. In those days, long before the Internet, it was a matter of reading what was available in libraries, subscribing to magazines, checking book reviews, and looking up sources cited in articles and books.

One of the things I read was *Militarism and Repression* by Michael Randle.[1] I had seen it in the catalogue for Housmans Bookshop in London, and bought a copy. For developing a social defence system, it was important to understand militarism and to be aware of methods of repression, because nonviolent defenders would need to deal with these methods. Among the references in *Militarism and Repression* was the article by Steve Wright that I read shortly afterwards.[2]

It wasn't until several years later, in 1985, that I first contacted Steve. That year I came across in my files an old article of his on alternative defence, from

1 Michael Randle, *Militarism and Repression* (South Boston: International Seminars on Training for Nonviolent Action, 1980).

2 Steve Wright, "New police technologies: an exploration of the social implications and unforeseen impacts of some recent developments," *Journal of Peace Research,* vol. 15, no. 4, 1978, pp. 305–322.

a 1981 newsletter. In my initial letter to Steve, I said I remembered his article about new police technologies, which had impressed me. I asked whether he was still working on social defence or alternative defence, and sent some of my publications. It was basically a letter to make a connection.

Before long, Steve wrote back offering ideas and suggestions for connections. At the time he was working for Manchester City Council as head of its Police Monitoring Committee's Research Unit. Although at this stage Steve was less involved with social defence, nevertheless he pointed me to the US Student Pugwash movement and to the Richardson Institute's work on alternative defence.

A few years later, in August 1988, I wrote asking Steve about any work he had done on police technologies. He replied saying "The most exhaustive piece I have written is my PhD thesis which is on 'New Police Technologies & Sub-State Conflict Control.'"[3] He also mentioned several articles he had written.

I had my university library obtain a copy of Steve's thesis. It was on microfilm. I remember spending several hours one afternoon reading through it on the library's microfilm reader. It was a massive treatment, with detailed information about technologies of repression. I was in no doubt about Steve's knowledge in the area.

In April 1990 there was a conference on social defence at Bradford University. I had never before been to Europe. The conference provided the incentive to make the long and exhausting trip. A couple of weeks beforehand, I wrote to Steve saying I'd be staying in Manchester one night and that we could meet at my hotel. And so we did, on Thursday 12 April.

Face to face, Steve was enthusiastic, committed and brimming with ideas. I asked Steve about publications about the technology of repression and for names of people researching in the area. He gave me a series of names of researchers and where each one worked, describing their contributions. Today they read as a who's who for figures and groups in the field: Richard Falk, Michael Klare, Amnesty International, Phil Scranton, Michael Stohl, Noam Chomsky and Edward Herman, Ian Ross and Ted Gurr. I wrote down the names on a piece of hotel note paper and later wrote to nearly every one of them. Judging by their replies, it was apparent that Steve was the central figure in the field.

In a subsequent letter I told Steve I had written to the people he suggested during our meeting in Manchester, and then written to others they suggested. What I found—no surprise—was that there was virtually nothing being done

3 University of Lancaster, 1987

on nonviolent resistance to the technology of repression. Because Steve was interested in seeing the network in action, I listed the responses I received.

- Richard Falk referred me to some of his work (which he said was "not directly relevant") and recommended Michael Klare.
- Michael Klare offered some general suggestions for sources, and recommended Bob Irwin.
- Michael Stohl recommended Alex Schmid and Michael Klare.
- Edward Herman offered a long list of books on the CIA, political police, etc.

In addition to Steve's suggestions, I wrote to two others.

- Peter Klerks was recommended to me by Giliam de Valk, who I met in Bradford. Peter sent highly useful information about Alex Schmid's operation, PIOOM.
- Bob Irwin, who had been recommended by Michael Klare, sent some extremely helpful comments and references.

These days, with the Internet, it seems quick and easy to find out what work is being done in an area. Before the Internet, the key was finding a nodal figure—like Steve on repression technology—and getting the names of others in the field.

There was an advantage in writing personal letters. Because they took a bit of time and effort to compose and send off, I think people treated them more seriously compared to the onslaught of emails and social media comment that began in the following decade.

In writing to Steve after our meeting, I told him that I was guest-editing some issues of the journal *Philosophy and Social Action,* including one on the theme of "Resisting state violence." I offered to publish one of his papers, and ended up using his long paper on the new technologies of political repression. First he sent hard copy, then at my request a disc with the article in Wordperfect. In an aerogramme posted on 6 December 1990, Steve wrote that the file was called Omega, and noted that he'd just set up "a new outfit called the OMEGA Foundation." Omega is the last letter in the Greek alphabet, and in physics it is the symbol for electrical resistance.

The Omega Foundation's goal was to collect information about the technology of repression—surveillance cameras, electroshock batons, leg irons, and so forth—and use the information to support campaigns against torture and other forms of political repression. It was thus about resistance to state power.

Getting Steve's article ready for publication in *Philosophy and Social Action* required checking lots of details, which we managed by post in an efficient manner.[4] Steve continued to send me suggestions for making contacts in the peace-research community. I told him about our small group Schweik Action Wollongong which was running projects about social defence. One of the projects involved interviewing people knowledgeable about telecommunications about how to resist an invasion or coup without violence. This resonated with Steve. We had a common interest in techniques that citizen campaigners could use to resist state power.

I wrote a short article titled "Science and technology for nonviolent struggle" and submitted it to *Science and Public Policy*.[5] The journal, like many in the social sciences, uses a double-blind refereeing process: submissions are sent to reviewers who write reports for the editor, and neither the author nor the reviewer is informed of the other's identity. Soon I received the report of an anonymous reviewer, who was very knowledgeable. From the content of the report I guessed that Steve was the reviewer, and also I recognised his typewriter. When I told him this—and thanked him for the review—he said he had recognised me as the author. It was a small world.

Much of our correspondence was about the possibility of finding sources of money to support our activities. I applied for a research grant on "Science and technology for nonviolent struggle" and Steve agreed to be a nominated assessor. My application was successful the second time around. Steve applied for a grant from The Joseph Rowntree Foundation that was successful, giving him more time to do the work he wanted to. In the following few years we wrote to each other about what we were doing on our projects. In 1994 we first started using email.

Some of Steve's letters during the 1990s included stories of his adventures in collecting information at so-called "security fairs," where companies tout their products to enhance "security," many of which relate to surveillance, crowd control and torture. Steve would figure out how to attend such showcases for the technology of repression, collect information there and use it for campaigning. Sometimes he fed information to Amnesty International; sometimes he wrote articles for the print media under the pseudonym Robin Ballantyne.

---

4 Steve Wright, "The new technologies of political repression: a case for arms control?" *Philosophy and Social Action,* vol. 18, nos. 3–4, July-December 1991, pp. 31–62, https://www.bmartin.cc/pubs/91psa/91psa_Wright.pdf

5 Brian Martin, "Science for non-violent struggle," *Science and Public Policy*, vol. 19, no. 1, February 1992, pp. 55–58.

A highlight of his efforts was playing a key role in exposing surveillance of global electronic communication by spy agencies. In 1996, New Zealand activist Nicky Hager's book *Secret Power* was published.[6] Through a remarkable feat of investigative activism, Hager exposed the Echelon system, a coordinated operation by spy agencies in the Five Eyes group (US, Britain, Canada, Australia and New Zealand) to suck up all electronic communications around the world—phone and computer traffic—and analyse it to enable tracking of topics and targets. Hager's book was known to a small number of people interested in government surveillance and spying, but did not reach a wider audience. In 1998 Steve, in a report to the European Parliament, drew on Hager's findings and exposed the Echelon system.[7] The story was taken up worldwide.[8] Years later, Edward Snowden exposed the latest form of global surveillance of electronic communication.

In 2001, I was studying political jiu-jitsu, the process by which violent attacks on peaceful protesters can trigger greater support for the protesters. Political jiu-jitsu is one of the stages in Gene Sharp's "dynamics of nonviolent action," which describes facets of nonviolent campaigns.[9] What puzzled me was that many violent attacks on peaceful protesters did not lead to political jiu-jitsu. With two colleagues, I had been looking at the Indonesian genocide of 1965–1966.[10] Surely mass killing of nonresisting civilians should cause observers to become concerned. My insight was that the perpetrators were doing something to inhibit the jiu-jitsu effect, and I came up with five types of tactics: covering up the action; devaluing the targets; reinterpreting events by lying, minimising, blaming and framing; using official channels to give the appearance of justice; and intimidating or rewarding people involved.

Another insight was that this same process could apply in other domains besides attacks on peaceful protesters. Torture seemed a prime example. Perpetrators carry out torture in secret, denigrate their targets as terrorists or

6 Nicky Hager, *Secret Power: New Zealand's Role in the International Spy Network* (Nelson, New Zealand: Craig Potten, 1996).

7 Steve Wright, *An Appraisal of Technologies of Political Control* (Luxembourg: European Parliament, Scientific and Technological Options Assessment, 1998).

8 For Steve's account, see "The Echelon trail: an illegal vision," *Surveillance & Society,* vol. 3, nos. 2/3, 2005, pp. 198–215.

9 Gene Sharp, *The Politics of Nonviolent Action* (Boston: Porter Sargent, 1973), Part 3.

10 Brian Martin, Wendy Varney and Adrian Vickers, "Political jiu-jitsu against Indonesian repression: studying lower-profile nonviolent resistance," *Pacifica Review,* vol. 13, no. 2, June 2001, pp. 143–156.

criminals, say the methods used are not all that harmful, blame rogue elements, refer complainants to courts, and threaten targets with further harm.

I invited Steve to collaborate on an article applying this framework to torture technology. He was enthusiastic. Over a period of months we negotiated the content of the article, wrote and revised it, and saw it published in *Medicine, Conflict and Survival.*[11]

Collaborating with Steve was worthwhile. He had a wealth of ideas and a giant reservoir of knowledge. Furthermore, he was attracted to the model I had developed and quite used to seeing things using the framework of tactics and counter-tactics. Indeed, thinking this way seemed to stimulate his creativity.

I learned two things about Steve and doing research. The first was that while he had a wealth of ideas, he didn't always check details. He would include information and references that looked all right, but I learned I needed to check them, because in a few instances corrections were needed. That was fine with me: I was used to such checking.

The second thing was that Steve was a procrastinator and binger. Like many writers, he would postpone writing until the pressure became great enough to stimulate a burst of effort. At some point, a friend of Steve's told me that Steve wouldn't finish his part of a collaboration unless given a firm deadline. Although our article didn't have a required completion date, I gave Steve a deadline and he did his bit.

Later, Steve told me about his experience writing his PhD thesis. He knew the material backwards but hadn't started writing his thesis, and eventually the university gave him a submission date: if his thesis wasn't submitted by that date, his candidature would be terminated. This turned out to be enough pressure to get him writing, and at a tremendous pace. He wrote his entire thesis in just six weeks. He told me about using the drug guarana, like caffeine but stronger, to keep going through thick and thin during those six weeks, and there was a finale of a storm and some other obstacle that just about derailed submission on the very last day.

Given that background, I should have been grateful that Steve was able to write anything at all in a joint paper, given that we were at opposite ends of the earth and I had only email as leverage to encourage him to finish his part of the paper. But he did.

---

11 Brian Martin and Steve Wright, "Countershock: mobilizing resistance to electroshock weapons," *Medicine, Conflict and Survival,* vol. 19, no. 3, July-September 2003, pp. 205–222.

In the following years, we had several occasions to meet face to face. Twice I visited him in England. In Manchester in April 2003, he showed me around the offices of the Omega Foundation. We talked at length about key people in the field, and where to publish articles. At least these are the main items in my pages of notes from my visit, no doubt taken in between Steve's stories. On a second visit in Manchester, he drove me to Leeds, where he had become an academic at Leeds Metropolitan University, where there was a conference and later a meeting of Praxis group. He later moved to Leeds and the university was renamed Leeds Beckett.

Steve made three visits to Wollongong. During the first, in June 2004, supported by my research grant, we had plenty of time to discuss a range of issues, and I introduced him to colleagues and activist friends. Steve gave a seminar titled "Mass torture and full spectrum dominance." It was filled with stories and images of frightful technological-political scenarios, some already realised and some looming in the future. Those who attended were greatly affected.

His final visit, in 2010, was for a meeting of nonviolence researchers; the biannual meeting of the International Peace Research Association was held in Sydney that year, and I supported a small group of nonviolence researchers to attend a nonviolence research strategy meeting in Wollongong afterwards. As usual, Steve sparked with lots of ideas, which was useful to challenge the rest of us who thought about nonviolence in more conventional ways.

After one of his visits to Wollongong, Steve's next stop was China, where he would be attending a security fair. He was well aware of the dangers he faced in some countries, and, before leaving, left me with every item he possessed that might be slightly suspicious.

Steve had an acute sense of the dangers that repression technologies posed in the hands of governments, police and militaries. He did what he could to alert a range of groups, and worked openly and behind the scenes to support laws, regulations and activist campaigns to control and delegitimise these technologies. His best possible legacy is a heightened awareness throughout various networks to carry on with efforts to rid the world of torture and repression.

Resistance to repression the Steve Wright way

Introduction by Brian Martin

Steve and I began corresponding in the 1980s. I saved all our letters, in either hard copy or electronic form. Many of Steve's letters contain fascinating insights into his efforts against repression technology and his thinking about strategy. Going through these letters, I've extracted passages that focus on investigating the repression trade and campaigning against it. Most details about our personal affairs and collaborative research are omitted. I've included extracts only up to 2005, covering the period when Steve was regularly visiting arms and security fairs.

Steve's letters were filled with typos. He obviously wrote at speed and didn't bother to correct errors. Most inaccuracies have been corrected here. Even though typos might be considered to give a more genuine picture of Steve's communications, they are distracting. Steve occasionally seemed to have kept his finger on the same key too long, leading to spellings such as "aavaailable." He often ended sentences with a long series of full stops .... I've replaced these with single ellipses ... which don't indicate that anything is missing, just that Steve finished a sentence with multiple full stops. In a few places, I've added explanatory text in square brackets or footnotes. Except where indicated, text here is taken from Steve's letters to me. I've included two of my emails to Steve, from 2002, to illustrate our exchange of ideas while developing a joint article.

Even though technologies have changed dramatically, much of the strategic thinking from decades ago has relevance today. If you are concerned about surveillance, social control and torture, there is much to learn from Steve.

8 August 1985

Thanks for your kind words on my earlier work. As you can see [from the letterhead], I am now working for Manchester City Council — as Head of its Police Monitoring Committee's Research Unit ... we watch the local fuzz!

I have moved more away for social defence in recent years only in terms of time devoted. After writing a pamphlet on the repressive side of civil defence tactics which included a section on alternative defence, most of my research efforts have been towards the export of repressive technologies and how to stop them. I can send you a copy if it would be of interest. There is a tie up of course, so much so that at one stage the Dutch government were going to fund my work as part of a larger study on civilian resistance. My theory is that certain new police technologies may severely undermine the viability of some of the traditional civilian resistance techniques—new pain and less lethal technology could subvert nonviolence training unless proper preparation anticipated the effects and creative countermeasures were evolved.

14 June 1991

After the gulf war ended, there was a tiny piece in the *Guardian* to say that Hiatt Handcuff boxes were found in Kuwait prison after the Iraqis fled. It struck a chord since I remembered past news stories where there was mention of western involvement or equipment reported at the site of some state sponsored atrocity soon after the regime collapsed. I am left thinking that if major humanitarian organisations such as Amnesty are to have any impact, immediately after a state terrorist regime falls, a task force needs to be dropped in to immediately check out the evidence of external collusion. We might argue about the structure of such a task force if it is to have both authority, legitimacy and credibility but in a publication such as yours, a powerful case can be made for the major international organisations to pay more than lip service to human rights rhetoric and recognise the importance of acting quickly when a torturing regime loses its grip.

14 January 1992

The most relevant action I'm currently involved in is with Amnesty International who tomorrow publish a book on business and the repression trade.[1] Our aim is to get Amnesty activists to write politely to companies asking for their policies for trading with human rights violators. It's a way of questioning business ethics, is non-violent though potentially economically damaging to the company and is a potentially powerful way in which concerned people in liberal democracies can directly intervene in stopping the flow of repression expertise and hardware to the torturing states.

1 Editor's note: Amnesty International. 1992. *Repression Trade UK Ltd: How the UK Trades in Torture and Death.* London: Amnesty International.

22 March 1992

Schweik Action sounds fun. Is your report on telecommunications for social defence out yet?[2] There was a related story in the March edition of AI [Amnesty International] British Section Group Newsletter. It concerned Andrew Brown, the Parliamentary Columnist on the Independent and referred to a feature in the American magazine CompuServe. His wife Caroline wrote to a Jamaican prisoner on death row. One day a telegram arrived saying "Appointed to hang on Thursday. Call Carl Rattray, Jamaica. Save Us. Ivan Morgan & Earl Pratt." With less than a week to act, letters were out of the question. The two men had waited on death row for 13 years but no letter campaign could be organised in a few days. The only form of long-distance mass pressure left to exert was a fax campaign. AI had fax numbers for the Governor General, the Prime Minister, the Foreign Minister and the Minister for Justice (Carl Rattay). Although Brown didn't know it at the time, AI USA had also posted full details in Library 15, Ethics/Human Rights of the Issues Forum on CompuServe. The day before the execution, several people reported that the fax machines of the Jamaican Government had suffered sudden catastrophic failure. The fax campaign helped to save the men's lives and Compuserve with its quick inexpensive faxing facility had helped enormously.

7 October 1992

MILIPOL was like a black & white TV cold war spy drama. I arrived in Moscow to be met at the airport by the organisers' lackeys. Sitting in their car, I was asked for my formal invite. This time it had not arrived—only a fax from Intourist [Russian tour operator]—so I was asked to meet the Frenchman in charge at his hotel the next day. A nerve-wracking drive followed but I made the connection and persuaded him of my bona fides. I was given the access card of his assistant to get past the KGB perimeter guards. It amused me to look at it and read my new designation of interpreter as I tried to recollect my 4 words of Russian. The fair itself had many foreign exhibitors and the bridgeheading by French, US, German and English companies was apparent.

I thought I'd done with such trips for a year but somehow the money emerged to attend the HURIDOCS conference on Crete. The contacts were amazing. One of the participants from Hong Kong said she knew of some local millionaires who would be interested in my findings from the ChinaSecure

2 Steve refers to Schweik Action Wollongong, a small group of which I was a member. We carried out community research projects: https://www.bmartin.cc/others/SAW.html.

exhibition to be held in Beijing. So at the end of July, I nervously made my way to China. In Tiananmen I found that the surveillance cameras were made in the US! Anyway, I managed to get some of my findings published in the *Guardian,* and I enclose a copy of the article for your files.

Finally, you asked about linking challenges to repression technologies with challenges to the state. I know something of the dangers but we are both aware that research and training in this area are nearly always learnt on the job at the worst possible moment and nearly all of the researchers fail to survive the process of R&D. This evolutionary process in situ needs to be avoided but even the more advanced approaches of territorial defence have flaws. The Yugoslav experience is now revealing the terrible price of attempting a violent response to a more violent state authority. At least some of the answer must lie in the path you are advocating in terms of non-violent training as a tactical approach. Such a strategy can allow proliferation of action not just restricting it to set battle fronts. It might be worth exploring the possibilities of getting a grant for this work from the United States Institute for Peace. Their latest brochure on solicited grants says they are specifically looking for proposals on conflict resolution training. They tend to take a conflict management approach and yours might be too radical. Yet the blurb does identify the need to train local mediators during dangerous periods of transition in places such as Eastern Europe, the former USSR, parts of Africa, Asia & Latin America. Grants available are 100,000 dollars and they are looking for materials and techniques which must be suitable to real conflict situations and contain an evaluation component. In any event it's probably worth sending off for the brochure. If you succeed, you can appoint me as a researcher and I'll come up with the anti-state repression bible of the 21st Century … the evolutionary equivalent of the air sniffing frog who invented a new survival niche to survive the hazards of being limited to the sea. I always remember that archetypal deviant fish when the going gets tough. Without it, all of what we know as civilisation would have been doomed so when people say we are naive—they should have talked to that fish.

17 September 1993

Whilst there is, as you say, no direct literature on this area [science and technology for nonviolent struggle], there is much that is there. For example the scientific material on riot agents often includes advice on decontamination which could be applied. There is also the work on IRA [Irish Republican Army] countermeasures which contains a vast store of possible technology which could be used without their violent ethos. This includes material on interception of SIGINT [signals intelligence] material using adapted B & W TV's; blocking of surveillance devices using field animals; detection of helicopters and SAS squads using stolen NATO infrared binoculars etc. I've one or two articles which I could send you if you are exploring this avenue. There is also the question of research as a tool of non-violent resistance which of course your own work is a case in point. In the early eighties, there was a conference in London on researching state structures. The papers were fascinating—particularly the material on the electronic nervous system of most state repressive systems. Of course all of this is vulnerable to technical interception and much to quite primitive destructive measures such as thermite—depending on whether your chosen ethos does not disallow violence against property. There is also a substantial literature on guerrilla TV using homemade equipment. Such counter broadcasting is to my mind a critical measure in creating counter-realities in any society under state siege. You could look at publications such as *Radio is my Bomb: A DIY Manual for Pirates.*

My own perspective on this subject is that most of the communities that have ever used countermeasures against state repression and state terror have done so spontaneously and that much of what you wish to reapply must be inspired by anecdotal evidence and stories including researchers and journalists that revealed hidden state structures since exposure on a bigger stage has produced useful chilling effects against repressive structures which have depended on secrecy. To find such stories, it might be worth going fishing. I would suggest the IPRA Newsletter, HURIDOCS magazine, PIOOM journal at Leiden University, JPR, JCR, and the new journal for non-violence which has just started in Europe.[3]

I can write to the latter since they are currently commissioning papers suggesting that contact you. There is also a magazine here, based in Hull, called *Lobster,* which just specialises in exposing dark state deeds. There are others but I guess the best way forward would be to write a short resume of what you are attempting to achieve—treat it maybe as an historic study for this purpose, of finding out how people have used countermeasures to resist state terror, on 1 page of A4 with contact numbers. I could circulate it here and you could circulate it amongst your networks and relevant computer bulletin boards.

3 IPRA: International Peace Research Association; HURIDOCS: human rights organisation; PIOOM Journal later ceased publication; JPR: Journal of Peace Research; JCR: Journal of Conflict Resolution. The new *International Journal of Nonviolence* was short lived.

Most of what you would get back would be dross but a small percentage would with luck be gold.

Omega's work of using technical systems to research companies is a good case of action at a distance.[4] We've found many well known companies which have a contaminated underbelly. For example Fiat makes mines, Kodak makes riot gas etc. There is some beautiful counterpointing of reality with advertising slogans here. Our chosen route, following an intersectional meeting of Amnesty International groups in London in May, is to get local AI groups to ask searching questions to their local merchants of repression. When they wriggle with plausible denials we now have data on 3000 companies to evidence our casework. The campaign begins in October to coincide with Amnesty's campaign on the disappeared. I'll keep you posted on how this little experiment works out—providing of course some company lawyer doesn't manage to sue us to pieces!

Re Schweik Action Wollongong and the opposition to bureaucratic elites,[5] I wonder if I told you or sent you material on Policewatch from my old police monitoring days. Our slogan was for a more accountable police force and it was deliberately written in the style of the *Sun* rather than the *Guardian.* I think it was incredibly effective — even the Prime Minister Margaret Thatcher read it because it was so direct. Its approach was to directly tackle larger issues through examples that everyone could understand, either through cause celebres such as the Stalker Affair or through inadequate policies such as the no-criming of domestic crimes against women. We did of course have the advantage of getting a copy of a glossy news sheet through every door in the city and the mass media would regurgitate our propaganda as news in itself which would echo to the walls of the city gates. Because it generated a policy debate within the local force chiefs, many of the policies we wanted changing have today changed along our lines ... I guess it is an approach which can be reapplied. Every bureaucratic elite is vulnerable to the challenge of ... "We demand greater accountability" ... particularly if it uses an economic line about how the way our money is spent. Any unwillingness to comply or acknowledge means that the press senses a story and the whole issue develops a critical mass. What I do think is important, as was the case in the related whistleblowers material, is to take possession of our victories and to create case studies of even partial victories whose fruit maybe

4 Omega refers to the Omega Foundation, where Steve worked. It was later renamed the Omega Research Foundation.

5 The result of the project was published several years later: Schweik Action Wollongong, *Challenging Bureaucratic Elites* (1997), https://www.bmartin.cc/dissent/documents/Schweik_cbe/.

came much later. Somehow we need to create a culture which accepts that it is not because life is difficult that we do not dare; it is because we do not dare that life is difficult. Ha! … but it helps when others like you dare too.

25 February 1995

It has been a while since we last corresponded so I thought I would drop you a quick note via the net to illustrate that our system [email] does work and to stay in touch.

Over the last year Omega have been involved on a Channel 4 Dispatches programme called *The Torture Trail* which was broadcast on 11 January 95. It involved secretly filming an undercover team's effort to buy £5m of electric torture equipment in the UK.[6] Caused a bit of a stir here: one of the companies was raided by the police; another company suspended its sales staff and the government were forced to admit that some British police forces had acquired 50,000 electronic riot shields as passive weapons for use against wild dogs in pre-planned operations.

Finally on Pepper gas. There has been an explosion of companies getting into this field now. Some of the interest has been accelerated by the US programme of research into non-lethal weapons. *Guardian* (16 Feb 95) reported that US troops have deployed chemical foam and sticky foam in Somalia. What is new here is that the companies are also selling antidotes to the chemicals which may be useful to your project. I see this as an indication of the severity of the pepper gas: the manufacturers need to decontaminate the police and vehicles of the personnel deploying it. But the antidotes are designed to be effective against all current riot agents.

9 March 1995

This is the way to do it [use email], use the technology we continuously advocate! I'm still a bit of a novice but this is nearly real time info and the chance of turn around within hours is there should we need it.

It is good to learn of your many projects. I like the idea of architecture that changes a community's perspective for the better.[7] Back in my hometown

---

6 Steve's published account: Robin Ballantyne, "Electro-shock weapons: the 'torture trail'," *Fortress Europe? – Circular Letter*, 31 (February 1995), [https://desexil.com/wp-content/uploads/2021/04/cl31.pdf]

7 Published later as Helen Gillett, Brian Martin and Chris Rust, "Building in nonviolence: nonviolent struggle and the built environment," *Civilian-Based Defense*, vol. 11, no. 3, Fall 1996, pp. 1, 4–7, https://www.bmartin.cc/pubs/96cbd.html.

of Newcastle, they have one estate, Byker, which was famously developed to keep the community together, encourage local pride and a sense of owning the territory. As its fame grew, media people have taken it up as a place to explore new ideas. There have been some intriguing results when local Geordies [people from Newcastle] had the chance of putting any artwork of their choice on the wall—anything from modern art to old masters. Geordies having a drink at their local clubs then discussed the merits of what they chose. But the people of Tyneside have been so screwed over by governments in the past that they have a fighting spirit that no amount of community re-structuring can destroy. Alas most of the architecture and design criteria I have seen in recent years have been concerned with designing out community solidarity, taking away defensible space and building in facilities which will allow police to take over in the event of a disturbance and control exits.

It is quite a difficult subject to get any consensus on in Britain. Fear of crime dominates every discussion about freedom and the majority of people would agree to anything if they thought their house had less chance of being burgled and their insurance costs would go down. Many cities have successfully mounted citywide surveillance projects and have claimed that these have reduced crime, although in most instances it is just a matter of displacement. The surveillance equipment manufacturers are advocating solutions based on neural networks which mean that individuals can be tracked during their stay in the city and their movements recorded and sequentially joined.

Britain has just announced it's testing new chemical foam for its police and it is just a matter of time before the new generation of less lethal weapons being evolved by laboratories like Sandia and Los Alamos in the US are put on display at various police and arms fairs. The new toffee gun has already had a public airing to bemused journalists in preparation for it being put on standby for the withdrawal of US troops from Somalia. In the event it wasn't used by the Americans, who are itching for a demonstration site in the South to demonstrate their new non-lethal warfare doctrine. Some of the historical work on disabling chemicals has been collated by colleagues and I will attempt to get their permission to put it on the network in due course.

15 March 1995

I still can't believe the potential for contacting a whole network of people through pre-set broadcast facilities. It will save much time later on if we get all the media numbers pre-loaded. It is reassuring that we could, in an emergency, send out a press release to the world's press and to all the relevant agencies as well as masses of supporting documentation. Through my previous work, I'm familiar with the need to gorge the press with organised well-written info. There is so much noise that they can ignore a great deal and yet time pressures mean that anything well written with accompanying pictures can be a lazy journalist's dream. It will be interesting to try out the theory in a limited exercise later in the year.

I've not seen the two books you referred to on surveillance but will now look out for them. What worries me in the UK is that just one or two gruesome cases such as the James Bulger child murder or a baby snatch can get every anxious parent saying I want any measure that makes this world more secure for me and the civil liberties dimension is an abstraction. On the same basis in the UK, we have had the issue of identity cards aired again—it will take the form of a smart card—maybe incorporating another facility such as a social security card or a driving licence with a photograph. What has been less publicised is the drive towards incorporating biometric data—any card that has pictures for official use in the UK will be machine readable by photographic image. It's part of the problem of imagining the dangers of these new technologies. It's being aware of how all the elements create something that cannot be seen in isolation. Each piecemeal improvement is rubber stamped and yet few take the time to see how such 'modernisation' is being plugged into systems and programmes which are malleable and can work to a very different range of agendas.

In Manchester, during my Police Monitoring Unit days, the Greater Manchester Police swore down thump that they were not red triangling gays and lesbians on their databases. (Our worry was that a homophobic chief constable such as the previous top cop James Anderton could signal a war on any sexual 'deviants' and the police on the ground would use their databases either proactively in stop and search operations, or that during a stop and search, prior knowledge of someone's sexuality would have a strong negative influence on what happened next.) So it was interesting to read in *Computing* 2 Feb 95 that GMP's operational intelligence system had been used to log information on homosexuals. The police line in response was fascinating: 'When the system was purchased, it came pre-loaded with certain personal characteristic markers including homosexuality...' So the manufacturers provide options, some of which are used and some of which are on standby. The British Mod [Ministry of Defence] is facing prosecution by the data protection registrar for holding similar data on sexual orientation on armed forces personnel (*Computing* 26 Jan 95).

In terms of countermeasures, *Computing*, 2 February 95, carried a piece warning MI5 that a major hole existed in Digital's DECnet networking architecture which allowed unauthorised access: Digital is a leading supplier to MoD and GCHQ [Government Communications Headquarters, UK spy body]. The report mentions a little-known MI5 group UNIRAS (Unified Incident Reporting & Alerting Service) which warns the intelligence agency about IT problems but on this occasion it took 4 months. The report recognises that hackers are very adept and very quick at exploiting such weaknesses. Alas both opposites are involved in the same process, the improvement of the overall system which often seems to be the long term biproduct of struggles against centralised and anti-democratic technologies. It appeals to my sense of humour that the astrophysicist Stephen Hawking has cogently argued that viruses by any of the extant criteria should be regarded as life forms. Subversive life forms: we have a long way to go before resistance programmes get that status or integrity in self-replication.

30 January 1998

Life here has been very busy. Pete[8] and I went to the European Parliament on related areas this week. He attended a seminar on Human Rights and the Internet, while I presented a report on 'An Appraisal of the Technology of Political Control' which if you haven't got already you can order from [details given]. It's free! So encourage your students to write in.

So far it's caused quite a stir since the report covers the USA NSA [National Security Agency] email, telephone and fax interception systems Echelon and Oratory systems—largely from Nicky Hager's book in New Zealand: *Secret Power* (published by Craig Potton). US Embassy officials were there to meet me when I first presented the report and GCHQ were urgently requesting copies … I guess it's put the issue on the agenda again. Glyn Ford has just done a piece for *Tribune* magazine called Watching all over the World …

Relevant to your own project, we covered a technology called Harlequin that maps all the phones that any one phone has been in touch with to visually represent friendship networks. Of course if the politics change then it is a generator of crude but effective arrest lists. Channel 4 did a visual piece on the report which spread the word further.

Other sections cover the new less-lethal weapons, prison technologies and the loss of accountability with privatisation and interrogation, torture and execution technologies. You might find the bibliography of use.

8 Pete Abel, key figure at the Omega Foundation.

Omega has secured funding to scan all of our documentation and company brochures into new computer filing systems. It means that if you requested info on companies we could give you thousands of documents and colour photographs on CD ROM—perhaps up and running by the end of 1998. It means we can feed journalists cutting edge stuff in real time—but we must also include a billing system in there ...

The project for this week though is UK exports of small arms and light weapons. We are working for Oxfam and will produce a final report over the next 10 days. Finally, I'll be in Kuala Lumpur later on this year. If our schedules permit, maybe I'll come to see you in Australia.

24 February 1999

Omega have just been granted $35,000 by the Rockefeller family trust but the rest of our funding is coming to an end. We have just asked Rowntrees for £140,000 over three years. The trustees preliminary meeting was here last Friday but the full meeting on the 14 March will decide our fate. We have never been more active or more effective yet Rowntrees have a policy of not giving continued funding. Wish us well, we might need a lot of good vibes to push us through on the day.

We have been doing quite a bit of work related to your project [on communication and nonviolent struggle], most recently via the Privacy International Big Brother awards ceremony and also with the Mark Thomas Show. The Big brother awards gave oscars to big corporate bastards and a lifetime achievement award to Menwith Hill [UK spy base]. We also gave Winston awards to those who had battled most effectively against surveillance.[9] It might be a good case study of the community fighting back. Tonite's show features Mark Thomas personally delivering the Menwith Hill award (a human head in tasteful gold being stamped on by a jackboot). In a daring hit on the base, he enters the citadel via hot air balloon ...

The last time we worked with him involved using cameras and a commercial shop front inside an arms fair where Mark set up a fictious stall selling spin doctor services to companies selling repressive equipment fingered by Amnesty and to countries with bad human rights records. The Indonesian high military command bit on camera, admitted torture and actually talked about hiring Mark. It was as if Hitler was persuaded to use Tony Hancock as his policy adviser. Mockingly surreal ...

---

9 Winston Smith is the protagonist of George Orwell's book 1984.

Another stunt of Mark's was to use Labour MPs' reliance on pagers for official guidance to trap them like sheep at their last party conference, beeping them all at once and asking them to call for more when Mandelson gave his speech. This stunt deserves an international following …

On a more academic front, the STOA report has spawned its own life and new work has already been commissioned by the EU parliament. I'm doing a chapter for a book on human rights and the internet and I will be speaking in Washington in April on some of the STOA stuff on Echelon. What has amazed me more than anything is that if radical groups like ours are given a policy voice at political level, then after a while it is not us speaking but the entire political machinery and the media go into overdrive. The internet has provided a very useful mechanism to multiply the impact of such initiatives to spread counter models and the reptiles in the media just feed on it.

(It's interesting that such communications interception networks are challenging environmentalists now. Just last week as the genetically modified debate took off in the UK, Friends of the Earth's phones went dead and Greenpeace's activities were stymied by a motorway interception when they were on their way to an action. Activists still do not understand how pervasive communication interception is with new interfaces on to GSM, mobile, emails, etc. being added all the time.)

19 July 2001

If you are intending to continue to follow up such resistance work, Omega is working with Relatives for Justice in Belfast to legally challenge the introduction of the new plastic bullet. I wrote a piece for the *Guardian,* 'A Shot in the Dark', on June 28th which covers the technical issues such a challenge might use. But I think we are perhaps just at the beginning of legally fighting back against such weapon systems. The European Court has recently ruled that the victims of plastic bullet usage in Northern Ireland had their right to life illegally taken from them, a judgement which has profound implications for challenging the misuse of this technology.

17 August 2001

The political situation is moving quite quickly here and we have had two new weapons introduced this year, the new plastic bullet and the advanced taser paralysing weapon. You might want some of this stuff for your files: the *New Scientist* piece about what I found when I walked into the Marine Corps HQ has been heavily sanitized by *New Sci,* but I thought I could bear the compromise for the worldwide audience it would reach. (The *Guardian* piece pressured other researchers to ask the Met [London's Metropolitan Police Service] if they were going to use Tasers and they went public—after which we challenged the safety assertions. (Brian Rappert has an amazing piece called "Moralizing violence"—have you seen it? It should be available on the statewatch.org site now.[10]) He's also done a piece on 'The Future of Non-lethal weapons in contemporary security policy'. I'll send you an offprint. We are very near to full deployment of these new weapons in a conflict like Macedonia or worse Israel (where they are already calling up reservists trained in maths and logic, which means they need their war planners at ready for a full-blown conflict with the Palestinians). In the meantime, I've been tracking developments in face tracking algorithmics and one system trialled in the UK has just gone to China. In these circumstances, I might leave the shell of Omega's largely surreptitious work and go more public whilst I still have a suitable time window. I'm thinking of re-entering academia—perhaps Leeds Met Uni where I can work with Eddie Halpin.

3 September 2001

Thanks for your encouraging words. I'm excited about the idea of working together more intensely next year.

Two factors might help this. I'm working with Eddie Halpin at Leeds Metropolitan University and have had preliminary discussions about beginning to work there part time in the department of informatics. Eddie has written about the use of communications technologies in resisting state violence, e.g. the B92 group in the former Yugoslavia and we have friends in Bangladesh who created the first web server for the country using two 286 machines but then had to invent a new language to give the local people access: Bangla.

So much is happening here, I'm beginning to wish we could create researcher clones. Colleagues at Omega have had a first bash at mapping the entire world's light weapons producers. This should go on line via NISAT later this year.

I'm working with Brian Rappert and Elizabeth Stanley and last month we set up an embryonic Critical Study Group on Non-Lethal Weapons. So much is surfacing in this area it is difficult to keep track. There's a 1st European Symposium in a couple of weeks in Germany which has many contributions

10 Also published in a modified form as Brian Rappert, "Moralizing violence," *Science as Culture, vol.* 13, no. 1, 2004, pp. 3–35.

on microwaves for use against humans and equipment. They include certain joint US and Russian initiatives which seems extraordinary.

Thanks for promising to send me a hard copy of your book.[11] I'll promote it here at all my conferences. (I'm doing one for the European Group for the Study of Deviance and Social Control later on in Venice this week. It's a critical paper on 'The militarisation of the police and the end of non-violence?' Don't worry though: I will contradict my own assertion saying essentially that after Genoa[12] we can expect more state violence and mass protests are 20th century—we need new forms. An interesting line came from George Monbiot in the *Guardian* about 'The Grannies From hell': elderly women going to live with Palestinian families in Israel which means any attempt to massacre will involve an internationalisation of the conflict as innocent foreign citizens become also illegally targeted—courageous stuff ...

If I get funding for telematics research, I would love to work on the jujitsu stuff you spoke of as a sub-project. I'm hoping to write for *New Scientist* again on algorithmic surveillance. All cameras including face and vehicle recognition are being linked up in London and this will be the template. Meanwhile the company Visionics who made the Newham face recognition system has just sold its system to China and it's also gone to Israel. In the meantime the CIA has set up one US company (In-Q-Tel) to invest in Safe-Web to fight cyber censorship in Beijing. Their software stops the Chinese censors determining where web surfers have been. Privacy International with Statewatch, ACLU and Omega had a conference earlier this year on surveillance by design which examined many of the paths to resisting such monitoring but change is moving apace. In Finland now they are beginning to conceive of using a person's mobile phone as their identity chip ...

10 September 2001

The Genoa G8 meeting and its fallout are still daily news in Italy and people can't quite take in that all their social and political rights were so easily suspended there. There is a wealth of new information on police tactics using agent provocateurs, stealing counter documentation from the media centres, engaging in pre-planned ruthless violence, etc. Plus lots of strange cameos. The police burst into one centre ready to beat those present to a pulp but were

11 *Technology for Nonviolent Struggle* (London: War Resisters' International, 2001), https://www.bmartin.cc/pubs/01tnvs/.

12 At the G8 meeting held in Genoa, Italy in July 2001, large-scale protests against corporate globalisation were met by severe repression.

thwarted by the presence of an Italian MP who gave them a severe ticking off saying they had no legal right to be there and to get out. This they did but then went on to attack the media centre but ambulances were so quickly on the scene to take the bodies away that protestors are saying that they must have been told to be on standby very early on.

What was quite odd about this protest in military terms was that the black bloc group of anarchists who were ostensibly the target of the police were bypassed when they decided who to punish. It was the much easier group of pink fluffy non-violent resistors who were so ruthlessly pulped.

The social resistance movement must examine what the required endgame is. If global protest groups take on the state head to head and mobilise at great cost to themselves, it's likely that all future G8 meetings will take place in areas where they can't easily assemble. Future protestors might need to begin to think through the dynamics of multiple gatherings over hundreds of sites but easier said than done … Yet even in bringing lots of people together in temporary places like in Genoa protestors run risks when pre-emptive policing raids take place …

Even as I write steps are being taken by activists to protest against DSEI (a big arms fair) in London's Docklands and a range of squats used by some protestors have been raided in a series of pre-emptive strikes. Usually this fair takes place near Franham and is really easy for the organisers to maintain security since it is so far away from normal life. Yet this time they have decided to hold it in the heart of the capital so many more people will attempt to protest. There is no chance that any of the sides involved will back off but it's curious that the authorities have given the organisers permission to gather at such a provocative fair in such an easily accessible place. We'll see.

13 September 2001

It looks as if we have gained access to the first EU Symposium on Non-lethal Weapons in ten days in Germany. The papers on offer foretell of a new generation of vortex ring and high-powered microwaves being deployed but this should give us a firm opportunity to quantify the level of progress they have made so far. Companies will be there promoting their wares, and wherever there is a company, Omega pricks its ears up.

It's like a game of electronic karma understood in the exact sense of every single act and thought creates repercussions which mate, conflict and co-operate with each other to synthesise systems which have enough strength and integrity to survive, replicate and pass their essence on. If you ever come to the UK, it might be worth introducing you to some of the former Provos who Buddha-like talked about the folly of going head to head with the state. These guys were honed down to bone and soul literally: their political work was done whilst they were naked, the writing materials a finger in the excrement on the walls of their cells during the dirty protest, and for a time the same people years later were doing the negotiation with their former adversary. At a micro level there are still many flaws since with this example the entire movement of all sides was permeated by other agencies with other agendas, and how to deal with such infiltration without the sanctions of death, kneecappings and the other fearsome paraphernalia of insurgent organisations is a moot point. Clearly it has to be both effective and consistent, otherwise those struggles just breed replicants of the old processes. Ironically the IRA and now the Unionists trained the RUC [Royal Ulster Constabulary] and the British Army to be the most effective in Europe and paradoxically, the RUC and the Army trained the Provos and the Ulster loyalist paramilitaries to survive all the weapons and state intelligence activities that were thrown at them.

I'll contact some of the people that were at our Vienna meeting for their website addresses. Some of the material reported was about agent provocateurs dressed like the black bloc anarchists and returning quite openly into police cars. This was new since they didn't feel it was necessary to hide anything from those present … but the record of what people saw was politically damaging. The activists appear to have been naive about the importance of the footage that they took to the authorities in maintaining a seamless official version of events. It's something your cyberactivism approach might develop: the need to get real-time digital images out onto a safe niche on the web away from official censorship.

Also the plain sensible approach of not concentrating all the most valuable evidence in one place where the authorities can steal it all on some mickey mouse pretext. It might also be worth looking at the Bstards, the Michelin Man characters that have so much padding that they can't easily be attacked or hurt by the police and are very visible.

28 September 2001

Brian Rappert and I, at literally enormous expense, gained access to the 1st European Symposium on Non-lethal Weapons earlier this week. There were several interesting presentations from manufacturers and government labs—particularly from the Netherlands—which focussed on anti-materiel applications which made me think of your work.

The key presentations covered the facility of even home-made microwave devices powered from between a suitcase or a small vehicle, to completely wipe hard drives or to mess up databank and communications systems. The effective distance varied from between 50 meters to more than 15 kilometres. Any cyberactivist caught in a major conflict guided by CIT [Computing and Information Technology] and sophisticated surveillance, tracking, monitoring and interception systems could be greatly assisted by such technologies.

Of course it's foolhardy to discuss such matters in depth just prior to the predicted Middle Eastern war we spoke of earlier this year. However, many of the companies are making commercial products to be fired against mobile communications platforms to wipe out their IT capabilities and relatively cheaply. The TNO people were configuring their devices using cannibalised microwave ovens together with commercially available satellite dishes which were directional. The technical data gathered was vital in terms of maximising certainty that a particular facility was no longer functioning.

15 November 2001

Events of September 11 have turned the surveillance world upside down. The failure of Echelon to discover bin Laden's handiwork means we get much more of the same. If you want to track what is happening in term of new surveillance powers in Europe, look up Statewatch.org and open up their observatory section.

I've just come back from Shanghai, so I'm wondering if you have seen Greg Walton's 'China's Golden Shield: Corporations and the Development of Surveillance Technology in the People's Republic of China'.

6 June 2002 (Brian to Steve)

Our first semester is coming to an end, so I have more time to think about writing. Here's a proposal for an article by the two of us on political jiu-jitsu and torture technology.

As discussed before, the basic idea of political jiu-jitsu is that when violence is used against a person who is nonviolent, this can rebound against the attacker. More generally, when the attack is disproportionate to the provocation, this can generate greater support for those attacked. The support can be from third parties, the camp of the attacker and the grievance group.

Torture is widely seen as inappropriate since the victim is relatively powerless. Therefore, to be seen to use torture can trigger a form of political jiu-jitsu. Torturers seek to inhibit political jiu-jitsu in various ways, for example by not admitting it in the first place. That no government admits to torture indicates the potential power of political jiu-jitsu in this area.

Our focus would be on inhibiting political jiu-jitsu through technology. Namely, torturers use torture techniques that don't generate as much outrage because their significance isn't widely recognised.

I can think of four case studies. There are undoubtedly many more, but four is enough for an article!

1. sensory deprivation
2. falanga
3. pepper spray
4. stun belts

These are used variously against prisoners (political and otherwise), "terrorists" and protesters.

In each case, we would describe the struggles involving science and communication. Specifically, authorities use the technique to cause pain and suffering that is not readily recognised as such by wider audiences. In order to counter this inhibition of political jiu-jitsu, grievance groups need to mobilise scientific experts, evidence, witnesses, language, etc.

The result of our analysis would be a series of recommendations for those challenging the use of innovative-technology-based torture techniques.

I think the easiest way to proceed would be for me to write as much as possible of the article, especially drafts of the discussion of political jiu-jitsu, the overall framework (introduction, conclusion) and whatever I know about the case studies. Then it would be over to you to add in material about the case studies, since you know so very much about them.

If you think this is worthwhile and you'd like to proceed, then let me know: 1. any comments on the plan for the article 2. your recommendation for a journal or journals.

I need to know the target journal and audience in order to write in a suitable style, referencing format and length.

Of course we could aim at more than one journal/magazine. Probably it's better to start with a more in-depth treatment. If we're satisfied with our analysis and evidence, we could then spin off shorter and more accessible versions. Ultimately it would be good to encourage activist groups to think strategically in terms of political jiu-jitsu.

6 June 2002

You've just caught me between journeys. I've just come back from Bulgaria, I'm on my way to China on Sunday and then on to Chicago before the month ends ... In the meantime I have a contract to write the consumer's guide to researching the repression trade with a July deadline and Omega is preparing the Northern Ireland Human Rights Commission work on plastic bullets and their proposed alternatives ...

So it's hectic, but I would never forgo an opportunity to attempt a joint article with you ... We are beginning to use some of your methodologies to legally attack some of the key companies and have set the dogs on one of the major UK distributers of MSP [Managed Service Provider] technologies with the result that their chief sales director has been arrested by the police and the company and its computers raided by the police. (I can send you some documentation on this. The inside story is much more intense.) In a further attack, we worked with a comedian to expose the loopholes in the EU licencing of firearms which was broadcast on Channel 4 TV—so humour can play a powerful role as ever ...

Taking these factors into account, it might be worth widening the scope slightly to get a richer set of case examples ... and take on some of the more professional human rights violators and their new technologies. My thinking is this: getting specific torture technologies tied to a specific violation is always hard especially when allegations of torture are involved. Company lawyers are part of each corporate and state defence strategy against your approach to political jujitsu and they need to be brought into the frame.

However, if we look at examples of state violence which involve torture and other cruel, inhuman and degrading treatments, then we can put the case in a much wider framework of international humanitarian law since according to the UNHCHR's police bible, the police force must be both proportionate, discriminate and minimal. (Have you seen this document? Maybe I can email it to you if I haven't already since it forms the basis in my mind of challenging future violations within a framework which is quite solid.)

Anyway, what I am imagining at the moment is the move from many-to-one torture which is still the most common, towards a new situation of mass punishment of few-to-many where the purpose is the gratuitous infliction of pain to anyone in a control zone, whether it is protestors, refugees, or mixtures of combatants and civilians. In the last few weeks we have been working with the Sunshine project in Texas attempting to get the documentation to look at the array of mass pain infliction systems currently being researched as part of the joint non-lethal weapons programme. Some of which include mass gassing with valium and other calmatives … These guys have no imagination in terms of what might happen next if a male army was allowed to rampage through a sea of comatose or semi-comatose civilians offering multiple opportunities for sadism and rape …

In some senses the act of research itself is a form of political jujitsu since it allows technical challenge to the assertions and smooth words of the military apologists. And even bringing this stuff out in the open is seen as an act of subversion because secrecy is part of the current landscape after September 11 and efforts are being made to close down documentation available from the National Academy of Sciences.

Such a widening might require a review of the case examples, the ones you suggest, namely:

1. sensory deprivation
2. falanga
3. pepper spray
4. stun belts

are certainly relevant. However, I would be hard pressed to come up with recent examples of sensory deprivation. Falanga is well documented but is a primitive technology; pepper spray is now well established and the wording of anything we wrote identifying a product would almost certainly bring a legal challenge which would have to be dealt with. Stun belts are interesting, not least because we have Muhammad Ali agreeing to be used as part of the campaign against them …

Off the top of my head, where would I go with examples? Well, we want success stories: examples of seemingly impossible targets, giants of domination and control which have been successfully attacked. We both agree that so little research has gone into countermeasures that whatever we write has to be writ large and inspirational and persuade those who can that they can make a difference … Just for the sake of argument what would my four examples be?

1. Echelon and global surveillance networks;

2. Electroshock, stun and restraint technologies;

3. Less-lethal weapons for punishment and control;

4. Legal systems and preventative systems to stop torture—and inhuman cruel and degrading treatment

How would I defend these choices? Well they ought to be both relevant and inspirational and preferably *new* and able to anticipate the struggles to come …

1. Echelon and global surveillance networks

Well, I couldn't resist the idea of targeting global surveillance systems designed to target dissenters and maintain economic inequality. Surveillance is used by all states to track dissenters and the anti-Echelon process is an example of how a small group of researchers have exposed and challenged these developments and how that battle will shift and adapt after September the 11th, particularly with the official statements made shortly afterwards saying that torture might be the only way of extracting information. And how will those friendship networks be located and targeted? We can mention the use of the Big Brother Awards, the Australian and New Zealand connections and the EU Echelon Committee …

2. Electroshock, stun and restraint technologies

There is a rich seam here. We have the wider Amnesty Stop Torture Campaign which has resulted in both EU and UN policy initiatives to prepare lists of torture technologies which need to be banned … Omega are involved in that process so we have the documentation. The restraint technologies, well we have battered the key companies again and again and are confident with the examples but the long term is to close them down—although they make all the UK police handcuffs too … The restraint belt stuff and the use of stun batons are well exampled by the prison in Arizona where the NIJ [National Institute of Justice] was using as a laboratory to test the utility of less-lethal weapons. An independent evaluator's report was seen as so damaging (they didn't tell him of their experimental status) they brought another evaluator in whose report was even more damaging and led to some far reaching changes … (Can you believe that this prison governor was making money for the private prison by selling online images from the CCTV in the women's shower areas to soft porn sites?!)

3. Less-lethal weapons for punishment and control

This section would enable us to look at pepper gas and plastic bullets which have been widely misused and the legal and policy challenges that have emerged out of them. It would also allow us to chronicle some of the legal challenges in getting documentation and the case against the US company selling tear gas to the Israelis even after they knew it was being misused for punishment. We can revisit the Patten Commission and examine how attempts at resistance also need a detailed technological assessment too if the claims of the proponents of these technologies are to be undermined by fact rather than by emotional outrage …

4. Legal systems and preventative systems to stop torture—and cruel inhuman and degrading treatment

I'm not so strong on this but where I'm coming from is that we do have a framework to stop people being tortured by states, to prevent cruel and inhuman treatment and with the World Court to bring perpetrators to account. Why doesn't it work? Well we have some examples of people arresting those like Pinochet who have been complicit in setting up torture systems but as yet no victory. Peter Tatchell was beaten up when he tried to arrest Mugabe … but the beginnings are there. Can we do an audit of the way that extant legal protections work or fail? And is there a need for a people's intelligence agency which can track what actually happens rather than the PR spin? What would a legal framework look like if human rights mattered? A three strikes and the CEO is out sort of approach for companies? I see this section as a shopping list of protocols and procedures for halting torture and human rights abuse if governments were serious and where the contradictions lie when states are charged with keeping us safe …

I had a tiny personal experience of this last week from a crooked money exchange in Bulgaria. The rate of exchange was 3 levs per pound but this outfit had reversed the buy and sell labels all in Bulgarian in a tourist area which effectively meant the rate was actually 2 levs per pound. It was a complete scam but most people just walked away.

I noticed how little money was given to me before the exchange was complete and said, I'm not happy with that rate, I do not wish to proceed. A heavy guy then arrived who spoke English and said that is the rate. We then exchanged arguments and his was that his boss set the rate and there was nothing I could do about it. The amount I was about to lose was small—about £10—but I thought about your jujitsu approach and decided to put it to the test. The odds were against me in that I was a foreigner actually doing sensitive research there so normally it would have been in my best interests to walk away. However, I thought if I give up then it's breaking a threshold and I will be tempted to withdraw in the future. So there is the question both of letting the sharks know that they could not always perform this scam and my reputation to myself …

So I said to the heavy guy OK, you'll do no more business here today since I'll inform every potential customer that you're a ripoff merchant and kindly ask them to go elsewhere … And I'll stay here for as long as it takes … 2 hours later they called the market security who arrived with guns and attempted to bully me into compliance except I was a foot higher. The bureau then closed … At this point I should have given up but decided to go to the police proper … this was a little risky but I wanted to see if my nerve would hold. I got there to find they didn't speak English but they were good humoured and with sign language they told me there was a separate agency charged with policing such scams: the Federal Bureau of Finance which actually licences the exchange booths. They also managed to say that a complaint from a tourist in a nearby resort had led to the exchange place being instantly fined 2000 levs. Great … so I went back to my original booth which had now re-opened. The look of horror on the guy's face when I resumed my place of turning away business was a joy to behold. I then said to him, I wouldn't want to be in your shoes on Monday. I'm complaining to the Bureau of Finance and I hear that just yesterday they fined someone in the next village that attempted to make this scam 2000 levs. It's probably not your fault, you were just following instructions from your boss—but he won't see it like that on Monday … you'll probably get sacked … it's a shame …

I was promptly given my money back and gained a renewed respect for non-violent direct action … If I'd have had the time on Monday I would have followed it through with a formal complaint to the bureau as well to add spice to the episode but there were other fish to fry …

8 June 2002 (Brian to Steve)

Your adventures and valuable interventions are always exciting to read about. Are you ever in a position to train others in your practical skills concerning the repression trade? (I wouldn't be very good at it but others would be.) There's a need for more investigator-activists like you!

I've taken note of points in your letter that I think are important for applying political jiu-jitsu to repression technologies, in particular the role of company lawyers and the idea of researchers as agents of social action.

After getting your suggestions about case studies, my preference now would be for us to pick a single area as the primary case study and to just mention others in passing. Probably the best case study for our initial purposes is your no. 2: electroshock, stun and restraint technologies.

A central consideration is whether there is evidence of mobilisation of opposition to the technologies following exposure of both their use and (e.g. via scientific studies) their harm.

Now some comments on the other case studies we've raised.

- Sensory deprivation: I included that in my list precisely because it's old. The acceptance of the term "sensory deprivation" suggests that this form of torture has been delegitimised. This could be mentioned as a brief illustration.
- Echelon etc.: this is a vital area to study but I think it's sufficiently different to be worthy of a separate examination. I'll think about how the analysis could best be applied.
- Less-lethal weapons of punishment and control: this would be fine as the central case study but I picked electroshock etc. in slight preference.
- Legal systems: these seldom invoke political jiu-jitsu. In fact, an analysis in terms of political jiu-jitsu *explains* why legal interventions are so weak. So this area will be included, but not as the central focus.[13]

Your story about the money changer is great. Your use of direct action (informing others) was the key. As soon as you tried to get officials to take action, that was something else—appealing to authorities—and less likely to be effective, at least in a corrupt or power-based system. In fact, the best chance of getting authorities to act is through direct action. Anyway, that's the theory. Congratulations on your insight and courage!

13 Steve and I had many more exchanges about our planned article. The material is most cogently presented in the published version: Brian Martin and Steve Wright, "Countershock: mobilizing resistance to electroshock weapons," *Medicine, Conflict and Survival,* Vol. 19, No. 3, July-September 2003, pp. 205–222, https://www.bmartin.cc/pubs/03mcs.html.

25 July 2002

As for torture jiu jitsu, I'll see what you say before making a final judgement but I'm a little uncomfortable with it since very few people have testified turning their minds and bodies successfully against these people. There are exceptions. Last year I went to an event with Mark Thomas where Kurdish dissidents were telling their stories with the line it was hilarious—and describing how they wore the torturers physically down. There is also the outcome with one of the electroshock sales people here in the UK who committed suicide after the second Torture Trail was shown. Pete here felt like quitting since he had never envisaged such an outcome. My view, which I had to be very clear about, was we simply held up a mirror to his actions and for the first time the guy made a moral decision. We didn't limit his options … His wife however was talking of taking legal action against the programme but didn't pursue it. In these glimpses I think there is a glimmer of understanding but I think torture jiu jitsu sounds beyond what we might be confident with achieving as a process of a regular basis. But I'll give it further thought.

27 August 2002

I'm preparing stuff on new disabling technologies for a special UN expert Seminar in October so the mind set will be appropriate—I'm looking at the emergence of new technologies for collective human rights violation. So much material is emerging on this now that it needs synthesizing. A paper has come to light via the US Sunshine project which is advocating club drugs and orphan pharmaceutical drugs as new calmative agents for mass tranquilization. They have even identified certain named receptor sites in the human brain to target chemicals to induce panic. Biotechnology will become increasingly important in the efforts of the state to deal with mass protest. I fear that the Iraq war will become the new testing ground since Saddam seems insistent about using the population there as mass hostages against US aggression—so to avoid being picked off by precision-guided munitions in the desert like before, the next Middle East war is likely to involve either mass casualties or hand to hand fighting against a mixture of combatants and non-combatants. It's a scenario the new US non-lethal warfare doctrine has been ostensibly designed to engage with. The outcome will probably be a bloody mess.

If it looks tight, I'll give you a referenced stream of consciousness piece which reflects my thinking and analysis. A prompt will usually work since when I work, I work fast …

21 January 2003

I'm moving away from the idea of using torture jiu jitsu—because the individuals being abused have so little power individually at that point. It's the network and later actions which affect the jiu jitsu of countershock. I think the countershock concept is much more powerful since it is not time bound; neither is it individualistic but process and network orientated. It encapsulates the idea that state terror spreads a shock wave for hundreds of miles but the process of countershock can spread resistance for thousands and focus it back on the state authorities from a multitude of directions. It can be street orientated, company orientated, or maliciously targeted at the communications network of a repressive state and it is a meme-like thing that can replicate and be evolved.

Inside our office we take the view that it's neither the policy nerd approach nor the activist approach that works. Legislation is important but if that is the endgame there is no audit, no check, no sustaining pressure. It's a question of both and more. In the case of electroshock, if we do achieve legislative change, we are not reliant on government to prosecute malefactors. NGOs and individuals can take action as they have in the UK. The countershock process is true jiu jitsu since it not only immobilises the perpetrators, it punishes the company, prosecutes individual stars and uses the press machine to whip up a media frenzy directed against people and companies and states of that type.

I shall be in Taiwan in the first week of April 5–9 and return date depends on availability of flights. (I'll be taking EC and UN stuff on torture technology regulations—have hooked up with friends who have promised to introduce me to the president, himself a previous political prisoner—the end game is to persuade him to ban Taiwan manufactured electroshock equipment, much of which is Chinese.) It would be such a coup to get that since if we target the major supplier states, many of the non-EU ones who will not be affected by the new regulation if it's passed, want to join the EC and their obedience to this regulation will be a condition of entry. South Africa is dependent on EU Aid and we can crank up the AI machine to put pressure on the authorities there. After Korea, if Taiwan goes that just leaves China and America and in the lead-up to the Olympics we can go into overdrive on China. America then becomes the number 1 pariah state.

3 February 2003

I've been trying to rethink some of your concepts and looking for examples of literal torture jiu jitsu. There are very few that I know of but one, a very remarkable human being who I've met twice, stays in my mind. He's a Tibetan monk, Palden Gyatso, who was a prisoner of conscience for 33 years. He told me he was tortured virtually every day—they starved him so badly, he ate his boots but when he was released (thanks to pressure from Amnesty International which he freely acknowledges in an interview with Annie Lennox) he travelled to see the Dalai Lama in Dharamsala. The Dalai Lama gave him permission to bribe the guards at his old prison and buy back the torture instruments used on him which he subsequently did. He has since travelled the world using these instruments to illustrate the human rights violations of the Chinese authorities, winning massive publicity for his cause. Look him up on the web—it's a tremendously humbling story but one which I think fits well into what we are trying to elaborate.

7 February 2003

So much has and is being done on these issues that it's easy to forget the victories and focus on the horrors than continue to come down the wire. The key I think from your work is that counter-shock is also a technology which can replicate and some of what we write is an instruction manual of standard procedures to do this jiu jitsu well and with the desired effect. I'll try to include a couple of examples where this hasn't always occurred and NGOs have completely fucked up. It's then a case of the opponent having the advantage and counter-counter shock. For NGOs this usually involves lawyers. No-one apart from activists or policy makers and the media use the term torture technology. Its seen as a smear in the industry and company lawyers are immediately put on the case. CAAT [Campaign Against the Arms Trade] after the Torture Trail managed to libel a company by sloppy writing. Omega fortunately had sufficient empirical evidence on the outfit COPEX to counter the libel accusation. In the end CAAT won damages from COPEX which they used to carry on the work—and I've not heard much of COPEX since the late nineties so the process left them much diminished. The case is an apt health warning but needs to be worded carefully to avoid repeating the libel or necessarily embarrassing the NGO. The key point is to provide a health warning, and encourage good and accurate reporting without being shocked, sued and put out of business, house and home by the commercial organisation being targeted …

6 March 2003

My timetable is pretty much finalised for the beginning of April now. I shall fly to Chicago on April 1, then leave for Japan on April 2, then to Taiwan on April 3–7. I think I might have told you about this journey but my goal apart from the usual peek at their security markets is to meet with either their President or Human Rights Commissioner to gain a ban on manufacture of electroshock weapons. The peculiar legal status of Taiwan makes this one tricky but the desired outcome is to get Taiwan to challenge the human rights record of China by banning the export of these devices on human rights grounds. The instruments to achieve this are ostensibly the EC draft regulation on torture technology and the UN draft document which I recently sent you. It helps that most of the manufacturing companies are actually Chinese. I'm not sure what the prospects are of pulling this one off but it's a pure leap of imagination in the dark and I guess no-one else is going to attempt the move so I shall …

Brian's notes on a visit to the Omega Foundation, 15 April 2003

Omega's attitude to surveillance is: "don't worry about it." Omega has been in existence since 1990. Companies and governments should know about Omega, but by their behaviour many obviously don't.

Omega's modus operandi: find a media angle such as a German tourist held in a Saudi prison using German manacles. The production details are vital, because general statements—for example, "shackles are used in Saudi Arabia"—are not news. The data are vital to protect against attacks, including legal action. Companies sometimes claim that they do not sell weapons to a particular country. Producing company brochures or documents from arms fairs exposes these claims as false.

Governments often use language to obfuscate their actions. For example, "No electroshock batons are sold to Saudi Arabia." Actually, the batons were given away, perhaps with backdoor payments or some other quid pro quo.

A woman made herself invulnerable to legal actions for defamation by having no assets, not being afraid of gaol, and having documents showing that her possessions were owned by others. For example, Pete had loaned her a toaster. Therefore, when the bailiff arrives, she shows the certificates showing that possessions are owned by others. (Information on this is shared among the participants. There is no single knowledge repository.)

Another idea: when personal items are put up for auction, two or more supporters go along and keep bidding by small increments, so auctioneers eventually give up.

27 May 2003

I've started sounding out the formal process for initiating legal change in Taiwan. They seem very keen to progress and it would be a good example for us. Taiwan sells a huge number of such prods to other countries which export them on. Since these countries like China and the US have human rights problems in their jails there is a logical case to ban such brokering and exports via them. Thus one simple single act can have a domino or cascade impact. It would be useful to think about this more deeply in terms of actions which are local and limited to meme-type actions which have a self-organising and replicating ability to reach out, influence and mutate to international levels.

The Germany visit provided so much new data. I think I have to find a way of getting some of it to you today whilst I remember. I'm specifically concerned by the human testing of the microwave weapon at 2km which caused heating. I think I mentioned that I asked about countermeasures and their black and white response was, "In the zone there are tourists and terrorists. Anyone who uses countermeasures like foil is not a tourist and we simply shoot terrorists." The other area of concern is plasma tasers. These can be used to spray a conductive aerosol which then allows lightning to be projected at the crowd. Curiously, the Russian presentation had almost exactly the same imagery including the same odd-shaped dummies. My suspicion is that the Russians are doing some of the basic science for Rheinmetall. There is a piece in this week's *New Scientist* on this quoting both Brian Rappert and myself but the presentations contain much more. Pete here pointed out that the aerosol would be subject to being blown away by wind so countermeasures would include wind making vehicles to literally blow back the conductive plasma.

The other technology there that drew my attention was a suitcase that could wipe out car electronics, disable computers, alarms, CCTV, mobile phones and any other electronics in the vicinity. A potential portable havoc machine on the high street, down a motorway or in a security installation or bank. I've not seen such an irresponsible invention for quite a while but one which could be of incredible value in times when peaceful challenge to an information-based tyranny was required.

I met Daniel Ellsberg in the early 1980's at a Pugwash student conference in either Yale or Princeton. I wonder if he gave a paper there because he was certainly at his most eloquent. What struck me at the time was the technology he used. Without the photocopier this act of backfire could never have been achieved and he was acutely aware of the significance of the this technology in giving him time to replicate his exposure of the Pentagon papers … and his kids without any training could aid the process, if my recall is accurate. Fascinating days … and useful because he was acting under acute pressure, with threats of exposure and worse so time was of the essence and safety better assured by mass replication of the new paradigm, initially to key individuals and selected media and through them to the world. A good example of a cascade via one specific initiation event.

Notice for Steve's talk at the University of Wollongong, 15 June 2004

Dr Steve Wright (Director, Omega Foundation, Manchester, UK)

Mass torture and full spectrum dominance

Since the days of thumbscrews and the rack of medieval times up to the "torture lite" now being served up for consumers at Guantanamo Bay, torture has been seen as a state service provided on a one-to-one or a one-to-many basis. Future exercises in "shock and awe" may change that pattern to an industrialisation of human rights violation through the advent of mass human paralysis using new laser, microwave, chemical and biological technologies designed to maim, mutilate and incapacitate but usually not kill. The technologies are now beyond the prototype stage and military scenarios to justify their use are, in part, already in the public domain. The key issue is who will control such technologies and how will human rights organisations deal with the flood of traumatised victims these weapons will create?

Dr Steve Wright is Director of the Omega Foundation in Manchester and a Visiting Professor in Informatics at Leeds Metropolitan University. He has researched the repression trade for 30 years, working closely with Amnesty International's International Secretariat to expose unsavoury deals, document the state of the art and where necessary undertake field research to reveal just who is colluding with whom. His 1998 report to the European Parliament led to the setting up of the Echelon Committee and a worldwide questioning of the politics of an apparatus capable of global telecommunications interception. He has a particular interest in the new generations of paralysing and incapacitating technologies and the prospect of their development ushering in a new era of mass torture and punishment.

11 November 2004

The Bradford conference was interesting on NLW [non-lethal weapons]—Jürgen Altmann has a German grant to do some scientific assessments which will be of enormous benefit to us in deconstructing the technics. For example the VMAD microwave system is meant to be self-limiting since it is allegedly just too painful to stay in the beam. However at this conference the pain impact on human eyes was questioned. Wouldn't a natural reflex response be to shut the eyes in response to the pain? Yes came back the answer. Well how would people then leave? Jürgen highlighted the contradiction. He said his preliminary assessment suggested there was nothing in the weapon's technical specification to limit human exposure to a certain level or a specific temperature rise. The implication was that blinded humans would simply continue to cook whilst they stumbled around in pain … One of our early tasks is to deconstruct the advertising around such weapons. All the proponents are incredibly sensitive to criticism. I was accused of racism at this conference after questioning the Israeli policy of targeting Palestinian children with both sub-lethal and lethal technology. (This fits your core hypothesis about attempting to rubbish opponents.)

Notice for Steve's talk at the University of Wollongong, 23 February 2005

Zapping the refugees: climate change and border control

New technologies under development are capable of inflicting pain on masses of people and could be used for border control against asylum seekers. Implementation might be rationalised by the threat of mass migration due to climate change, nuclear disaster or exaggerated fears of refugees created by governments. We focus on taser anti-personnel mines, suggesting both technological counter-measures and ways of making the use of such technology politically counter-productive. We also outline several other types of 'non-lethal' technology that could be used for border control: high-powered microwaves; armed robots; wireless tasers; acoustic devices/vortex rings; ionising and pulsed energy lasers; chemical calmatives, convulsants, bioregulators and malodurants. Whether all these possible border technologies will be implemented is a matter for speculation, but their serious human rights implications warrant advance scrutiny.

Dr Steve Wright is Visiting Professor at the Praxis Centre, Leeds Metropolitan University. He has researched the repression trade for 30 years, working closely with Amnesty International's International Secretariat to expose unsavoury deals, document the state of the art and where necessary undertake field research to reveal just who is colluding with whom. His 1998 report to the European Parliament led to the setting up of the Echelon Committee and a worldwide questioning of the politics of an apparatus capable of global telecommunications interception. He has a particular interest in the new generations of paralysing and incapacitating technologies and the prospect of their development ushering in a new era of mass torture and punishment.

Second variety

Janneke Schönenbach and Olaf Arndt

I. In Mancunia[1] – a personal remark

When in 2000 the writer Darius James presented us with the printout of a comprehensive appraisal, published by the EU Parliament's Scientific and Technological Options Assessment (STOA) Department, which bore the unwieldy title An Appraisal of Technologies of Political Control, our first thought was: this is "conspiracy theory".

The EU could not possibly have commissioned a non-governmental organization to paint such a dystopian picture of our future. The name of the group of authors (Omega Foundation) reinforced this view. If this was not "fake news", which was to be read in the 1000-page report, then good night, Europe!

We drove to Manchester. We wanted to know what was really behind it.

In the cramped office of a brick building from the "workshop of the world"-epoch, a bearded man rolled back and forth on a kneeling chair between his alleged 270,000 documents: Steve Wright.

Amongst the first things he spoke about was a commission by the European Parliament (EP) to conduct a series of three-year studies for the Human Rights and Democratic Governance unit, on the task of tracking the "armourers of torturers" through research work. The findings were subsequently published from 2001 in: "Future Sub-Lethal Incapacitating and Paralysing Technologies", as well as "The role of sub-lethal weapons in human rights abuse".

Wright said of this period of his work and life (in an email to the author) that it was:

> *So scary I didn't want to retain so much of the memory of the field experience though the policy continues to pulsate. I had to attend a committee of experts earlier this month being confronted by a possie from a top Pharma company worried about whether their exports of anaesthesia were going to be affected by our ban on execution drugs.*

1 Mancunian is anything from or related to the city of Manchester in particular: The Manchester dialect, also known as the Manc accent.

The fact that the EU solicited critical opinions on such issues and projects, which it funded with another unit, was new to us. Meanwhile, through Steve we envisioned for the first time the shiny façade of democracy and the laboratory of atrocities behind it.

A short time later we were hanging out downstairs in front of Omega's monstrous archive/bureau, in a fish and chip booth that had a deep fryer in which one could have easily baked three or four whales at the same time in bread dough. The cod that emerged from the waves of boiling oil was of appropriate proportions and delicious. This brought us to Steve's second favorite topic: food. "I'll stuff you with curry" was a sentence that was to come true in every respect that evening on the famous Manchester "curry mile".

A five-storey Chinese restaurant with an estimated 800 seats was the next meeting point with Steve the next day. Everything that was exotic, super-hot and extra-spicy and in at least one respect enormous fascinated him immensely.

The chap produced dazzling pictures without interruption: stories from a pre-war Afghanistan, a very young Steve, naked, dressed only in a floor-length fur coat, riding through the mountains on a horse freshly bought from the Taliban, were as much a part of the repertoire as the cheeky disarming of an FBI officer at a security conference in the US. A proof photo exists! Regardless, Steve was never big-headed or self-indulgent. The swagger and horror stories were an exact expression of the vitality that made him grow beyond the ordinary in his scientific and political work. His tangible horror at political grievances and weapon mis-developments was contagious and never abated.

When we returned home from Manchester a few days later, everything around us had already changed. Every page of the report was suddenly filled with life. We perceived the world differently.

This was only reinforced when we met Steve over and over again in Ettlingen. Down there in a part of Southern Germany that seemed to be pacified by prosperity, the Institute for Chemical Technology of the Fraunhofer Society hosted its Biennials for "Non-Lethal Weapons"—a trade show, carefully disguised as science, for all kinds of exotic prototype "boutique weapons" to shock, paralyze, torture and incapacitate. During these "holistic conferences" (from the self-image of the organisers), we could see all the latest batons behind the buzzwords and learned a great deal about incapacitation by extreme pain and inducing sleep. The Mantra, recited by chairman John B. Alexander, was that: "when you wake up and realise that you are not dead, you will be grateful to us".

Steve had elevated "conference" to a special way of life. We do not mean the agonizing, day-long endurance in poorly ventilated halls, which—already at the 9am lecture—were bursting with the sweat of the participants in their synthetic shirts. The special way of life developed in the evenings, for example in the Erbprinz, an exclusive restaurant located on the other side of the Bächle (the "little beck").

Because Steve wanted us to, we sat at a table with the cloned guys from MI5 and GSG9. Or in a wine bar with the Russians who had supplied the drugs for the gas operation in the Moscow Musical Theatre siege. Why should we also squat with the NGO frat boys? After all, we wanted to hear something new, not what we ourselves thought about the whole show. The jackets of the state functionaries lay crumpled on the old German-toned corner bench and the synthetic shirt sleeves were rolled up to better pack the German beer. Steve tickled out all the essential information about future defence technology projects out of people in the evenings, while he himself only talked about his favourite topics: food, good wine, travel. The guys flowed out. They would have loved to have a cool friend like Steve.

The willingness to talk blatantly about anti-human rights projects did not stem solely from the self-assurance that these projects would mean the ultimate "humanisation of warfare". To vary Benjamin's famous phrase, here you could "feel the wind blowing from the future"—but there were no Angels of History in sight: everybody was in the mood for departing into the wastelands of authoritarian democracy. One was allowed to be satisfied. After all, the German government had alimented these events.

The schizophrenia of such verbal contortions, which conflated "war" and "humane", resulted not least from the sense of community: among their peers, in the society of those belonging to the "conference" way-of-life, with everybody constantly jetting around the globe, every member felt safe. Here, contradictions could be healed, the irreconcilable could be thought together. Terms such as "holism" (meaning the holistic nature of the strategies of violence) and "revolution" ("revolution in military affairs") circulated—as a meaningless mockery of all social liberation movements.

If military and police representatives already generally live and act in the feeling that their version of reality will prevail in the end, regardless of political course settings or counter-movements by civil rights activists, then this feeling of omnipotence increased even more when the worldwide community came together over Saumagen (speciality of Palatinate: "stuffed pig's stomach") and Obstler ("eau de vie", mixed fruit brandy).

Steve's role was a risky balancing act, which perhaps only did not lead to the fall because the parties needed each other: on the one hand, he played the one who belongs, knows everything, from whom one need have no secrets. He played and won: they accepted him.

On the other hand, the representatives of state power wanted to know the arguments of their opponents in order to be able to include them in their "road maps". It was an ostensible give and take, a crude deal that was already pushing the limits in purely physical terms—after 10 hours of sitting in the conference room—when we continued to sit until ultimo, because the likelihood of tongues coming loose increased with every round of schnapps.

Steve's great achievement was to always maintain his integrity.

The lectures the next morning; you had to get through them. Highly attentive despite sleep deficit; everything had to be documented, and linked to what had been said in the pub the night before. How Steve endured all those years, decades, and how he managed to summarise what he heard, condensed to the essentials, to present it the next day in London to the "small arms" working group of Amnesty, to the ICRC in Geneva or at Pugwash, and why he was not shot for what he did (repeatedly exposing the arms lobby), remains an eternal mystery to us.

Our friendship lasted for almost twenty years, until Steve's death. There has not been a project we have thought up since then that did not involve his thoughts. From a cooperation for a robotic theatre on the topic of "drones and autonomous weapons" (2018 at the Kunsthalle Mannheim), a jointly written text was then created as a preview of our next cooperation, which now sadly must remain a plan.

Steve's typical way of writing cannot be reproduced in this text that follows, because it is partially a re-translation of the German version. But his style of thinking (in short fragments that were shot out like bullets) and his ability to immediately fascinate everybody around him with his barrage of ideas is clearly noticeable.

Steve was a great visionary. He taught us to fearlessly confront the horrors of the 21st century, a Philip K. Dick type of technology; out of control.

II. AI - Future selective assassination as a government service?

"The prospect of machines with the discretion and power to take human life is morally repugnant".[2]

The upcoming 5G communication and a multitude of smart, sensor-based, autonomous devices already in mass production, which are "autonomous", i.e.: controlled by algorithms, have brought the promises of a technical ecosphere full of "intelligent machines", which have been circulating for decades, within reach.

Seventy years ago, such an "intelligent ecosphere" was sketched lifelike as science-fiction: Second Variety is the title of a 1952 story by Philip K. Dick. The plot: in the near future of a Third World War, artificial intelligence (AI) has become decisive for war. Both world powers have upgraded autonomous killer robots in an arms race. In the end, the apparatuses have become so "humanoid" that not only are the "real" soldiers no longer able to distinguish them from their comrades, the fighting machines themselves also have their problems with it. The mission of all three existing "variants" is the same: sneak into the heart of the soldiers, penetrate their positions and kill everything humanoid there. The dystopian narrative ends with Dick's typically sarcastic hope; the protagonist watches as the robots' various clever versions begin to destroy each other and die.

When we started talking about autonomous killer robots, we found ourselves musing about a DARPA programme of research to make robots hunt in packs for "uncooperative humans"—like dogs to the tune of who let the dogs out. Few thought then that a sci-fi notion of putting behaviour into these systems, that most of us would find terrifyingly obnoxious, could ever translate into real life. Yet we are now all collectively coming further into range.

Why? Well, such software is infinitely malleable. Other Dick-style robots were already on the battlefield as "buddies". They can lift up a wounded soldier and carry him back to base. "Comfort" women and men are being designed with artificial intelligence to mimic sexual partners, while autonomous vehicles now being manufactured for the civilian market are being aggressively marketed as the next revolution in military technology on land, sea, air and in space. But

2 UN-Secretary General António Guterres, 25th of September 2018. The full quote is available at: https://www.un.org/sg/en/content/sg/speeches/2018-09-25/address-73rd-general-assembly

not all these autonomous robotic systems look like robots and some exist in cyberspace to facilitate new capacities to go hunting—based on the twin hi-tech powers of individual and collective identity recognition amalgamated with precision geo-location.

Second Variety serves as a provocative blueprint for some further reflections on the societal consequences of AI. This is less about the specific characteristics of a special code called "AI" than about the people who feed their machines with it—and their attitude towards society.

Core criteria of our civilization—such as democratic principles, sustainability, compatibility with basic and human rights, the right to work, the certainty that a state will never torture its citizens, in short: humanity—should be used as a benchmark for the evaluation of the predicted technical changes. For this reason, we put three theses at the end of the text, the answers to which should be linked to the obligation to act.[3]

The kalashnikovs of tomorrow

> *If any major military power pushes ahead with AI weapon development,*
> *a global arms race is virtually inevitable,*
> *and the endpoint of this technological trajectory is obvious:*
> *autonomous weapons will become the Kalashnikovs of tomorrow.*[4]

With the end of the Cold War, cybernetic technology, previously a tool to logistically manage and guarantee the balance of power, has obtained a new role. But behind what can be called the economical shift of cybertech—a manifest demilitarisation—and along with opening the iron curtain for global trade, a new kind of warfare has entered the stage: "AI war", using autonomous weaponry systems, that, according to Noel Sharkey, once activated or launched, decide to track and select its own targets with no chance to be stopped by human intervention.

In the early post-war phase, artists and designers working for the defense complex sketched the future soldier as an operator of digital tools for remote control—with a helmet, wired gloves and inside a war room shielded with screens. The front of this war was "inside", rather than "out there" at the border.

---

3 In the sense of the "global ethics" Steve taught us.

4 Autonomous Weapons: An Open Letter from AI & Robotics Researchers, July 28th 2015, signed by Stephen Hawking, Noam Chomsky and 20,027 more scientists around the globe: http://futureoflife.org/AI/open_letter_autonomous_weapons#signatories

Operating from a distance does not necessarily mean that war this new war—which is called "asymmetric" now, since another enemy unknown to the classic combat scenario came into sight –was taking place in faraway countries. With "new threats" such as migration, terrorism and crisis-induced civil unrest, AI war was coming home. The putatively neutral operation executed by an algorithm came under the suspicion of incorporating a new kind of violence—that a fatal decision, the one about life or death, was now partially in the hands of a machine.

The drone ecosystem

Since the introduction of the technology, the estimated number of people intentionally killed with drones surmounts 5500. For every one suspected terrorist, there are 28 certainly innocent civilians—that is not only a high collateral damage coefficient. It is certainly also the tool that is unique in the history of mankind in terms of the physical separation of executioner and executed, the separation of guilt and punishment. Never before, under conditions of the rule of law that function in principle, has the sentence been executed so far in advance of a guilt analysis. Never before has an unlawful act of this kind been so firmly anchored in the state's instruments of action. Certainly, there are precursors to killing on suspicion in exceptional historical situations, such as revolution or war. But it does not seem unreasonable to claim that digitization, which allows distant execution from the war room, favours this structural change. The "huge opportunity" seized by the USA to remove disruptive factors in the political "ecosystem" and to divert attention from its own guilt is a fundamental violation of human rights. The method of target identification and tracking unites search engines, databases and the actors at the computers in a process that only from a greater distance looks clean.

Governing by lists

Jutta Weber (2016) states that the "disposition matrix", a killing database, is the main tool with which the US government conducts its global "war on terror" and through which targeted executions are increasingly institutionalised. The "materiality of the databases and the algorithms of thematic or personal data analysis" are subject to a "technorationality based on recombination" that favours the "production of possible future targets for a data-based killing apparatus in which human and non-human decision-making processes are intimately interwoven".

Targeted killings have so far mainly taken place in Afghanistan, Iraq and Libya. Outside of conventional war theatres, drones are used to kill in Pakistan, Yemen, Somalia and Syria. Many scientists like Weber are therefore working on strategies to ban so-called lethal autonomous weapon systems (LAWS). Their worldwide largest alliance is called the International Committee for Robot Arms Control (ICRAC).[5]

Through the technical principle of using databases and algorithms for path and target decisions, a strong non-human component is added to the human decision. Through the intermingling of the decision-making levels they become, as Weber says, "opaque", or deliberately inextricable. Ultimately, through the resulting disclosure of legal foundations and personal rights, autonomous vehicles and "lethal autonomous weapon systems" are structurally more closely linked to each other than is obvious at first glance.

Database as a new norm

At the end of September 2017, Stiftung Warentest warned against "connected cars" and the carmakers' apps; they are "data snoopers".[6] Anyone who switches on the apps would become a "transparent user". E-call, the obligation to equip all new cars with an emergency call system via a mobile phone sim card from 31st March 2018 onwards, would open the floodgates to data leakage. In Tesla, for example, the "Customer Privacy Policy" already announces that information "may also be obtained from third parties, such as public databases, marketing companies, garages and social media like Facebook.[7] The onboard camera also plays a part in data collection and transmits information to authorities or employers "if required".[8]

The policy of lists and their screening is fundamentally changing our way of life, which has so far been based on human autonomy and decentralized individuality. It puts centrally controllable life in its place.

Weber's attested opacity, the inextricable data jungle that grows around us, blurs the boundaries between suspicious and unsuspicious action. One is potentially guilty of deviating from the norm of the database.

---

5 https://icrac.net/2014/06/banning-lethal-autonomous-weapon-systems-laws-the-way-forward/

6 https://www.test.de/Connected-Cars-Die-Apps-der-Autohersteller-sind-Daten-schnueffler-5231839-0/

7 https://www.tesla.com/de_DE/about/legal

8 http://www.spiegel.de/auto/aktuell/stiftung-warentest-auto-apps-sammeln-viel-mehr-daten-als-noetig-a-1169811.html

It is therefore questionable whether the use of autonomous devices is at all compatible with our ethical ideals and legal requirements for self-determination. Technical autonomy could easily lead us to an unconditional militarisation of the civilian.

"Find, fix, finish"

With a comprehensive autonomization of private and goods traffic, a NATO project from the mid-1970s is once again coming to the fore; that of satellite-based universal planning of all movements of goods and people, on which several generations of US presidents have worked. Ronald Reagan projected it into space, Bill Clinton wanted to use it to find and neutralise the USA's enemies around the globe within five minutes, Barack Obama perfected the 3F ("find, fix, finish") program. All the effort in vehicles, logistics and control technology—according to Virilio (1978), the only reason is "to challenge every human movement on earth". The regime of drones, propagated by the USA as the only efficient protection of Western societies, illustrates this idea impressively.

Communism questioned freedom of movement because it believed it knew better than its citizens what was useful to them. In order to position itself against this, industrial capital has suggested to the citizens of the Western hemisphere that good is only what gives them the greatest personal advantage. The most useful thing is the acquisition of complex, extremely expensive means of transport.

Neoliberal financial capitalism, the economic system belonging to the authoritarian-military, post-democratic state and its autonomous vehicles, believes that movement must be better controlled. For those who move freely are difficult to control and thus hardly subordinate to the omnipresent sales interests.

The machinic milieu

Under the "computational regime" (Rossiter & Zehle, 2015) and with the disintegration of the borders between the civil and the military, weapons turn into tools. They "migrate" into all day life and thereabouts become indistinguishable from non-violent digital hard- and software.

This is why we feel the need to build a strong system of ethical and social criteria, to prevent the unperceived proliferation of cyberweapons and thereby strengthen the distinction between the military and the civil, which is essential to a well-functioning democracy.

With all advisable respect for the need of security and a well-fortified society, civic empowerment must imply that we all benefit from keeping the digital drawbridge down.

If democratic states introduce a "total" machinic milieu which fulfils the pledge of security, they tend to replace compassion, one of the biggest show stoppers in the theatre of economical operations, with efficiency.

The "soft" (as in software) milieu carburises racial segmentation—for the sake of fortifying a definition of property and wealth that crystallises in a mainly industrial approach to a societal problem.

Gated communities

Algorithmically controlled weapons systems will no longer be exclusively used in the "war on terror". They are already on their way to the arsenals of modern democracies and will be used as part of the EU's "smart border programme" to control the 50,000-kilometre Schengen border, in order to repel the flow of refugees from Africa and West Asia.

Therefore, this project investigates the appropriate societal countermeasures and tries to enable visitors to qualify their opinion about the topic, encouraging them to take up a position for a more humane future.

In times of crises, the urge for protected spaces and exclusion is an epidemic. It seems only a hop, skip and a jump from gated communities to digital fortress walls circumferencing whole continents by means of drones, robot hunting packs and powerful IT hubs connecting all. Then, borderland is all over, in airports, malls, at home, around the estates of the new rich.

This is not a dystopian vision, but cited from the present EU science and research programmes such as Horizon 2020, or the already operational Talos robotic border-guard funded by an EU research programme. In conjunction with the daily dose of dramatic images of the sheer endless streams of refugees crossing into Europe and the moral panic that is ensuing as we speak, we witness a rapidly expanding set of new industries dedicated to either private or state security and political control, or to yielding new arenas for war in cities or asymmetric defence along borders.

What we call the "digital age" takes physical shape under such conditions. The welfare promise associated with "algorithmic reliance" unveils as a scramble for "solutions" that cannot be made without dismantling the current world economic order, structural violence and the flow of wealth from poor to rich.

That is why, as renowned philosopher Saskia Sassen (2014) argues, the new concept of "expulsion" is replacing everything that has previously been termed as "inequality".

Imagineering the new warfare

Such concepts of security are highly imaged using glossy DVD movies and power point presentations, quite simply because the politicians making decisions on whether or not to provide financial support rarely have the scientific and technological expertise to make an informed decision.

New varieties of internal security warfare are emerging with Hollywood "imagineers" on the payroll, projecting dreams of technological omniscience. At a time of economic crisis, such programmes are more challenged but since some of them are devoted to dealing with foreign infiltration, terrorist and counter-riot risk factors associated with the economic downturn, their institutionalisation into our future social fabric seems inevitable, whether in war, or prisons, at borders, or in the hands of the riot police.

From wire to data

Of course, there is a lot of extremely sophisticated hi-tech on the horizon—nevertheless, current solutions will mainly be standard military and police fences, weaponry, riot control and surveillance. Why do we nevertheless need to look into the future already today?

Tools and weapons for digital security management are the crystal ball of the fortune teller which visualises the way we conceive ourselves. With good cause, "avantgarde" is a military term: we are testifying a seismic shift from wire to data, from projectiles to immaterial stunning and stopping technologies.

Brutally "smart"

The adoption of "smart" digital tools masks the brutal responses to current societal catastrophes, branding them as "life-saving surgical operations". By turning migration into a "technical problem" and Europe into a fortress, both the financial world and the weapons industry seem to consider it best: if the problem can be technically fixed no changes are needed to the Constitution. Inside the fortress, the existing status quo of law and order remains untouched.

Migration industry

In addition to this, the rash of holding centres and warehousing rapidly being assembled is all based on European Parliament money; this is what Lampedusa expert and professor of intercultural communication, Heidrun Friese (2015), calls "the migration industry". Through a special kind of "capitalist sorcery" (Stengers & Pignarre, 2015), hi-tech push-backs, sci-fi style police rearmament, border control with drones and robot hunting packs, plus containment, turn out to be a giant money-making machine.

Data with no prejudices

The former head of the BKA, Horst Herold, has called dragnet investigation, or Rasterfahndung—a very early form of digital security management or computer-assisted profiling—the most fair or "just" criminal detection method ever. He thought that digital data management will erase prejudices from police investigations. In the late 1970s, he might not have foreseen targeted assassinations from 20,000 km distance, with an operator on the joystick and pre-programmed collateral damage. He would not have believed that data-access might turn out to be a bigoted and highly biased trick to save oneself from feeling responsible for out-of-favour behaviour.

Both the fast-paced redistribution of wealth euphemistically called "hi-frequency trading", and the new IT-driven arsenal for automated monitoring, identifying and paralysing or killing people, are two sides of the same coin; the organised dispossession of all less-organised people. Insofar data is genuinely racist, the new tool to manifest class divides, the most cold-blooded instrument to select who is in and who is out.

The technopolitics of exclusion

In light of the adverse environmental and societal effects of the long history of exploitation of humane and natural "resources", a process which was dramatically accelerated in the age of cybernetics and fuelled in a breath-taking way by moving from an analogue into a binary world, the ruling class decided to adopt the very means that sharpened the conflict and pulled the digital drawbridges around Europe's 50,000 km long Schengen border.

The have-nots which knock at the doors obviously lack that of the must-haves: they have no papers, no money, no access. Egalité, once one of the three main liberating keywords of the French Enlightenment, becomes a trap for 99% of the inequal.

All this enables the political decision-makers to hide behind their shiny technologies. The immanent violence of the algorithm, which always seems to "decide" on the side of fairness in its stoical way of equalising all individual fate, is invisible at first glance.

The technopolitics of exclusion manifests the political will to select the dispensable personnel from the project of Civilisation. To give it a more humanitarian sheen, they are sorted out by (seemingly) clean criteria that any machine can scan.

Execution as a government service

We might ask whether a new norm is emerging, that of "whatever is feasible becomes necessary". In an era of so-called fake news, the truth is more likely to emerge from contradictions, especially against claims that only bad guys got killed. The Bureau of Investigative Journalists website has been very helpful in the past, and they have done a great deal to deconstruct US SAG reports from Wikileaks to reveal the scale of official lying, when it comes to murdering civilians using drones. Even the pope can have a role, since earlier this year he came out categorically against any form of execution as an affront to human dignity.

Indeed, Europe has a specific policy of opposing the death penalty and all imports and exports of associated instruments. Well, if a drone is specifically programmed to execute a named person or group of people based on gender, race, sexual orientation or dress, then no should mean no, but will it?

In practical terms, this means looking for evidence of "affordances" regarding future robot killing. What needs to be in place for it to be a feasible reality, so each gap between potential innovation and future deployment becomes less and less? We might identify: a precise architecture of surveillance for guidance; accurate geo-location tools; accurate identity recognition through vehicle numberplate, face or other biometric data; working algorithms to separate good guys from bad guys in terms of set ID, behaviours, sexual orientation, ethnicity; additional corroboration—for example digital search of mobile phone contents from a distance—and so on.

It's the algorithms, stupid

Yet surely the idea of autonomous weapons technologies is decades off? We have not yet gone through the looking-glass into the world of "Black Mirror", or are we? Many existing drone systems work on having a human "on the loop" rather that "in the loop". In other words, they are semi-autonomous already, merely seeking human permissions as part of a legal fiction for accountability's sake.

The aforementioned ICRAC is working on legislation through the UN to ban such technologies before they are ever deployed. The worry is that such deployment will happen through a myriad of breakthroughs or "affordances", which make what was once impossible entirely doable. Often such breakthroughs will be secret, although where they do break into the open—such as Google staff quitting because their company was cooperating with the Department of Defense to share harvested face images to help program drone targets—they must be challenged.

Other weapons companies are gearing their weapons up into neural networks linking body cameras and neuro-muscular incapacitating systems. When the weapons are switched on the cameras automatically record. It is a short step away to make the opposite process work, so when the face recognition cameras see someone on their database, the weapons are automatically switched on, or a drone launched. The company concerned is international, with a finger in most EU and international police forces and military units—while also being highly litigious—and is already buying up AI assets and, of course, setting up responsible ethics committees (hopefully devoid of the usual white collar mercenaries).

Follow the money

We all now need to look carefully into the new economics of border control currently being prepared and planned by the EU. The British NGO, Scientists for Global Responsibility (SGR), reported on a rapidly expanding EU Defence fund with a total €13 billion planned for 2021-2027.[9] Restrictions against using this for border defence and autonomous weapons research were reportedly removed by the Council. This was later followed by an announcement over the summer that the Commission will now be asking for 30% more. The funding is in addition to the large national military budgets and a further even larger fund for joint European military operations. The SGR highlights the lack of appropriate governance; being outside of formal EU structures, it would avoid treaty restrictions on funding such military activities.

We need to develop effective opposition to arcane EU defence budgets that few are watching but that will yield a paradigm shift in capacities, if they are not effectively challenged and blocked.

---

9 http://enaat.org/wp-content/uploads/2018/11/181115_ENAAT_JointStatement-DefFund_FINAL-with-signatures.pdf

Auditing future security proposals as if people mattered

At the time of writing, a further new report on "hothouse earth" was published, warning of the dire effects emerging from a 2-degree climate changed world.[10]

Indeed, even a glimpse at today's news might support such a dystopian view. Heatwaves across Europe, Japan and even the Arctic; climate induced breeching of a dam in Laos; devastating and deadly fires near and around Athens which have seen people rushing into the sea, now Portugal and California. For many of us these are just harbingers of the much worse spasms to come. All the while, the drum beat of securitisation spells out a different message.

However, we need to guard against the deepening psychic effects of ever more securitisation: nearly a million prescriptions were issued to kids in the UK for anti-depressants last year. Just yesterday, the BBC reported that self harm by girls in the UK doubled last year.[11] Of course, it is not just in the UK but across Europe and beyond. As austerity budgets cut meaningful social, educational and welfare expenditures, a whole new generation are facing starkly difficult times.

Our challenge is to devise solutions or alternatives which might spark hope, without necessarily "sugaring the pill". It is about choices and encouraging all generations to care about and to question the security options they are offered. The focus of meaningful culture in such difficult times is to provide an early warning and to empower resistance. Current security measures often represent a protection racket for the already secure, whilst the dispossessed get diminishing returns. Essentially, it is a morality tale of citadels, sentinels and ever shifting and increasingly dangerous boundaries. It is no coincidence that part of the EU deal with Turkey was to rid Europe of inconvenient migrants. Turkey's response was to build a wall with Syria with lethal automatic robot machine guns, every 300 metres.

How can we tell that story?

Maybe, rather than writing academic texts, we need to invent autonomous robots that hunt the manufacturers of these weapons and related components to their elite lairs with a return to sender mission? Or hacker-like research activists who reveal the shareholders in those companies that build the walls and the drones from Israel to Mexico? Or maybe a morality tale where young people are encouraged to no longer work for the military but to sign up to

10 https://www.bbc.co.uk/news/science-environment-45084144

11 https://www.bbc.co.uk/news/newsbeat-45082767

a Hippocratic oath for scientists and engineers? The academics and scientists will research and publish fine papers on the logics we now face but few will read. Many more will engage with artistic endeavours, performances in public space, die-ins. Our hope is that these informed encounters will help persuade all generations to support a greater people's involvement in auditing proposed "security solutions".

Our challenge as ever is to learn to think in a new way—as if all people mattered.

Humanity

When we carefully listen to the sound of autonomous technology, we perceive echoes of Zygmunt Bauman's (2000) liquid modernity and the notion—in his book Wasted Lives: Modernity and its Outcasts (2004)—that a whole class of people are being designated as flawed consumers. The horror here is that as in the sci-fi movie Soylent Green, it is as if we have evolved technologies to consume us since more money can be made from that process. Think migrants, political cowardice, detention camps and the rise of political hyenas demanding the end of humanitarian treaty obligations.

Such is the notion of a "toxic masculinity"—personified by the likes of President Trump but becoming a role model for the siren voices from the right, preaching that we could become great again if it was not for "them". Where is the caring dimension which marks us out as human, focusing on power with rather than power over?

Losing humanity comes with a tremendous price to pay.

III. Appendix: AI white paper

Assumption 1

The talk of AI has already had a lasting impact on our lives, although AI has hardly been used in practice to date. It will influence our everyday life even more intensively the more areas of life it penetrates.

AI has the best chances of becoming the "fifth cheap"—according to the theory of global ecologist Jason W. Moore.[12] Moore speaks of "four cheaps", without which capitalism could not function, and he means quasi-free labour, and quasi-free energy, food and raw materials.

12 See: https://jasonwmoore.com/

Confidently, we can therefore already now consider AI as the resource of the future. The question that needs to be asked about assumption 1 is: What is the goal of AI?

Upgrading AI to an acting subject is intentional and should be placed in contrast to the labour force as an autonomous agent.

Assumption 2

Because "nature" only exists in our heads, natural intelligence can easily be replaced by artificial intelligence. As Bruce Sterling (2000) suggested, physical substrates belong to the "good old-fashioned future" and therefore are "dead media".

In any case, almost everything that exists today and may appear like nature is made by us from what we have received "for free" at some point.

If assumption 2 is correct, artificial intelligence will not only replace today's "reality" on a large scale in the future. AI will inevitably also become political, just as Jaron Lanier claimed two decades ago about virtual reality.

The question that needs to be asked in connection with assumption 2 is: What kind of politics does AI make?

Assumption 3

One of mankind's fantasies of omnipotence is that everything that people invent is controllable. Added to this is the mistaken belief of geoengineers; what we may have broken, we can repair with the same logic inherent in man-made destruction.

The Faustian temptation to find out how to breathe life into dead matter in order to subjugate an "artificial intelligence" has found expression in countless immortal literary texts, from the "Knopfgiesser" anecdote in Ibsen's Peer Gynt to Meyrick's The Golem, to Shelley's Frankenstein. In every single case, things are getting out of hand.

Assumption 3 is thus: this is what will happen with AI. "Neural networks" and "self-generating", "learning" code could prove to be the new monsters.

The question that needs to be asked about assumption 3 is: What must "meaningful human control" look like that does not let a massively spreading AI become a dangerous revenant?

References

Arndt, Olaf; Stefanie Peter, and Dagmar Wünnenberg. 2000. *Hyperorganisms, AI and Society*. Hannover: Internationalismus.

Bauman, Zygmunt. 2000. *Liquid Modernity*. Cambridge: Polity Press.

Bauman, Zygmunt. 2004. *Wasted Lives: Modernity and its Outcasts*. Cambridge: Polity Press.

Friese, Heidrun. 2015. "Border Economies – The Nascent Migration Industry". In: Cecilia Wee, Janneke Schönenbach, and Olaf Arndt (ed's). *Supramarkt*. Sparsnäs: Irene Publishing, pp.195-220.

Rossiter, Ned, and Soenke Zehle. 2015. "Parametric Politics – Imperial Infrastructures and Systemic Dispositions". In: Cecilia Wee, Janneke Schönenbach, and Olaf Arndt (ed's). *Supramarkt*. Sparsnäs: Irene Publishing, pp.325-336.

Sassen, Saskia. 2014. *Expulsions: Brutality and Complexity in the Global Economy*. Cambridge, MA: Harvard University Press.

Stengers, Isabelle, and Philippe Pignarre. 2015. "Needing People to Think". In: Cecilia Wee, Janneke Schönenbach, and Olaf Arndt (ed's). *Supramarkt*. Sparsnäs: Irene Publishing, pp.463-491.

Virilio, Paul. 1978. *Fahren Fahren Fahren*. Berlin: Seite 53.

Weber, Jutta. 2016. "Keep adding. On kill lists, drone warfare and the politics of databases". *Environment and Planning*; Society and Space. 34(1), pp.107-125. https://doi.org/10.1177/0263775815623537

Imaging war and the regional defence economy

Dave Webb

Working with Steve was always quite an experience! I was always amazed and impressed at how much information he retained and could pull up when needed. Unfortunately, my memory is nothing like as good and I apologise in advance to anyone for any important event I have forgotten, left out, or got wrong, in what follows.

Steve possessed an amazing mixture of information, stories, contacts. His background in Science and Technology and Peace Studies was crucial in establishing our research centre and the peace studies courses that emerged at Leeds Metropolitan University. There is not space to go into it all but there are a few memories in the following.

Those first steps

It was Eddie Halpin who introduced me to Steve, and I soon discovered that we had common interests in the possible uses and misuses of technology, in peace, conflict, human rights and also in Menwith Hill.[1] Menwith Hill is the huge U.S. spy base just outside Harrogate in North Yorkshire, run by the U.S. National Security Agency (NSA) which is responsible for signals intelligence (SIGINT) activities. The base is part of a global system used for the interception of electronic communications, both military and commercial.

Information from a range of satellites is downloaded there via a large number of highly visible dishes covered by white 'radomes'—which gives them an appropriate eerie futuristic look. The satellites themselves are used either to relay signals—electronic messages—of all kinds (from phone, fax, email, etc) or to intercept them. The information gathered is then interrogated by powerful computers to find communications that may be of interest to U.S. security, military or commercial interests. Selected data is then passed on to the NSA HQ at Fort Mead in Maryland for further processing.

1 https://yorkshirecnd.org.uk/campaigns/menwith-hill/

Long before the Snowden revelations that implicated Menwith Hill in the huge U.S. global spying operations network, Steve had been researching into ECHELON, a now out-of-date code name given to the NSA's interception capabilities. He was author of a Science and Technology Options Assessment (STOA) Report for the European Parliament in 1998 called *An Appraisal of Technologies of Political Control.*[2]

Steve loved to stir things up a bit and this report certainly did that. One of the sections was on 'Developments in Surveillance Technology' and mentioned the work of Nicky Hager, Duncan Campbell and others who had helped uncover the details of ECHELON which implicated Menwith Hill in illegal U.S./U.K. surveillance activities. It also mentioned a report by 'Statewatch' on how "the EU had secretly agreed to set up an international telephone tapping network via a secret network of committees established under the 'third pillar' of the Maastricht Treaty covering co-operation on law and order". A follow up STOA report by Duncan Campbell, *Interception Capabilities 2000*,[3] was approved and presented to the parliament in Brussels in February 2000. In this report, Campbell described how the spying being carried out was also used to benefit U.S. commercial interests by intercepting competitors' bids for big contracts. Steve and Duncan's reports led to the European Parliament appointing a committee of 36 MEPs to further investigate the ECHELON system in July.

The events on September 11 the following year put an end to further investigation, as the case was made that the use of the global surveillance system, including Menwith Hill, was needed in the search for terrorists and terrorist organisations.

When we first met, Steve was still working for the Manchester based 'Omega Foundation', and Eddie was keen to include him as part of a research group we were putting together. So, through the Faculty Research Committee, Steve was established as a visiting professor and together we developed the 'Centre for the Study of Information and Technology for Peace, Conflict Resolution and Human Rights'. The aim of the Centre was to "create a multidisciplinary research group within the University who share common interests located within the Faculty of Information and Engineering Systems" at Leeds Metropolitan University, and included a number of fellow travellers from different departments around the University.

The Centre eventually became 'the Praxis Centre for the Study of Information and Technology in Peace, Conflict Resolution and Human Rights', which

2 https://cryptome.org/stoa-atpc.htm#4.

3 https://www.cyber-rights.org/interception/stoa/interception_capabilities_2000.htm

was launched on 26th March 2004, during an afternoon seminar under the heading, "The Pledge for Peace for Children: Reality or Hope?" It was opened by the Vice-Chancellor, Professor Simon Lee, and Tony Bryant, Professor of Informatics and head of research in the faculty. It featured a talk by a friend and colleague of Steve's, Rae McGrath, a founder of the Manchester-based, Nobel Peace Prize winning organisation, 'Mines Advisory Group' (MAG). Rae spoke on "A practical vision of the reality of children of war, the explosive remnants of war and the results that follow". Other speakers included Andrea Khan, Policy Analyst and Researcher, Advisor on Children's Rights to the Senate of Canada; Rebecca Peters, Director of the International Action Network on Small Arms (IANSA), and Pam Dawes from Manchester Aid to Kosovo.

From here, we initiated or joined a whole range of projects. As we said at the time, (mostly in Steve's words I think), we were:

> *Adopting the premise that, in the 21st century, democracy can only work if there is a body of informed opinion with sufficiently honed information tools to efficiently challenge new security policy making – especially dis-information policies which seek to go beyond the limits of the law.*

We would attempt to examine:

- New technologies and their uses
- Privacy and data protection
- Civil liberties and the consequential effects on:
    - Civil Society and
    - Democracy and Governance
- Information usage and flows between NGOs

By this time Steve had a full-time job in the faculty and we were also developing new Peace Studies courses at undergraduate and postgraduate level.

Steve was always interested in the students and getting to know them. He was always ready to help and advise them on their work and future development. His stories and connections came in very useful too. He was also always out to shock and surprise them a bit, in order to motivate them into becoming involved and active. I still have a collection of some of the pictures of arms, torture equipment and possible future weapons technologies. He would slip one or two of these use in presentations to wake people up a bit.

He would often mention his work on Arms Fairs—where he would go undercover, pretending to be a customer, or just blag his way through the entrance, and gather information and take photographs of the range of deadly weapons and torture items that were on offer. He was also a friend of Mark Thomas and had worked with him for a TV programme that Mark was making about arms fairs. So, one day when Mark was appearing in Leeds, Steve was able to arrange a meeting and then persuaded Mark to come along to meet and entertain the students, which he did in his usual brilliant style.

Among the projects that we were involved in a couple stand out in my memory which are good examples of how Steve liked to work. The one I would like to focus on was developed from a common interest on how different academic disciplines viewed, researched, and portrayed war and conflict and also how individuals, the media and commercial entertainment industries view and interpret war experiences.

Imaging war: Intergenerational perspectives

This was a European Science Foundation (ESF) funded International Conference held at Vadstena, a historic town on the banks of Lake Vattern in Sweden, from 3rd – 7th September 2008. I cannot remember exactly how we came across the ESF project to fund international and interdisciplinary conferences—I think Steve in particular was always looking for ways to add to our contact list and encourage cross disciplinary exchanges. This was always a major aim of the Praxis Centre in any case.

We applied to the ESF using their submission form in 2006 and I think it was mostly Steve who wrote the following in the section 'Project Aims':

> We have entered a time of highly technological warfare, where over half of the world's research and development is now military and an ongoing revolution in military affairs (RMA) is changing the rules and weapons that will be used to define our common futures in a global society.
>
> Yet most of the public are getting their information on the implications of these developments, not from learned scientific or technological treatise but from the media, film, literature, computer games and simulations. The way that war is imaged varies considerably between artists, scientists, urban geographers, media theorists and indeed between generations. Given the controversies which form our daily news about the "War on Terror" and the projected need to give up our traditional human rights and civil

liberties, it is essential that we understand the role of the war imagers and their critics. There are many lenses to tell the story, including political, PR and weapons procurement; media journalism (which leaves out as much as it includes), games, stories, and literature.

This conference seeks to explore what these various cultures are saying to each other and how organised knowledge systems, scenarios and stories are used to legitimate or deconstruct new paradigms on war and its consequences.

The conference seeks to explore dissonance and common ground between the image builders and the image consumers; the weapons manufacturers and the story tellers; the politicians and the children. Given its timeliness and originality, we anticipate a wide audience for such an event and are seeking to include as many of the relevant dimensions of the topic as possible. We also wish to encourage different generations to participate and hope to open up some of the plenary sessions to the wider local community to enable them to engage with the scientific and cultural dimensions that the conference will provide.

We had learnt a lot about working with different groups and individuals from various subject areas from a one-day symposium that we had organised with Kristyn Gorton, who was soon to move on to the University of York and now is a professor at the University of Leeds. The symposium was held on 5th November 2007, so we had to call it 'Remember, Remember'! The aims were pretty much the same as for the ESF submission and we did manage to obtain a bit of, mainly internal, funding to support it.

One of the speakers at the symposium was Stephen Graham, then a Professor of Geography at the University of Durham; he and Steve had known each other for a while. Steve thought we should have two professors involved for the ESF Conference, so I was proposed as chair with Stephen Graham as vice chair, with Krityn as member so the organising committee.

There was a call for papers and we sent out invitations to some selected experts. There were some very interesting abstracts submitted from academics and professionals from around the world, who shared a common interest in the ways in which war is imaged, imagined and presented in, for example, film and photography, computer games, and the news media.

The Conference went very well. The setting was beautiful by the lakeside, in a wonderful hotel that was once a castle, built originally by King Gustav 1 in

1545 to protect Stockholm. The resources available were excellent, including a range of social areas and a bar which provided many opportunities for participants to meet, chat and exchange information and ideas. This was the kind of environment that Steve liked, giving him a chance to mix, get to know people, relay a few of his tales and make connections.

We spent some time looking for a Keynote speaker and eventually secured British War Correspondent Kate Adie. Kate happened to be in Sweden—she broadcasted 'From Our Own Correspondent' from there—so did not have too far to travel. She gave a very focused and personal talk, drawing on thirty years of reporting on wars in many locations, and also shared generously from her rich experience with colleagues outside the conference room.

Colleagues from widely differing disciplinary backgrounds, from countries that included Nigeria, Argentina, Sweden, Columbia, Brazil, the US, Bangladesh, Australia, Lebanon, France and Portugal, as well as the UK, contributed to many rich discussions and the sharing of ideas, theoretical frameworks, fears, hopes, predictions and experience.

An important aspect of the conference was that of "intergenerational perspectives". Sean Sutton, a photographer working for the MAG, told some powerful stories, illustrated by wonderful photographs, of his experiences with groups of all ages in post conflict zones. Similarly, Shahidal Alam (founder of the *Drik Picture Library and Pathshala: South Asian Institute of Photography,* and founder chairman of *Majority World*, a global community that provides a platform for indigenous photographers, photographic agencies and image collections) showed some fascinating photographs and film clips to illustrate how conflicts in Bangladesh and Sri Lanka affected young and old.

Before the conference we were taken to two Primary Schools in Linkoping by Anahi Otby, who teaches there. We were able to talk to the children there of their ideas and impressions of peace and war and were able to take some of their work (pictures, reflections, etc) to the conference where it was presented by Anahi. In addition, Johan Thomas from the Swedish Student Pugwash Group gave his impressions of "Youth Perceptions on Presentations of War and Conflict", discussing how the use of web-based technologies was potentially changing the way that young people interact with national and international events, including conflict and war. Ian Kaplan, another PhD student from Leeds Met., displayed some of his excellent photographs and gave a fascinating presentation of his experiences working with teachers and students in the Conflict Zone in Karen State, Burma.

Rachel Muir, a PhD student in Peace Studies from Bradford, spoke of her experiences as a humanitarian worker in Bosnia, while others spoke about humanitarian work in other places, including Angola. Several speakers drew on their personal experiences as the victims of conflict, including Ayeray Medina Bustos, one of our PhD students, and her twin sister Anahi Otby, who with Osvaldo Cesar Gasparini, spoke about the years of oppression in Argentina. Osvaldo, who has written a book about his experiences,[4] spoke movingly about being imprisoned and tortured for eight years in Argentina.

As we noted in our final report:

> *An important feature of Imaging War was the wide range of disciplinary and experiential backgrounds present, which included participants from film, photography and journalism; cultural studies and literature; physics and engineering; applied ethics and peace studies. The range of expertise and experience was equally varied with presenters and participants from frontline war journalism; the development of computer games; the critical analysis and appraisal of technologies of warfare - both past and future, along with others who had lived through and suffered as the result of war and conflict or had been involved in humanitarian work in conflict zones.*

Many new connections and contacts were made, enabling interdisciplinary and international cross-fertilisation of knowledge and ideas.

We were approached by three separate publishers who were interested in publishing papers presented at the conference, and a special issue of the journal *Peace Review*[5] was used to publish a useful and interesting collection which gave just a flavour of the rich discussion and interaction that took place:

- 'Truths' and 'Re-Imaging' in the Reconciliation Process" by Seidu Alidu, David Webb and Gavin Fairbairn;
- "Critical Analysis of New Weapons Technologies" by Jürgen Altmann;
- "(Un)Covering the Silence During the Argentinean Coup d'État" by Ayeray Medina Bustos, David Webb & Gavin Fairbairn;
- "Tracing the Logics of Contemporary Digital Media Culture" by Patrick Crogan;

4 *Dias de Prision: Memorias de Sierra Chica, Caseros, La Plata U9,* by Osvaldo Cesar Gasparini, Editorial Dunken, Buenos Aires (2008)

5 *Peace Review*, Volume 21, Issue 2 (2009) https://www.tandfonline.com/toc/cper20/21/2?nav=tocList

- "Remediating War in Iraq" by Kristen Daly;
- "War's Mental Health Legacies for Children of Combatants" by Aida Dias & Luisa Sales;
- "Empathy, Sympathy, and the Image of the Other" by Gavin Fairbairn;
- "Imag(in)ing Tomorrow's Wars and Weapons", by Charles Gannon;
- "Restoring the Story" by Gillian Huebner; and
- "The Meaning of the Peacelines of Belfast" by Emily Ravenscroft.

Steve, more than most, recognised the importance of individuals and organised groups to challenge norms. He could see that the military and their friends in government could not necessarily be trusted to work for the benefit of the common good. There have been occasions when this has happened, and these have been inspiring example of what humans can achieve. However, much too often there have been occasions when self-interest, corruption, sleaze and short-sighted greed have resulted in human and possible global catastrophe. Steve continued to work to support those who speak truth to power and question the motives and methods of those in control. He did this for as long as he was able—his contribution was so important, and his presence is sorely missed—our struggles will be that much harder without him.

Reflections on the work of Steve Wright

Hendrik Bullens

It was at the very beginning of the 1990s, right after the end of the Cold War, that our ways crossed for the first time. That time can be remembered for the unprecedented spirit of optimism, invigoration and confidence in a better and more peaceful future, which was shared by many. Catchwords indicating the high hopes, great expectations and new political ground of the time may be recalled here: cuts to military budgets; disarmament and de-militarization; destruction of conventional and mass destruction weapons; downsizing of the defence sector, thus creating a peace dividend for arms industry conversion towards civilian purposes; common non-violent security, sustainable development and global peace.

However, Steve and I belonged to the rather small group of people who had difficulties in sharing this downright euphoria (notably among the peace research community), of which we were very sceptical. Both of us had been working on the Military Industrial Complex (MIC) and we realized its unbroken power and kraken-like networks, against which President Eisenhower in great foresight had warned in his farewell speech. While particularly peace research increasingly focused on (mostly short- to mid-term) resolution of internal conflicts, Steve and I preferred to look at the bigger picture: Steve in terms of the interplay of neo-liberalism, militarism, arms- and repression-technologies; while I dealt with adaptation strategies of the state and the MIC during those times of (temporary) budget cuts. At the time I was a convener of the Security & Disarmament Commission, which published several books on these topics that Steve made contributions to.

To us, the growing discrepancy between the dumping of outdated and obsolete ordnance (sold to the public as 'disarmament') and the skyrocketing investments in new so-called intelligent weapons—military- and other security-technologies which were needed in a changed security landscape to wage what was called 'low-intensity conflicts and internal wars'—was too obvious. These new types of armed conflict were, as Steve wrote:

Largely fought with light weapons and small arms [...] Correspondingly the international arms trade is changing with a decline in the overall value of large weapon systems transferred, but with analysts forecasting quite large increases in the production, trade and transfer of low-intensity warfare equipment, training and technologies (Wright 1997, p. 93-94).

Today, this shift may have been balanced or even reversed, particularly since the Trump administration, but it was typical for the first decade after the end of the Cold War—and this became Steve's main area of research. Behind all this was the fact that although the armed wing of the MIC, NATO, had lost its 'communist-arch-enemy-in-the-East', and therefore actually also the justification for its existence, there was no iota of questioning the continuation of its political *raison d'être*, let alone its dissolution. It was these stirring developments that undoubtedly shaped Steve's professional concerns and career.

Following on from Steve's PhD research into 'New Police Technologies and Sub-State Conflict Control', he was certainly the right person to become head of the Manchester City Council's Police Monitoring Unit in 1985, where he gained and applied first experiences. In 1989, Steve moved to The Omega Foundation as its new director.

In this capacity he worked with the UN Register of Conventional Arms, UN Office of Disarmament Affairs (UNODA), UN Institute for Disarmament Research (UNIDIR), UN Small Arms and Light Weapons (SALW), the European Commission, Amnesty International and other NGOs engaged in Human Rights violations and torture. Steve's innovative contribution dealt with the production, sales and trafficking of weapon-, torture-, execution- and surveillance-technologies, finding new sources, ways and techniques to collect and analyse hitherto widely missing data. These activities resulted, for instance, in the establishment of the OMEGA Data Base Project and his report on *Technologies of Political Control* for the Science and Technology section of the European Parliament (STOA). Notably, the latter led to political debates in Europe about the dangers of mass surveillance by the US NSA—long before the Edward Snowden leaks.

This work also needed a new type of investigation method, as Steve wrote:

Research on light weapons if it is to be accurate requires a newer and more risky kind of field research, entering the market place and the murky world of arms dealers, black markets, arms fairs and physically monitoring the often interchangeable trades in arms, drugs, and even toxic wastes (Wright, 1997).

As noted earlier, these were Steve's research topics when we met for the first time at the beginning of the 1990s. It was on the occasion of conferences and sessions of the European Peace Research Association (EuPRA) and the International Peace Research Association's (IPRA) Security and Disarmament Commission—one in Budapest, another in Malta, as far as I recall—when our cooperation and friendship began. At that time, power point presentations were non-existent or very rare, and Steve used a slide show accompanied by oral explanation, always in free speech—I never saw him with a written paper.

What he presented was the exciting state of affairs in a field research project on the tracking of the MG 3 general purpose machine-gun, produced and traded by the German-based company Heckler & Koch. Hundreds of thousands of these guns have found their way, both legally and illegally, across the world to conflict regions. In an engaging and virtually furious way, Steve depicted and presented how he had been tracing the illegal trafficking of thousands of MG3s—from the arms fairs and the company to an arms dealer, transported via secret distribution channels and dubious middlemen, to the final customers. Steve recounted how he was verbally and physically intimidated by Heckler & Koch representatives, how difficult it was to trace down the deal, as well as how he had received numerous anonymous phone calls threatening him if he would not stop the project.[1]

Furthermore, it was through such talks and discussions that I learned about Steve's own interpretation and wording of Karl Marx's concept of dialectical contradiction. In discussions about the question of whether the then-changes in the arms industry were rather quantitative decreases or qualitative increases through improvements, he used to answer: "It's never 'either-or' – but always both and more".

Steve also oftentimes addressed the need and chances for a substantial and true conversion of the arms industry, or more precisely: how these chances were not used and even mis-used. In the same paper he referred, for instance, to 'Pseudo-conversion', or what we might refer to today as 'fake-conversion' or 'alternative conversion'. That was at that time the prevailing form of civil product-diversification in the arms industry, albeit without replacing and decreasing the military share of the product-line and turnover. Steve wrote:

1 *Note*: In 2019, Heckler & Koch was sentenced to pay Euro 3.7 million because of the illegal export of 5,000 semi-automatic guns, rifles and according ammunition to crisis-ridden Mexico to be used in regions of counterinsurgency; Heckler & Koch employees involved received prison sentences.

Indeed, many of the major arms companies also run parallel police/ internal security equipment manufacturing operations and much diversification is already taking place. Such cross-fertilization of technologies is creating a policing revolution and speeding up the process of para-militarising the police whilst disguising the nature of the overall process [...] if Heckler & Koch sells variants of their submachine guns to police forces rather than the military, the official record indicates a diversification towards civilian purposes whereas in reality it is nothing of the sort. This masking of the trade in weapons for internal control has led to the current Omega project (Wright, 1997).

A later important impact of Steve's work was the 1998 European Commission's ban on the export of torture- and execution-technologies from the EU. Later, Steve was actively engaged in the International Committee for Robot Arms Control (ICRAC). In 2009, Steve became a Reader in Politics and Applied Ethics at Leeds Metropolitan (now Leeds Beckett) University. As well as teaching his main fields of expertise and Conflict and Peace Studies, together with his colleagues he established the MA program 'International Human Rights Practice'.

In Steve's blog post 'Going full circle…', Steve looks back on his 50 years of experience with the UK's arms-, surveillance- and security-industries and the MIC. As a young boy he worked at an arms factory which employed some 25,000 workers. Because of decreasing Ministry of Defence orders, the owners and government were considering conversion towards producing powerhouses and other forms of energy instead. However, the idea was finally dropped in favour of fully-automated production of modern battle tanks, at the cost of huge job losses with merely 100 people remaining from the workforce. His blog concludes:

The same engineers making tanks have vast experience in marine engineering and are situated in a region which has the densest concentration of wind energy in the UK. So much could be achieved if only we had more joined up thinking and political leaders with vision and ambition.[2]

At our 2014 and 2015 conferences in Istanbul and Norway, Steve impressed with his predictive knowledge: lively presentations on current developments in surveillance-, repression- and border control-technologies. These are now not only used during upheavals or mass-protests but increasingly against the

2 https://leedspage.wordpress.com/2016/03/11/going-full-circle/amp

millions of refugees fleeing war or hunger. He demonstrated the use of so-called non-lethal weapons which oftentimes can severely injure and even kill people. He showed how (killer-)drones and micro bio-robots, infra-red cameras and even gene-technological surveillance devices are used to distinguish and identify protesters according to gender or ethnicity.

Steve and I remained in close contact, at conferences, workshops and via email. He never gave up; in 2019, he was in contact with Palestinian protesters whom he advised on how to deal with the repression- and control-tools of the Israeli military and police, as well as on tactical issues of resistance.

References

Wright, Steve. 1997. Tracking the Trade in Light Weapons and Related Technologies: The Omega Database Project. In: Hendrik Bullens (ed). *Arms Industry at the Crossroads: Conversion, Restructuring and Arms Trade in Europe.* Mosbach: IPRA Security and Disarmament Commission Paper 8. Available from: https://catalogue.sipri.org/cgi-bin/koha/opac-detail.pl?biblionumber=16777

A spy for peace

Steve Wright

February 2005, previously unpublished

Introduction

This is a note to Brian Martin from Robin Ballantyne [Steve Wright's pseudonym] on the techniques of field research best suited to perform investigative study of the players involved in the military, security and police business, better known as the repression trade. The note is intended for researchers interested in the mechanics of such field research. It aims to provide a practical guide on how to enter such market places; the best modus operandi to undertake such research without drawing too much attention to the researcher; how to best prepare for a visit; what to look for and how to record it; how such field research findings should be analysed and reported and how to compile an up-to-date arms dealers diary so that future security fairs can be investigated and assessed.

Why spy?

Most information about the trade in military, security and police equipment transfers is out of date. Arms fairs are a rich source of up-to-the-minute data since they act as a showcase where companies and governments can show off the latest in technology and trumpet to future buyers the special products and innovations which lie on the immediate horizon. Documentation on many products including associated technical information may only ever surface at one particular arms fair. Such data can and has proved vital in undermining corporate denials about being involved in a particular branch of the security business.

Apart from certain sensitive destinations such as China, entering arms and security fairs is not spying. The best way of thinking about it is gathering data from a specialised trade show. This is less dramatic than thinking of such work as James Bond type penetration but more appropriate to get the researcher into the appropriate mind set of seeking company product information. The key reason for being in such a venue is to gather product and technical information on transfers, colluders, traders and buyers and to ensure that any assertions about specific weapons and technologies can be backed up by documentation. Denial is quite common in this area of business so it is important to ensure that sufficient documentation and photographs are taken to support a researcher's perceptions that a particular deal, event, transfer happened and is significant.

Thus the most important activity at the fair after safely getting in and out is making a record of those present and their most relevant products and activities which can be used by other researchers keen to uncover more evidence on particular transactions and security support networks.

Preparation & modus operandi

When a novice researcher enters an arms or security fair for the first time, it can be a bewildering and slightly scary moment. Even someone who has immersed themselves in the literature of arms and human rights will find the dazzling marketplace of stalls selling everything from armoured vehicles to electric shock devices somewhat confusing. So preparation is key.

Many arms exhibitions put their maps and product lists online in advance of the event. It is worth checking that the first day is not one limited to VIPs or press especially if it is a foreign event where every day spent abroad is precious and resource intensive. It also needs to be said that many more fairs are advertised than take place and it is not unusual for an event to be cancelled or postponed. Therefore before committing resources to travelling, double check either the website or with the organisers or their foreign agents that the event will take place as planned.

To go to such an event, one will need an identity. To pretend to be what or rather who you are not takes a tremendous amount of subterfuge and simply is not worth it. The best modus operandi is to go as a security consultant and say you are moving into new areas and are seeking new clients. That way your passport confirms that you are who you say you are. That is important at a venue where your passport is sometimes required to confirm identity and it avoids adding unwanted paranoia given that usually such events are crawling with military police, state security and intelligence officers. Being a consultant in a new area serves two purposes. There is no need to hide your ignorance, which is genuine, and it gives you a real opportunity to ask lots of interesting questions. The dealers love this opportunity to show off their knowledge since after the initial rush such events nearly always involve long periods of tedium for the sellers. The consultant tag also gets the vendor's interest since you say you are looking at developing new markets for new clients and therefore it makes economic sense for these business people to see you as a promising business contact. Later on, when you want documentation, brochures and photographs, your ID also is self-explanatory — i.e. you are ignorant of their products and need as much material as possible to show potential clients.

What will be expected is a proper business card. An absence of a card with email, telephone, address and fax numbers will draw suspicion. The best option is to get a set professionally made up with a PO Box number and a suitable security consulting logo. You can arrange for your normal phone to have a different ring for a new line if required or invest in another line just for your investigative purposes, for example a mobile number that you only answer for that link.

Many security and arms fairs will take place outside your home country, outside your normal language zone and may even be in a different continent. It is worth taking such considerations into account when preparing. Since English is the main lingua franca of these events, if you speak English you probably have enough communication skills to get by. However, should the reason for doing field work in a particular country require precise details of a specific technology in a language which you are totally unfamiliar with, say Turkish, Russian or Chinese, then do hire an interpreter and use them as part of your introductory repertoire.

If you are travelling long distances to another country where the climate and food are vastly different from your country of departure, ensure that you allow yourself sufficient time to wind down and adjust. Nothing is more stressful than having to go directly to a security expo after being on a 12-hour flight. It is much better to have had a couple of days acclimatizing, to have checked out directions to the venue and to know roughly how long it will take you to get there and back and how.

The field visit — How to get in, what to look for

There are essentially two ways to gain entry to an arms, police and security fair: (i) pre-book on an official invitation proforma or via the organizing company's website; or (ii) just turn up on the day and register on site.

For the new researcher, the first approach has the benefits of making the journey secure. If you are say heading for a security fair in one of the world's hot spots, say in the Middle East, it is more comforting to show them a letter of acknowledgement or a formal invitation from the organizers, The only disadvantage to this formal approach is that it signals your plans to whoever may be watching on the international telecommunication highways.

The second approach has the disadvantage of uncertainty — you never quite know if you will be refused entry or not. However in my experience of twenty years of visiting fairs, I have never been turned away at the door. In fact I have had sufficient encouragement at some entrances to try my hand at getting a press badge. This requires a little nerve if you have no press bona fides but the advantages are substantial including special press information packs, an impressive badge and a virtual carte blanche to photograph anything which moves.

Once you are in, the first impression is one of blooming buzzing confusion. The first thing to do is to buy or acquire a show guide giving a map of all the show halls and the position of various country pavilions and stands together with a timetable of any special events such as VIP visits or equipment demonstrations. Then move to a coffee sitting area and pick up a daily show guide if one is available. The sitting areas are important places to sit and people watch without drawing attention to yourself. Lots of deals are done here and one of the important things to watch out for is invitees: who is there, what status they have and from what countries. Sometimes the press packs give lists of visiting delegations and these might be important later on. For example, what was the UK government doing selling arms in Jordan at a fair attended by the Iraqi high military command?

The coffee corners are good spots to earwig on deals or commercial conversations. If you are a newcomer, this is a free space to mark out your priorities in terms of interesting companies and their whereabouts on the official map. It is really easy to miss critical stands if the fair is a large one covering several sites so an important first step is to mark out a series of walks. Begin in one corner and methodically track each series of stands line by line making your way slowly and methodically down the entire length of each hall. Make marked notes on any stalls which you may wish to return to later.

Gathering & documentation

The amount of documentation available at each stall is limited to what the stall holder has physically brought with them. As a rule of thumb this will gradually run out over the duration of the fair and will usually always be used up by the last day. This is especially true if there are public open days or if the fair has a day open to military staff and their families. The key to ensuring maximum documentation is to get into the fair on the first day it is publicly accessible and get in there as early in the first day as possible.

The best tactic is to work the fair in the first hour it is open and siphon off as much documentation from all the stands that is relevant to your field of interests. Be aware that not all the documentation will be on display. Some companies have a limited number of heavy duty catalogues for their best potential customers. On the second more thorough run through the fair when the crowds have settled down a bit, revisit the key target stalls and ask for further documentation.

It helps here if there are more than one of you since one can hold the camera and the other can do an interview. These interviews may be the only time you get proof positive that one company is enabling another for example to produce its products under licensed production.

Photographs or video material are potentially valuable in identifying people, products and procurements. Some of the stands themselves will contain material and claims which will appear nowhere else. Do not be afraid to ask searching questions or just to leave the camera running all the time in case you pick up conversations taking place at each stand that you would otherwise be too nervous to video.

It has also to be said that many stands are vacated at lunch time leaving a wealth of company info and contact lists including videos, etc. Such stalls sometimes provide a golden opportunity to liberate a vital jigsaw puzzle piece in an investigation but be prepared to be dumb about what is meant for the public and what is not.

Try to get photographs of key salespeople, key new products and key customers — especially if VIPs are in the assembled throng. The closer you can get the better. If you do not understand how a particular weapon works, ask and photograph the salesmen or woman telling you — you might just capture the only explanation of that technology before it goes public.

Doing the analysis

Once you are back to base, write down as much of what you saw as you can possibly remember including the equipment you photographed. Your short-term memory may be quite good but much will fade within a few hours of attending the fair. Note the most salient details, connections and the contradictions, e.g. representatives from torturing or embargoed states buying stuff; leg irons and torture technologies on stands; innovations which change the way that internal wars are fought; new technologies which enable human tracking or extra-judicial execution. Also look out for invitations to new fairs.

Attending one of these events is like being on the *Readers Digest* competition list — once you're signed up you continue to get further invitations forevermore.

Map out the links between local connections and their corporate owners overseas and see if new ways are being evolved commercially to get around any arms embargoes by using subsidiaries.

Applying the research

Some items from the fair may be "hot news" — a particular deal or innovation — and that should be relayed to media contacts as soon as possible, especially if you have managed to secure photographs or video footage.

Some material is particularly relevant to specific NGOs such as the country teams of Amnesty International. Sharing information enables a jigsaw puzzle piece to be provided to an ally who could not otherwise have access to that documentation. Otherwise store everything. In the past, denials from companies or even threats of legal action have been obviated because documents secured at a security fair contradicted the company's official line and they backed off.

An arms dealers diary

Even a simple search of the web will reveal a long list of annual arms and security events on virtually every continent. Familiarise yourself with this list to ensure that you are aware of what is coming up. Sometimes these events happen in ways which contradict stated government policy or highlight hypocrisy — foreknowledge enables you to tip off a friendly journalist to secure the angle.

Going full circle…

Steve Wright[1]

Half a century ago, believe it or not, I used to work in an arms factory. It wasn't just any arms factory but the famous Vickers-Armstrongs on the banks of the Tyne, in Newcastle, seen by many as the original template for factories mass producing weapons, from 1842.

Lord Armstrong was an entrepreneur inventing hydraulic cranes to power the business of mass-producing large guns and tanks. His German style chateau, Cragside in Northumberland, entertained other arms dealers like Krupps in style – it was the first building on Earth to have electric light—pioneered by the first lightbulbs manufactured just up the Road by Swann, The factory is part of Geordie legend featuring in the 1862 Anthem of Tyneside, the Blaydon Races.[2]

Last month I went back. Actually, during my time there, I was just a kid, and no; I wasn't a junior arms dealer! My original job was rising at dawn and selling morning papers to the wraith like assembly workers, making tanks. For them it was hard, dirty engineering work. And thirsty—there were more pubs along the Scotswood road then anywhere else in Geordie land.

Five decades later, I am attending a briefing by Pearson Engineering. Two years ago because of a loss of MoD contracts, the then BAE systems owned factory went bust. Then in August 2015 there was a phoenix-like resurrection of tracked vehicle fitting out on the banks of the Tyne. This time the factory is ultra-clean, machine tooled production, high precision assembly by the Reece Group of companies. It is a much smaller workforce of over 100, a far cry from the 25,000 people who worked there at its peak. Indeed, almost everyone I spoke to on my journey to the factory had a close relative who used to work there.

Nowadays, the markets for this kind of arms production are seen as very volatile. My interest is in the impact of the associated sub-component business on the North East economy. Was this the answer to the Government's claim to be building new Northern Powerhouses?

1 This article was originally published on 11th March 2016, at: https://leedspage.wordpress.com/category/uncategorized/posts/

2 https://www.youtube.com/watch?v=6PrMaVjHS74

Sadly not. Coinciding with the rebirth of the Armstrongs site was the demise of the Five Quarter Energy Plan which would have created over 500 new jobs in the region, which had been promised government support to produce cheap energy. But the government subsequently welshed on the deal.

How different the North would look if government investment and industrial support in the South was matched pound for pound in the North. What is really needed is a new form of Marshall plan to finance, train and reinvigorate Northern Industries and not just ones working in the defence and security sectors. The same engineers making tanks have vast experience in marine engineering and are situated in a region which has the densest concentration of wind energy in the UK.

So much could be achieved If only we had more joined up thinking and political leaders with vision and ambition.

Techno-politics of exclusion

Steve Wright and Tessie Humble[1]

Introduction

If we are to adequately anticipate and accurately judge the likely trajectory of global responses to climate change, a working assumption should be that over the next fifty years, most political responses, will neither be just nor sufficient. Considerable work has now been achieved in mapping out relative vulnerability. (See, Scheffran et. al, 2012, parts V-VII) For several nations this may mean the end; others will be faced with substantial internal migration and for the most affected, a mass exodus to foreign shores, as people struggle to find continuity. All such scenarios remain contested and are part of the growing "securitization of climate change discourse" (Scheffran et al., 2012, part III).

We assume that preparations to meet these challenges will be wholly inadequate. States will be panicked into emergency measures and deep clamps on freedom of movement. Past analyses have treated such scenarios as environmental disasters. We see such scenarios being reframed as emergency planning options, which are already being re-structured into military driven national security/ crisis planning options. What can we expect if climate change policy responses are handed over to the military at a time when continuity of energy, water and food supply chains, can no longer be guaranteed? The essay presents evidence that many military organisations are now working on responses to climate change, from a state security rather than a human security perspective.

What does this entail? Essentially, two interrelated processes kick in: one informatics based; the other focussed on technologies for systematic physical exclusion of unauthorized citizens, based on a wide variety of emergent coercive capacities. States already now have tough systems at borders to prevent anyone without documentation passing and these are becoming increasingly sophisticated with various biometric recognition, surveillance and tracking capabilities. Face recognition and vehicle tracking systems originally designed in response to the "war against terror", can be rapidly re-orientated towards climate change refugees. Such people will not be officially designated as such

---

1 This article originally appeared in Cecilia Wee, Janneke Schönenbach and Olaf Arndt (eds). 2015. Supramarkt. Sparsnäs: Irene Publishing.

since the general derogatory label of illegal immigrants will facilitate a legal exclusion response because climate change refugees have no legal status.

This essay presents evidence of the security paradigm shift amongst major military powers to encompassing climate change as a major security threat. Similarly, the military, police, media entertainment, university security complex is already reframing its capability set towards new measures to ensure border security and zone exclusion. This new capability sets already include non-human algorithms and robotic elements for patrolling long borders. Indeed, a wide variety of sub-lethal weaponry has emerged which either can be fired directly at crowds by security personnel, or remotely operated by machine intelligence. But how probable are such deployments in a climate change context?

Furthermore, we explore the reconfiguration of the major manufactures of intelligent fencing systems; unmanned aerial vehicles (UAVs), robotic security and patrolling systems, as well as lethal and sub-lethal weapons technologies and doctrines, to meet the demands of these new markets. That is perhaps the core contribution of our text. It aims to analyse and reveal the level and extent of corporate collusion in building new exclusion systems as joint-market profit-making ventures, with a range of state clients. It will build on the picture of what we know already of who has built what and their partnerships and what models they are proposing for future crowd management, disaster control and perimeter protection, along critical conduits and borders.

The essay ends with a discussion of some ethical dilemmas of how to respond to such technical fixing of the second order effects of climate change, namely:

- To acquiesce which may be tantamount to collusion;
- To engage in research activism to reveal social and political consequences of existing fence systems like those recently erected in Libya and Bangladesh; or,
- To devise counter technologies which facilitate migration despite the official policies of exclusion.

Such uneasy ethics will be at the core of any future, intelligent NGO response to climate change induced mass migration. Do we build resilience into modern architectures and infrastructure or a fortress?; will we evolve a human or an inhumane menu of future solutions?; who is deciding such agendas for us and what drives them?

Reframing climate change as a security issue

Interest in climate change as a security issue is relatively new.[2] Initially, the focus was on the prospects for violent conflict in the wake of climate change, and then the fuller security implications began to sink in (UN, 2009). It was only in the last decade that such issues were framed in national security contexts, initially in the U.S., when a report for the Pentagon on the potentially catastrophic impacts of *abrupt* climate changes (by Schwartz and Randall, 2004) was leaked to the press.

Professor Dave Webb, of the Praxis Centre, has critically analysed this suppressed Pentagon Report in terms of "Thinking the Worst" (Webb, 2007), in terms of both scientific veracity and political agendas. The terrifying scenarios presented include severe drought with 10% of Europe moving to a different country; storms destroying coastal barriers; border skirmishes in Bangladesh, India and China, to direct confrontation between Saudi Arabia and China bringing US forces into the Gulf in direct confrontation—all before 2030.

In this future, deaths from famine, war and weather-related disasters are predicted to run into millions. Webb questions the plausibility of this study and its impact: was it a call for saner more sustainable agreements on climate change, or a national security agenda? "This sort or thinking and practice are very indicative of a situation in which human rights, international law and democratic processes are peremptorily sacrificed so that governments can continue to exercise complete control" (Webb, 2007, p.68).

Brausch and Scheffran (2012) have highlighted the different interests of policy makers with regard to national, international and human security perspectives. Thus, the US national security perspective was on whether or not the US military could continue to operate despite severe climate change impacts; the UN Security Council were primarily concerned about climate change as a threat multiplier, with the capacity to massively exacerbate existing conflicts and polarization (UN, 2007), and human rights NGO's were concerned whether the poorest communities, living in the most vulnerable regions could be protected from ensuing violent conflict and their overall lack of resilience.[3]

Within Europe, this *securitizing* move found support but opponents said the matter should be considered not by the UN Security Council (UNSC), but by the Economic and Social Council (ECOSOC) and by the UN General

2 For an excellent discussion, see Brausch, H.G., & Scheffran, J. (2012) Climate Change, Human Security and Violent Conflict in the Anthropocene, in Scheffren et. al. (2012), pp.3-21.

3 Ibid, p.6-7.

Assembly. Taking it to the UNSC transformed the issue from a development and environmental issue to one of international security, invoking very different lenses for viewing and addressing what should be the most appropriate international response.

During 2007, the Intergovernmental Panel on Climate Change (IPCC) released its 4th report (IPCC, 2007), which marked a turning point in both scientifically evidencing the reality of human induced climate change and identifying a wide range of specific vulnerabilities. By March 2008, the Council of the European Union released a paper on 'Climate Change and International Security' (European Council, 2008). Subsequently, over 23 counties have designated climate change as a threat—and formally identified as policy, means to counteract in national security strategies (Brzoska, 2012).

Paralleling this state re-scoping of climate change as a national security policy priority was the post-9/11 policing and security revolution. This dimension of melding post-9/11 crisis planning, with the financing, management and policing of migration, has been relatively neglected. An honourable exception has been the cutting-edge research work undertaken by Statewatch and TNI. New homeland security ideologies have reframed refugee policies within overarching counter-terror concerns.

Such policies saw the financing of new information management systems at borders and beyond. Ben Hayes' work for TNI and Statewatch in identifying the move from migration controls, to social controls, has been definitive. He has documented the 1990s process of creating immigration buffer zones in Central and Eastern Europe, initially to those countries wishing to join the EU. Such zones have subsequently grown according to Hayes, to encompass a neighbourhood that stretches from West Africa to Central Asia (Hayes, 2009). Instrumental in this process is the work of the specially created EU border management agency, Frontex, which he has documented in creating a "Southern Maritime frontier" and a "host of joint police and naval missions to combat illegal immigration by sea" (Hayes, 2009, p.33).

Hayes explained to one of the authors that the EU is exporting border security measures through technical support and the establishment of migration management systems, as well as creating a presence in third countries to intercept irregular migrations. Lavenex and Wichmann explain that externalisation usually focuses on technical operational support and capacity building (Lavenex & Wichmann, 2009, p.92). Intrinsic to advocating for the expansion and implementation of border security operational systems is the European Security Research Advisory Board (ESRAP) and Framework Programme for Research and Technological Development, currently at FP7 (Hayes, 2009). As a result of such measures, Guild argues "the borders of Europe have moved" (quoted in Geddes, 2003, p.13). Powerful new exclusion zones have been facilitated by creating high tech barriers on the perimeters of the buffer zones, as well as co-ordinated information management networks using Automatic Fingerprint identification (AFIS) systems supplied by companies such as Motorola, integrated into the real time EU wide database known as EURODAC. Ben Hayes further explores the evolution of international migration policies since the 1980s—including contemporary plans for the warehousing of refugees in poor regions.

Probabilities, scale and extent of induced migration[4]

In many senses the level, extent and speed of climate change and its real impact on levels of internal conflict and migration will remain contested. It does not matter: security resource expenditure and prioritisation is neither based, nor ranked, on an objective calculus of relative risk.

To engage in a comprehensive study of the implications of border securitisation on climate-induced migration, the very notion of Climate Induced Migration (CIM) must first be considered. The difficulty of identifying climate-induced migrants is a core issue surrounding the ambiguity of the 'climate-refugee'. Dr. Burridge, a Research Associate at the International Boundary Research Unit (IRBU) at Durham University, told one of the authors: "A climate change refugee does not particularly exist, or cannot be identified directly as having migrated for this reason" (Humble, 2011, Interview 3, Paragraph 10).

Whilst CIM has been extensively theorised and forewarned (see Myers, 2002; GHF, 2009; Renton et al., 2009), Burridge explained that attributing climate change as a causality to migration is difficult, if not impossible, thus making identification of climate-induced migrants problematic or even implausible.

The UK Foresight Report explains that incidents of 'spiked' weather events, such as storms, are likely to cause displacement, however, gradual environmental degradation will cause migration (Foresight, 2011). This is likely to both create and be compounded by an array of other environmental, social, economic and political factors (Foresight, 2011). Such factors include water scarcity, salinization of irrigated lands, deforestation (Myers, cited in Castles, 2002, p.3), ineffective government responses, ethnic disputes and economic problems (Myers and Kent, cited in Castles, 2002, p.4), amongst others. Therefore, this

4 This section draws strongly on Humble (2011)

great difficulty of "disaggregated causality" (Brown, 2008) presents a risk of making the climate-induced migrant an intangible figure, supporting Burridge's argument. This raises the question of the plausibility of constructing legal, or other operational definitions, and/or frameworks for recognition and protection of the climate-induced migrant (Zetter, 2008) to support legitimate migration and ability to seek refuge. Purkayastha and Scott informed one of the authors that the issue of CIM was essentially one of vulnerability and marginalisation that already exists as an integral part of society in many regions in the world. Purkayastha, an expert on border security struggles in the Palestinian territories, explained: "Economic migration predates climate change effects. The climate change effects will only amplify what already exists on the ground – very large disparities without a hope of its redress "(Humble, 2011, Interview 7, Paragraph 7).

Here, Purkayastha fundamentally attributes the root cause of migration that falls under CIM to severe economic inequalities and that climate change serves simply as an aggravating factor on such pre-existing stresses. Scott took this point further by arguing:

> *My honest feeling is that this whole discussion about climate change and migration is a red herring, that it's a diversion and, that the core problem of this question is one of vulnerability and the historical production of vulnerability and vulnerable populations [...] it would be the result of poverty, it would be the result of any host of policies that might account for impoverishment and the production of particular populations too, so to attribute migration to climate change I think misses that really key point (Humble, 2011, Interview 2, Paragraph 3).*

Climate change is already creating a more hazardous effect in developing nations than the global north, because of the former's generally warmer 'starting temperatures' (GHF, 2009) and their lower capacities to respond to risk (Baker, Ehrhart & Stone, 2008). With 40% of the world's population living in socio-economic poverty (GHF, 2009) and having limited capacity for adaption or resilience (Baker, Ehrhart & Stone, 2008), their socio-economic vulnerability to climate change is accentuated. Therefore, a strong relation can be drawn between pre-existing social or economic vulnerabilities and the extent that climate change affects communities' survival capacity and need to migrate.

This discourse is already being reified, as migrations attributed to climate change are being increasingly reported (Brown, 2007). For example, the Internal Displacement Monitoring Centre claimed in 2011 that 42 million people were displaced due to environmental factors in the Pacific and Asia alone.[5] A critical and commonly held viewpoint on the discussion is that regardless of the different causalities involved, who will be affected, how many and when, global migration flows will definitely accelerate as the effects of climate change increase (see: Webb, 2007; Brauch, 2005).

Migration as a security threat

A recurring theme is the concept of migration being considered as a security threat. Maria Martin of Statewatch, who writes extensively on the legal and human rights aspects of migration, provides invaluable insight on this:

> *So this very notion of what is the border made for and what does the notion of security and protection mean, I guess that's the core of it, because based on that you have for instance in Europe the development of the legal framework of the notion of cross border crime, it is crazy to see that everything that crosses the border is perceived as a potential threat. It could be a human threat […] There is a suspicion about everything. And the basis will be to track the threats and to prevent them from entering, whether that be at the fence or whatever location (Humble, 2011, Interview 5, Para 6).*

Martin explained that state border security is based around how threats are understood and conceptualised, which she argues in Europe is increasingly focussed on 'cross-border' crime. Guild argues migration and security studies have become 'subcategories' of international relations (Guild, 2009). As the migrant becomes classified under state-defined security terms, the figure becomes alien and more easily regarded as a 'problem' or 'threat' (Guild, 2009), and as Bigo argues, become caught in a "continuum of insecurity" (Bigo, 2002, as quoted in Guild, 2009).

Underlining Martin's argument, these notions of 'suspect sub-categories' enable us to understand why more and more people attempting to immigrate may be blocked in the current geopolitical context. If all human traffic is viewed as a potential threat under a 'guilty until proven otherwise' attitude, the role of border security is to intercept all immigrants, regardless of their needs or intentions, allowing only those who can prove their wealth or innocence to enter. Burridge echoed Martin's statements, arguing that migrants are clustered together with high-risk social groups:

5 See Asian Development Bank (2012).

One of the most significant problems I see is the conflation of migrants and asylum seekers or refugees with that of 'threats', criminal, terrorist, or otherwise [...] Every few years or more frequently, immigration bills try to get put through by the government [...] So in Arizona there was, I have a blank on the name of the Bill, [SB 1070], it was essentially increasing the criminalisation of migrants from being present in the US (Humble, 2011, Interview 3, Paragraph 9).

Here Burridge explained that migrants were not only considered as threats but were being portrayed as acting illegally. White argues similar sentiments, saying that immigrants are perceived as threats for varying reasons, most commonly through being portrayed as having "terrorist or criminal intentions" (White, 2011). Burridge exemplified this by arguing that laws are being implemented in the US, such as the SB 1070 legislation,[6] that essentially legalise treating all perceived migrants with the suspicion of acting illegally. This ultimately creates a reality where everyone that is associated with the notion of 'migrant'—prior to or post-border crossing, asylum seeker, refugee or those simply believed to look like migrants—is being regarded as a threat that must be intercepted (Martin and Wright, 2006).

Castles and Miller explain that international migration has become greatly politicised, arguing the migration-security nexus has materialised as a point of central importance for both national security and within global governance (Castles and Miller, 2009). Conclusive to Martin and Burridge's arguments is the shift of migration from being understood as a historical aspect of human behaviour for social and survival needs, to that of the migrant being a threat against which the nation-state must secure itself (Smith, 2007).

The numbers game

Jakobeit and Methmann (2012) have done an excellent job of deconstructing the politics of the climate change induced-migrants numbers debate, which they rightly see as highly politicized. They argue that the issue is complex and there are different types of migration which might be permanent or temporary, over a long or short distance. Their analysis reflects on traditional creative adaptation

6 SB 1070, full name Arizona Senate Bill 1070, gives the legal power to law enforcers to stop and detain anyone who they have 'reasonable suspicion' of being in the country without the correct legal documentation whilst verifying their status. This bill was been highly controversial and concerns of racial pro-filing have been raised. See: State of Arizona, Ministry of Citizenship (2010).

and coping mechanisms for dealing with existing climate change variations, in places like West Africa, which use circular migration. They examine the wide disparity of estimates in existing studies trying to quantify future numbers of climate refugees, which vary from 50 million (UNU-EHS, 2005) to 250 million (Christian Aid, 2009). Mocking such estimates has become part of the climate-change deniers' arsenal. But for the purposes of this chapter, they do not really matter. Manufactured perceptions are more vital to future securitization agendas than any scientific accounts. Future arrangements will be focused on 'illegal aliens', 'terrorist networks' and 'bogus asylum seekers'. Why you want to cross borders is less important than proving you have the correct paperwork to avoid being jailed.

All modern states now have well-oiled systems of tackling illegal migration, particularly given that many such would-be migrants into Europe, for example, are non-Christian. In these xenophobic times, Muslims are increasingly subject to enhanced attention, state security prejudice and paranoia, linking that religion with heightened security-risk status. Even though scientific communities may understand the need for sustainable solutions, the behaviour of security forces in on-going economic, political and military crises has underlined just how far we are from achieving such governance.

Poverty, water, food and fuel scarcity are part of a system of global 'structural violence' (Pilisuk 2008). Very poor people will bear the brunt of the consequences of climate change and they may rightly accuse their political leadership of corruption and being unmoved by the peoples' fate and suffering. The convergence of such perceptions can provoke a security crisis that will despatch thousands or even hundreds of thousands of people on to the streets, as in Egypt in January 2011.[7]

Most future climate-induced conflicts are unlikely to be pure types but will consist of a complex amalgam of causes and consequences. Serious work is now being accomplished to firmly establish causal correlations between various forms of climate change and the precipitation of internal conflict.[8] One constant, however, is the convergence of the crisis-policing technologies deployed and the corporate entities which will profit enormously from supplying them.

7 See: http://www.bbc.co.uk/news/world-africa-12308243 (31 January 2011).

8 See Scheffran et. al..(2012) and Science - https://www.science.org/doi/10.1126/science.1235367

Varieties of security control: techno-fixing popular response

The border exclusion technologies facing all migrants amongst many others include: concrete walls, sand walls, virtual walls, monitoring and sniper towers, cameras, land radars and wireless telecommunication, as well as infra-red surveillance, carbon dioxide probes, fingerprints and personal data identifying technology and storage networks, and the arms carried by border guards (Humble, 2011). According to Hayes (2009), Europe is moving towards a "high-tech techno-security paradigm" of border controls. This is being increasingly described as the 'fortification' of Europe (Geddes, 2003; Martin, 2012; Pécoud and Guchteneire, 2006), The report *NeoConOpticon* argues that the EU is moving towards "full-spectrum dominance" through the bolstering of both technological and physical surveillance systems and barricades (Hayes, 2009), designed to make its borders increasingly impermeable.

This information is in-line with the multitude of techniques and task-specific border management systems reported to be employed under the EU security agenda (see Statewatch, 2006; Hayes, 2009; Hobbing, 2010). Hobbing explains that Frontex, the security agency responsible for the management of the EU's external borders and interception of irregular migrants, is critical to the EU's Integrated Border Management (IBM) system (Hobbing, 2010). EuroSur, a surveillance system that covers land and maritime borders, has become an integral part of this, which seeks to achieve "full situational awareness" of external borders (Hayes, 2009). Other operational systems include Rapid Border Intervention Teams (RABITs), employed to help member states in "exceptional and urgent situations", such as mass influxes of irregular migrants (Hobbing, 2010), as well Eurodac databases, previously mentioned which now collect fingerprints of all migrants entering the EU (Martin and Wright, 2006).

We can anticipate that new enhanced border-control measures will also be accompanied by advanced crowd control initiatives. There has already been massive funding for future security technology innovations in the wake of 9/11. These can be rapidly redeployed for internal security use, just as we saw in the wake of the 'Arab Spring.' Variants of these riot technologies such as water cannon, kinetic energy weapons, irritant gases such as CN, CS, CR, and tactics using wedge formations, and riot shields were first evolved in former British colonies then further refined by the British Army and the RUC in Northern Ireland in the seventies. Since then, new neuro-muscular incapacitation devices, such as the 50,000 volt Taser, have proliferated across Europe and beyond.[9] All

9 See Wright (1998) and Omega Foundation (2000) for a detailed analysis and examples of proliferation and abuse.

these riot weapons essentially act as force multipliers enabling smaller groups of security personnel to control greater numbers of people. They can raise significant civil liberties and human rights issues when misused or deployed in conjunction with lethal weaponry (See Omega Foundation, 2000, Appendix C).[10]

New control ideologies and the revolution in military affairs

The emergence of new capacities to immobilize individuals and crowds using, weapons which have either pain induction, maim functions or paralysis effects, has not happened in a vacuum. Even before 9/11, the US Military in particular was re-orientating towards a different type of warfare where unconventional opponents would be operating within urban terrain amongst ordinary civilians.

New military doctrines emerged to justify this reframing as part of the so called 'Revolution in Military Affairs' (RMA) and the notions of so called "full spectrum dominance" contained in the United States Space Command (1997) document, Vision 2020. These doctrines incorporated new information and targeting tactics, as well as new weaponry designed to be used against both combatants and civilians (Halpin et. al, 2006). The new weaponry was promoted by the likes of Col. John Alexander, who advocated the notion of a non-lethal set of alternatives for 21st century warfare (Alexander, 1999). With Sci-Fi writers Janet and Chris Morris and Alvin and Heidi Toffler (1993), Alexander managed to persuade the US DoD to set up a new programme of work exploring this new form of warfare—The Joint Non-lethal Weapons Directorate (JNLWD)—of which he became the first Director in 1996.[11]

Post 9/11, the JNLWD, based at the Marine Corps HQ at Quantico, has become the engine of soliciting and approving new sub-lethal technologies, border protection and exclusion systems and directed energy, punishment at a distance weapons. Their official wish-list,[12] leaked by anti-secrecy site 'Public Intelligence',[13] includes:

- Lasers and heat beams designed to disperse crowds;
- Nausea-inducing sound waves targeted at scuba divers;
- The Impulse Swimmer Gun, is described as being able to "suppress underwater swimmers and divers";

10 http://www.bo.cnr.it/www-sciresp/OLD/GdL/Genova/crowd_control_STOA_annex.pdf

11 http://jnlwp.defense.gov/

12 See http://www.bbc.co.uk/news/technology-16415007

13 http://publicintelligence.net/

- System designed to move people through an area by emitting a "heat sensation" causing "involuntary movement";
- Electro-muscular pulses which "substantially increase" the time a hostile person can be incapacitated;
- A portable system which emits high-powered microwaves capable of stalling a car engine at a distance;
- An unmanned, airborne vessel equipped with a microwave-emitting device capable of preventing a ship's propulsion by causing "electrical system malfunction".

So called 'Non-Lethal Weapons' (NLW) technologies have subsequently globalised,[14] and form part of the new arsenals of military, police and special forces as their various roles and tactics converge (Davison, 2009). Their key role is to provide enhanced coercion without the public opprobrium that might accompany any state use of lethal force. Amnesty International (2003) has identified their deployment with many human rights violations including torture. Increasingly, such weapons are used in conjunction with other coercive tactics including small arms (Omega Foundation, 2000).

Sub-lethal public order and perimeter control weapons

The proceedings of the regular European non-lethal weapons symposia in Ettlingen, Germany, provide one of the best show cases to learn about such weapons and the standard operating procedures advocated by their proponents.[15] Critics of such alleged 'non-lethality' raise their potential for torture and mass human rights violation. Landmine Action was one of the first NGOs to report on potential configurations of some of these weapons for mass exclusion and perimeter protection, as new weapons were researched for replacing antipersonnel land mines in the wake of the Ottawa Treaty Ban (Doucet & Lloyd, 2001).

Some of these using direct energy sound like science fiction (see Moore, 2000; Hambling, 2002), but there has been a relentless search for technologies which can bridge the gap between 'shout and shoot' over several hundred metres. The Raytheon pain-beam based on a millimetre wave device, which

14 See Bradford Peace Studies Non-Lethal Weapons reports,Editor's note: See https://bradscholars.brad.ac.uk/browse?value=Non-lethal+weapons&type=subject or search for 'Bradford Peace Studies Non-Lethal Weapons reports'

15 Editor's note: original link defunct. But see for example: https://publica.fraunhofer.de/entities/mainwork/ec4487ce-7a5c-4f8c-ae59-05a87c93d70f/details

heats up humans to over 130 degrees, has been championed by the JNLWD[16] and prototypes fielded, albeit without operational use yet because of perceived controversy (Authur & Wright, 2006). However, Raytheon has already advertised related devices like the Silent Guardian, which are based on notions of "tuneable lethality" but promoted as harmless.[17]

Others showcased at Ettlingen, like the 'Taser Shockwave' which projects 50,000-volt electrified darts over a zone of five metres or so, are now in production.[18] Zone paralysis can be induced by a wide variety of mechanisms including laser and sound (Altmann, 2008; Hambling, 2011). The Russian authorities in 2002 used anaesthetics as a counter-terror capture approach in the Moscow Theatre siege against Chechen rebels but over 130 people died (Klotz et al., 2003). The British Medical Association has warned of the dangers of attempting to use drugs as weapons (BMA, 2007).[19] Work is continuing on refining such so called incapacitants, including work by Czech anaesthetists to add a time-released antidote,[20] and the US military have already field tested micro membrane balls that release agents only when trod on, with an obvious potential for border control. The BMA itself has warned of the dangers of nightmare developments in targeting chemical and bioweapons by genotype—so called ethnic weapons. These remain distant but breakthroughs in synthetic biology, mapping the human genotype, work on the 'human diversity project,' have brought such prospects closer.[21] Brain modelling has allowed a firmer grasp of the prospect of a new generation of incapacitants targeting the brain's own bio-regulators (controlling breathing, heart functions and levels of induced anxiety); dangerous breakthroughs which Bradford University's Professor Malcolm Dando has consistently warned about and indefatigably researched (Dando, 2001; Wheelis & Dando, 2005).

Yet many states are now using more everyday 'wide area' riot control agents such as CN, CS and OC to incapacitate large numbers, delivered from a bewildering array of devices including mortars, grenades and via special backpacks and water cannon (Crowley, 2013). During the Arab Spring, we saw

---

16 Editor's note: Original link defunct, but see: https://jnlwp.defense.gov/Portals/50/Documents/Resources/Publications/Government_Reports/JNLWP_ST_Stratgic_Plan_FINAL_Distro_A.pdf

17 Editor's note: Original link defunct, but see: https://www.theguardian.com/tecnology/2006/oct/05/guardianweeklytechnologysection

18 http://www.youtube.com/watch?v=9bzTJbMBuxk

19 For a discussion, see Wright (2007a)

20 http://mondediplo.com/2007/08/12bioweapons

21 See Dando (2002, in Lewer, 2002)

significant misuse of such devices to punish protestors whilst ushering them into more lethal firepower. In enclosed spaces riot agents will kill, although at the time of writing this has not stopped the Turkish authorities for example firing chemical irritants into tents or, in one instance, into a crowded police van where all 68 detainees died of asphyxiation. Such misuse of sub-lethal weapons is illegal under international law, but without adequate enforcement systems that will not stop ruthless authorities from treating their citizens in terms described by sociologist Zygmunt Bauman as 'disposable' people (Bauman, 2003).

Already, we see evidence of states treating whole groups as expendable during emergencies, for example the urgent needs of black residents in New Orleans displaced by Hurricane Katrina, who were afforded less priority than public order policing: "An already divided city was turned into a battleground between gated green zones and raging red zones" (Klein, 2007). In 2005, Morocco flew out planeloads of refugees from Senegal and dumped them in a minefield after they attempted to reach Spanish enclaves by storming razor wire fences.[22] More recently, Australia has said it will not take asylum seekers arriving by boat but will instead redirect them to Papua New Guinea.[23] Such countries will shirk their 'responsibility to protect' unless public pressure intensifies—but immigration and asylum are now such 'loaded' terms, the danger is for tipping points to go the other way towards supporting policies of exclusion. The relentless pace of innovation in new technologies of political control will see many security companies cashing in on climate change, as the capacity for large scale people containment and dissuasion increases.

In these contexts, it is vital that NGOs follow initiatives such as Bradford's Non-Lethal Weapons Project (Davison, 2009), which examines the 'state of the art'; Amnesty International, whose *Pain merchants* (2003) and *Terror Trade Times* (2002) mapped out corporate collusion by security technology providers in arming the torturers; and the work of experts assembled by Maslen (under the Geneva Academy in 2010 to examine the technical, ethical and legal dimensions of these new control capacities), evaluating their impacts within the frameworks of international Humanitarian Law.[24]

Such technical and legal contexts will become ever more important in challenging future vertical and horizontal proliferation of these systems, because any re-orientation of this security control capacity towards technically fixing

22 http://news.bbc.co.uk/1/hi/world/africa/4326670.stm

23 http://www.bbc.co.uk/news/world-asia-23358329

24 https://www.geneva-academy.ch/research/our-clusters/past-projects/detail/20-non-kinetic-energy-weapons

the 'problem' of climate-induced migration, will require neither new policy, nor new legislation. Anyone crossing borders because of climate change will increasingly find themself facing the hi-tech border fences described in the next section. Others will end up in long term refugee camps at the border, or if and when these overflow, in massed crowds rioting because of failed food, water, energy and health systems. If they become embroiled in associated public order conflicts they have no special legal status; except as a potentially illegal migrant or a looter. The exodus of refugees from Syria, at the time of writing, gives a stark snapshot of scale—two million people leaving the country (half of which are children) and five million internally displaced. How would such numbers be handled if repeated across many continents, at the same time?

Building active exclusion zones: the role, function and activities of corporate primes

Over the last twenty years or so, we have seen an acceleration of the pace of states building hi-tech boundary fences at critical borders. So much so, that the politics of exclusion now form a backdrop to contemporary culture. In September 2013, The Guardian asks 'Are you hemmed in by a fence or a separation wall?[25]' Hollywood explores the dispossessed being left in an inhospitable sprawl whilst the elite get to enjoy the bliss of extra-terrestrial *Elysium*.

The reality is a more relentless emergence of gated elite communities now being explored by urban geographers such as Stephen Graham at Newcastle University. Graham identifies the emergence of a much more brutalised militarised urban policing to enforce apartheid scale inequalities in places like the occupied Territories of Palestine. What has already emerged according to Graham, is an ideology of a militarised urban battlespace (Graham, 2009, 2010). The requirements of policing this space are serviced by a tiny number of multinational military conglomerates or "primes" who see an extraordinarily lucrative market opportunity for diversification into security walls and weaponry.

Accelerating 'intelligent' border construction

In an interview with (Humble, 2011), Ben Hayes described borders becoming increasingly restrictive, particularly surrounding the West, through implementing policies and advanced border control technologies:

25 https://www.theguardian.com/world/2013/sep/16/people-walls-stories-pictures-videos

[a] legacy of 25 plus years of tighter and tighter border controls in the west, the export of those controls and this [...] 'we've got to keep tightening the borders, ever tighter, ever tighter, ever tighter', we've done all the legislative stuff in Europe and now here we are going for this Euro, sort of, super high-tech techno-security paradigm with every kind of satellite, surveillance, censors and drones and all the rest of it (Humble, 2011, Interview 1, Paragraph 9).

Hayes explained:

Go back to probably about 10 years ago, where they first did the action plans on, I think it was 6, targeted countries that were seen to produce lots of refugees and migrants bound to Europe and that included Iraq, Afghanistan, Sri Lanka, and basically ever since then the EU has been providing either through its own programmes or through technical assistance from the member states have been providing support for border control, technology development, liaison officers, all of those things, so I would guess they have a presence in dozens of countries now globally dealing with immigration (Humble, 2011, Interview 1, Paragraph 1).

In Humble's (2011) study, several of the participants argued that the transfer of border controls is often to nations who traditionally had in-effect highly porous borders. For example, Wirsching argued:

In Africa (at least in Western and North Africa) since EU migration and border policies are increasingly externalized they lead to similar tendencies in Africa that did not exist before the EU migration and asylum policies in 1999 when there was [any] hardly border monitoring between artificial nation states (Humble, 2011, Interview 8, Paragraph 4).

Wirsching emphasized that the 'externalisation' of EU migration management has resulted in states who previously afforded limited attention to border controls, now implementing localised cross-border security measures and migration restriction, in order to stem the flow of migrants towards Europe (Humble, 2011). Hayes took this point further, arguing a domino effect of border securitisation:

[When a country] introduces border controls, strict ones, it inevitably has a knock on effect on the country next door, and it is that country that is then identified as a transit country, the receiving state then starts putting pressure on the transit country, saying "hey, guess what, you've got to tighten up your border controls", and [...] spreading miraculously through

the world, through this sort of twin processes of technical assistance and technology transfer (Humble, 2011, Interview 1, paragraph 5).

Hayes suggests that the spread of border securitisation is not just the result of formal externalisation policies but also comes from political pressure and thus transfer of border security measures. If correct, an assumption can be made that this domino effect is not restricted to particular regions, but can materialise anywhere that nations put emphasis on securitising borders and blocking migrants.

Resourcing the new architecture of hi-tech border control

Information on border security in Humble's study was greatly focused on Europe, America and their neighbours, suggesting that border securitisation has seen greater proliferation in and around Western states, which the weight of comparative literature also indicates. Pécoud and Guchteneire (2006) support this, claiming it is Western nations that are increasingly fortifying themselves against the rest of the world. However, the participants also mentioned non-Western states which are employing enhanced border security, and accumulatively, named 28 international borders across the globe with securitised borders.

Post 9/11, global government, according to Visiongain (quoted by Hayes, 2012), spent $178 billion in 2010 alone, with a forecast global spending on homeland security over the next decade of some $2.7 trillion. Within that, border security was scheduled for an estimated spend of $15.8 billion in 2010 and biometrics associated with identification management to top $11.2 billion in 2015 (Hayes, 2012).

Hayes (2012) underlines the role of large multinational defence contractors, or "primes" in servicing that market. In Europe the five big mega defence conglomerates, EADS, BAE Systems, Finmeccanica, SAFRAN and Thales, are core. In the USA, the huge military systems corporates are Lockheed-Martin, Boeing, Northrop Grumman, Raytheon and General Dynamics. Given the growing importance of biometric borders, IT conglomerates such as L3 Communications, Hewlett Packard, Dell, Verizon and IBM in the US, and Eriksson, Indra, Siemens Diehl and Sagem in Europe, have all become key players in many recent initiatives. Few other corporates could manage the enormity of the security contracts implemented post 9/11, but according to Hornqvist, they bring with them an associated mindset "that correspond more closely to military logic: neutralising, knocking out and destroying the enemy" (Hornqvist, 2004, p.35). Graham (2010) also warns of the dangers of blurring the lines demarking civilian law enforcement from military power. The resultant polarisation lends itself to creating enclaves of securitised privilege for "those who are risk-free and in need of protection to live, work and play—as well as enforcing the rules in archipelagos of human disposal, warehousing and incarceration" (p.90).

Within Europe the new security agenda was operationalised with an annual €200 million budget by the European Security Research Advisory Board (ESRAB) in April 2005, which set the EU security research priorities programme, via FP7, for 2007-2013. Hayes' (2010) report for TNI and Statewatch, *Neoconopticon,* expertly demolishes the processes which operationalise this programme, from bringing in big business to setting up a trusted "group of personalities" to create a "Homeland Security" style policy framework to police Europe's future. Hayes found that within that agenda, nearly half (50%) of the projects eventually approved were contracted to organisations, either servicing the defence or security sectors.

Hayes then maps out what has emerged as a militarised approach to immigration control, through maritime initiatives such as CHENS (Chiefs of European Navies 20 year vision for their future role); the European Border Surveillance System (EUROSUR), which includes an expansion of border surveillance into space via the Maritime Security Service Project (MARISS) which was led by Telespazio (Finmeccanica-Thales joint venture co.) and included EADS, Astrium, Qinetiq, SELEX-Si and Starlab (2010, p.37). Also included in the FP7 programme was the €20 million TALOS project, designed to integrate autonomous border control systems based both in aerial vehicles and in ground robots. *NeoConOpticon* provides the first crucial attempt to get a handle on the reframing of border security architecture now emerging and the significance of such incremental steps as "interoperability" to create a flexible system of security capability sets. It identifies the industry-university-policy partnerships which facilitate this overall securitisation. In Europe's case, it details how this will be managed by the newly created border management agency Frontex—whose war on migration covers the coast of Africa, the war zones of the Middle East and the many inconvenient islands in the Mediterranean.

For the "primes" these contracts are immensely lucrative. The EADS contact to install surveillance equipment over 9000 kilometres of Saudi Arabia's borders, including deserts, mountains and borders, will yield between €1.5 and 1.6 billion.[26] The Boeing contract covers both borders the US has with Canada and Mexico—some 7,500 miles. The 3-year contract is worth €2.1 billion and

26 Defence News 1 July 2009

includes many commercial partnerships; not least we are told by the BBC, with an Israeli company that makes cameras which can spot people 14 kilometres away.[27]

Is there any trend here for Pariah states like Israel to export expertise and tacit targeting knowhow built up via its illegal occupation of Palestine, to other control zones? Prof Stephen Graham certainly thinks so: "What was striking [...] is that Israel's military and security technology, doctrine and expertise have rapidly been mobilised and generalised as part of the US global war on terror" (Graham, 2010, p.228). He quotes Michael Evans: "Significant theoretical analyses were completed by RAND Corporation scholars, focusing on the technical and tactical peculiarities involved in conducting military operations inside cities" (Evans, 2007). Graham goes to quote an extraordinary account of US soldiers being present in IDF uniforms during the final stages of the massacre associated with the Israeli clearance of the Jenin refugee camp during April 2002.[28] This anti-democratic 'liveware' transfer of working knowledge is potentially corrosive.

One of Humble's (2011) interviewees confirmed such corporate links between Israel, the US and the RAND Corporation in building the Mexican fence:

> *There is a huge military industry that lobby and need investments and walls [are] becoming one of the so-called home wall security-industry investments. So when you talk about the wall here in the West bank [it] costs Israel around 2million dollar[s] per kilometre. For example in 2005 they said they'd need around 500 million dollar[s...] of high-tech for the wall, from cameras, to sensors, to wireless telecommunications, to check points, to metal detector and all of this, so imagine all of this goes to the high-tech industry, the military and the semi-military high-tech industry (Humble, 2011, Interview 3, Paragraph 3).*

And it's not just fences being bought and sold. When Brazilian Jean Charles de Menezes was executed in a London tube on 22nd July 2005, by a dum-dum bullet fired into his spinal cord by a Metropolitan Police Firearms Officer in plain clothes, few were aware that this so called Kratos technique of assassination had been a product of Met-Israeli security liaison. In future, attempts to resist containment actions which go beyond the law, ascertaining the roots of any corporate and ideological origins of associated policy and technology, will become increasingly important.

27 BBC, 21 September 2006.

28 http://news.bbc.co.uk/1/hi/scotland/1937048.stm

Global border securitisation[29]

The highest intensity of border securitisation is largely clustered around Europe, America, the Middle East and southern Asia. Territories with similar developments include North Africa, Central Asia and Russia and other isolated cases exist elsewhere. The borders of America are becoming increasingly fortified, with the US-Mexico border having multiple layers of security deployments. A virtual wall of surveillance is being constructed along the Canadian border and the Maritime area between the South East and the Caribbean is strongly guarded. Europe is also becoming increasingly impenetrable, particularly the maritime borders to the South. The Greece-Turkish land border, which is reported to be the route taken by 80% of undocumented migrants entering Europe (Vandystadt, 2012), has Frontex deployments (BBC, 2011), and Greece has begun to construct a fence along a portion of the crossing. To the North West, barriers also exist intermittently along outer European borders with Russia.

In North and West Africa, Morocco has increasingly guarded borders with Algeria and so does Mauritania with Mali. Morocco has a 1,500-mile-long mixed sand and stone barrier lined with mines along the Western Sahara territory, and Libya recently bought a €300 million security contract with Finmeccanica[30] to securitise all its borders. In the south, electric and barbed wire fences secure the Zimbabwe-Botswana border and the Zimbabwean–South Africa border respectively.

The Middle East has a large number of highly secured borders, most notably between Israel and the Palestinian Territories. There is a highly secured barrier under construction between Oman and the United Arab Emirates and between Saudi Arabia and Yemen. Meanwhile, in 2009 EADS Defence and Security[31] was contracted to securitise all of Saudi Arabia's borders. Carney, Milkian and Hoelscher (2011) coined the term 'Fortress India', referring to the heavily guarded 1,790-mile border fence around Bangladesh, parts of which are electrified (Wright, 2012). India is also deploying border securitisation across its borders with Pakistan, Tibet, Burma and the Kashmiri region. Pakistan has plans for a mine-lined fence with Afghanistan, but the extent that this will be realised is uncertain due to economic factors (Nation, 2010). Central Asia

29 These sections draw extensively from Humble (2011)

30 Finmeccanica is an Italian-based company that manufactures aerospace, defence and security technologies. See Finmeccanica (2012).

31 EADS Defence and Security is a European- based, internationally operating company thats works in security and aerospace technologies. See CTW (2012)

also has some fortified border security zones, such as between Uzbekistan and Kyrgyzstan, and Uzbekistan and Afghanistan.

Further East, Russia has an extensive low-security barbed wire fence along its borders with China and Mongolia. Both of North Korea's land borders are becoming increasingly highly secured, while Brunei and Limbang, and Malaysia and Thailand, both have heightened border security between their respective shared borders.

An extensive network of maritime security systems guard Australia's northern sea border. As Mark Levene has argued: "We live in a world of nation-state; formerly porous frontiers are now inviolable borders" (Humble, 2011, Interview 6, Paragraph 6). Here, Dr. Levene summed up the views given by the majority of the participants in Humble's (2011) study; that state borders are becoming increasingly impermeable. Our world is riddled with international borders that are increasingly difficult to pass, indicating evidence to support Jones' observation that this is the most "bounded and ordered world" we have yet experienced. Nevertheless, many zones still retain their traditional permeability, a point recognised by one of Humble's expert participants, Purkayastha, who argued:

> *I do think that border issues or border controls are actually increasing. Even then, there is a significant difference in terms of formal controls [...] In most developing countries, there is talk of increasing physical controls, [but] the actual borders are quite porous. [...] The rhetoric does not yet match the actual controls (Humble, 2011, Interview 7, Paragraph 1).*

It is clear that Purkayastha's assertion is fundamentally correct. The majority of borders in Africa, as well as the regions of South America, Central America and South East Asia, remain without bolstered security deployments, indicating the ability for people to move between states with relative freedom. Furthermore, Purkayastha argues that where border securitization has been introduced outside of the West, this has not resulted in borders being sealed off in practice.

Nevertheless, the assertion that most international borders remain permeable for now needs to be caveated. Firstly, as Dr. Hayes and Wirsching demonstrated, through the transmission of border controls, agendas of border securitization can shape border security in neighboring states to countries far removed. This is exemplified by the activities of the EC's Border Management Program in Central Asia (BOMCA), which aims to increase capacity building of border management in the region (EC, 2012). This can have a further informal regional 'knock-on effect', as discussed by Dr. Hayes. Additionally, as previously illustrated, the highly lucrative security-industry complex holds a strong vested interest in the intensification and expansion of border securitization and in a "paradigm-shift" towards states militarizing borders (Smith, 2007).

Importantly, the timespan of this border securitization development should be considered. Over half of the identified securitized borders developed enhanced security in the last 12 years alone, demonstrating a very recent growth. A new paradigm of border securitization is *emerging*. This is not the end of the narrative, but the beginning. The next section envisions what we might anticipate, if the current processes of militarization continues.

The permeability of securitised borders varies greatly, as do the consequences: forced 'lock-in', discussed earlier by Maccanico, such as with the Palestinian Territories (Jones, 2011) or increasingly dangerous migration routes, or both, depending on the border security as well as the crisis and the involved individuals' personal circumstances, which Warner, Olivia and Stal explain, determines who migrates and in what numbers (2008). According to the World Bank, as presented at COP 17 in Durban 2011, a five degree rise in temperature can be expected if we continue at our current rate of greenhouse gas emissions (World Bank, 2009). Such a rise may mean whole regions would become uninhabitable due to events like sea-level rise and desertification (GHF, 2010). In such a scenario, the migration 'push factor' in many regions may be very difficult, if not impossible, to remedy.

Borders as battlespaces that see: towards automated exclusion

We now live in an era of ubiquitous surveillance, especially in urban areas. Post 9/11, this surveillance capacity has been significantly upgraded. As military level systems have entered service, security is increasingly defined in national security contexts, and a politics of insecurity, risk, suspicion and prevention (Bigo, 2012).

Military surveillance systems are blanket rather than refined. But post-9/11, urban warfare doctrine has melded such distinctions. Military planners now envisage fighting in hostile mega cities of the urban South; how can military forces function in places where there might be no GPS communications or high buildings which obscure real threats? Graham analysed the emergence of a new raft of research and development by US military laboratories to render the complex city scapes transparent through advanced surveillance technology (Graham 2009, 2010). The US Defence Advanced Research Projects Agency

(DARPA), for example, sponsored initiatives such as 'Combat Zones That See' around 2003, with sci-fi notions of tracking whole populations through motion analysis via ubiquitous sensors, number plate recognition and face recognition programmes, and a 'Visibuilding' programme which allowed state agencies to look through buildings for human activity. Within this framework, surveillance capacity was coupled with automated armed, self-deciding robotic systems. Even nature is being harnessed to provide added surveillance capacities on land, sea, air and space (See Haggerty & Trottier, 2013).

Such scenarios were fictional prior to the Iraq insurgency, but subsequently we have had inklings of just how much has changed in terms of military capability sets. Over the summer of 2013 for example, the Guardian made a steady stream of shocking stories based on data provided by former Booze Allen analyst, Edward Snowden, that the US Military Intelligence's National Security Agency (NSA) was surveilling all social media through a programme named PRISM.[32] Post 9/11, we know that most UK cities have a so-called ring of steel around them—an urban CCTV surveillance and number plate recognition system which can play back every entry into the city zone. Post-2011 summer riots in the UK, the Guardian revealed that the Met Police were using a system from Leeds based company Datong plc., which could gather information from mobile phones over a 10-square-mile radius.[33] The city even has litter bins that can track mobile phones.[34] Post-9/11, surveillance has been enhanced at special major events like the London 2012 Olympics but also across many urban spaces, although especially at ports and borders.

Borders are some of the most intensely surveilled places on Earth. As pinch points we might anticipate substantial expenditure in upgrading capacities at borders, from biometric systems of social sorting, to watching systems that can spot anomalous behaviour. Hayes (2009) catalogues what he calls full spectrum surveillance, facilitated by what he terms a "digital tsunami". He cites the UK data retention scheme which has enabled the British police to get access to telecommunications a staggering 519,620 times in 2007. It also granted capacities from "undetectable bugs, tracing technologies and 'spyware'", to granting "cross-border powers over multi-nationals service providers" so states can conduct "foreign communications surveillance" as easy as domestic surveillance (Hayes, 2009, p.43). Other significant developments identified by Hayes include:

32 http://www.theguardian.com/world/prism

33 http://www.theguardian.com/uk/2011/oct/30/metropolitan-police-mbile-phone-surveillance

34 http://www.theguardian.com/world/2013/aug/12/city-london-corporation-spy-bins

- Calls for improved "situational awareness"—with the European Security Research and Innovation forum (ESRIF) encouraging the private sector to find new ways of fusing data gathered by a vast array of sensors "based on ground, air and space.";
- ISCAPS project on surveillance of public spaces;
- The Probant and HAMLET projects on the tracking of persons;
- The TRIPS project on surveillance of railway stations;
- EUROCOP project on geospatial information for pedestrian police officers;
- SUBITO programme on "real time detection of abandoned luggage" (p.45);
- HUMABIO project which uses behavioural analysis for human monitoring and authentication, using a network of cameras;
- SAMURAI project on "detection of suspicious and abnormal behaviour";
- INDECT project on automatic detection of threats;
- ADABTS project on "Automatic Detection of Abnormal Behaviour In Crowded Spaces" (led by Swedish Prime, FOI and Dutch prime, TNO) (p.4).

To name but a few. But the most significant developments are probably the two satellite-based surveillance developments Galileo And Kopernikus. This massively expensive project, with Galileo alone costing an estimated €3.4 billion, facilitates a myriad of satellite tracking functions. Kopernikus will provide the backbone for ground-based sensors and Unmanned Aerial Vehicles (UAV) to monitor people and the environment.

According to *NeoConOpticon*, the EU has supported at least a dozen UAV projects under various framework research programmes, including BSUAV and WI-MA2S, for border surveillance (Hayes, 2009, p.55). Elsewhere, the use of armed UAVs by the US across borders in places like Pakistan and Afghanistan on assassination missions, has sparked enormous controversy.[35] A crucial concern for NGOs such as Human Rights Watch (HRW) and ICRAC is the prospect of these systems becoming fully autonomous.[36]

We already have semi-autonomous precursor operations, or so called signature strikes, where targets are chosen automatically because they resemble

35 See Doyle, 2012

36 http://icrac.net/

similar situations where the use of lethal force could be justified. Although such terminator scenarios sound like science fiction, the rapid justification and escalating deployment of the US drone-led assassination strategy shows how quickly things can change. South Korea has already fielded the armed Samsung SGR-1 robot on its border, the demilitarized zone with North Korea.[37] Whilst the SGR-1 has autonomous surveillance functions, it needs human permission to open fire on live targets.

Other less intelligent killing systems are more autonomous. For example, the lethal 'self-healing' minefield uses a neural network to reposition mines if a border zone is breached.[38] Another variant which can be either lethal or sub lethal is Metal Storm's virtual minefield, which designates where 'mines' are on a virtual map held by a surveillance system which could be anything from an UAV or even a satellite. Cameras react to any physical breach by launching multiple mortar strikes to the designated spot.[39]

The security vulnerabilities of long interstate borders or parts of critical infrastructure can be used to justify 24/7 surveillance—a thankless and relentlessly dull albeit critical task which will always be presented as ripe for automation, either by ground-based or UAV robotic systems with either surveillance, guns or both. Already we have inklings of intent. The Pentagon made a call for contractors to provide a "multi-robot pursuit system" that will let a pack of robots "search for and detect a non-co-operative human." According to Wright, "What we have here are the beginnings of something designed to enable robots to hunt down humans like a pack of dogs. Once the software is perfected we can reasonably anticipate that they will become autonomous and become armed."[40] That was way back in 2008. Just this year (2013), *New Scientist* reported on drone systems which could tag those found in unauthorised spaces (Hambling, 2013)—again setting off unsavoury images of tracking and hunting down uncooperative humans.

Of course, the 'battle-spaces that see' mentioned above also include ordinary citizens armed only with a mobile phone camera, and instant access to worldwide social networks. Eyewitness images of lethal robots running amok in a crowd of refugees, with all the Hollywood associations with terminator, could destroy any semblance of public justification. However, we can anticipate

37 https://www.cnet.com/news/korean-machine-gun-robots-start-dmz-duty/

38 http://www.theregister.co.uk/2003/04/11/the_selfhealing_selfhopping_landmine/

39 https://www.ideaconnection.com/new-inventions/metal-storm-virtual-mine-field-03248.html

40 http://www.newscientist.com/blogs/shortsharpscience/2008/10/packs-of-robots-will-hunt-down.html

PR spin-doctors far more easily justifying sub-lethal options based on 'harmless weapons', even if they are not.

Again, we have inklings of future configurations. In 2007, irobot struck a deal with Taser International to mount their neuro-muscular incapacitation weapons on its military robots. Taser's shotgun fired wireless taser projectile, XREp, was initially seen as a natural tool for military robots on guard duty—but was recently withdrawn because of technical limitations. We can logically anticipate such technical setbacks to eventually be overcome. It is a similar story with directed energy weapons, such as the micro-millimetre wave active denial systems (nicknamed the 'pain beam') and Ionotron's shock inducing UV lasers, and the pulsed energy projectiles (See Altmann, 2008). So much money has been invested in them, we can anticipate both further miniaturisation enabling robot systems to carry such weapons, or their larger scale static deployment at borders and around critical infrastructure. Currently, drones within the US can only be used for surveillance, but the Electronic Frontier Foundation has uncovered proposals to weaponize them with less-lethal weapons.[41]

Powerful directed energy systems capable of shocking would-be migrants very long distances away are already now beyond prototype stage, and can be made autonomous and victim activated. Adverts for Raytheon's Silent Guardian,[42] coupled with drone surveillance to automatically track would-be illegal aliens, state agencies under duress could decide these form a logical continuation of current policy. Investors will enjoy the benefits of cashing in on climate change security fixes, as state after state adopt '21st century border control solutions'. But we could and should evolve alternatives—as if people mattered.

Conclusion: Towards resisting containment

None of these predictions are necessarily deterministic, despite state-security orientated border control options being massively funded at taxpayers' expense. In the long run, as Biermann and Boas (2008) suggest, what we actually need is a global protocol to protect climate refugees. Instead, we are liable to get two vastly different political economies of containment: one based on petty criminal black-market dodges to get across borders with professional human traffickers; the other, grandiose hi-tech so called geo-engineering schemes, or Plan B.

Already, we have evidence of criminal gangs exploiting migrants' need to leave Morocco for Spain, whilst the authorities turn asylum seekers back, allegedly

41 http://www.slate.com/blogs/future_tense/2013/07/03/documents_show_customs_and_border_protection_considered_weaponized_domestic.html

42 Editor's note: Original link defunct, but see: https://www.theguardian.com/technology/2006/oct/05/guardianweeklytechnologysection]

with resources provided by the EU.[43] Similarly in Palestine, black economies have grown up around the Israeli containment wall.[44] Ordinary people must find a way through, but at a cost.

In September 2013, in a speech to the annual British Science Festival, Astronomer Royal Lord Rees argued for some form of geo-engineering, which means some kind of planet-scale intervention to either cool the earth or soak up carbon dioxide.[45] The context is our failure to prevent $C0^2$ emissions continuing to rise. Rees says he is pessimistic about our ability to contain further rises—already running at 400ppm in May 2013:

> *If the effect is strong, and the world consequently seems on a rapidly warming trajectory into dangerous territory, there may be a pressure for 'panic measures'. These would have to involve a 'Plan B'—being fatalistic about continuing dependence on fossil fuels but combating its effects by some form of geoengineering.*

Rees is sanguine about the risks of such an intervention and the potential nightmare unanticipated consequences. But if establishment thinking is between containment and geo-engineering, NGOs must create a critical mass of thinking in support of other alternatives which are more sustainable, and do so on paltry resources. At the time of writing, there are already numerous geoengineering projects, some of which have been mapped by the ETC group.[46] Already evidence has been presented that Russia is pushing for future IPCC reports to have a section in support of "planet hacking". This is despite the UN moratorium on geoengineering which was agreed at the Biodiversity conference in 2010.

A key contribution has to be research activism, since far too few people are au fait with the whole area of security planning options. Hayes (2009) advocates new forms of research activism which will lead to substantial reform of the EU system of governance to prevent it becoming even more militarised. *NeoConOpticon* is a contribution to this debate and some of the NGOs concerned about these developments, including Statewatch and CIES, helped formulate a new series of ethical and societal checks and balances on the way all

43 http://www.theguardian.com/commentisfree/2013/sep/02/eu-ignoring-rights-abuses-morocco

44 http://halshs.archives-ouvertes.fr/docs/00/73/63/29/PDF/An_Undocumented_border_economy.pdf

45 http://www.theguardian.com/science/2013/sep/11/astronomer-royal-global-warming-lord-rees

46 http://www.theguardian.com/environment/graphic/2012/jul/17/geoengineering-world-map

future security research is funded by the EC. Graham (2010) advocates "counter geographies" to confront the new military urbanism, first by information but also with confrontation creative cartographies which create a public dissonance between what is being planned and the "official version". A key emphasis is on non-violence and art to shock people out of their passive somnolence, of the kind advocated by organisations such as EPKOT, who do public performances using full scale robotics and curate agi-prop events—embedded art in the name of security.[47]

Other NGOs such as HRW and ICRAC have undertaken a worldwide campaign for a new arms control regime to prevent the deployment of autonomous killing systems. These partnerships have been remarkably successful. Using ICRAC's expertise to provide heavyweight intellectual muscle (Asaro, 2012) was far more effective when married to HRW's (HRW) campaigning expertise and world wide networks. Following the publication of HRW's report on Losing Humanity (HRW, 2012), the joint campaign was launched in London, in April 2013 at the Amnesty International offices and quickly secured world-wide publicity, including the backing of Christor Heynes, the UN Special Rapporteur on Extra-judicial Killing, who warned of machines killing humans without supervision.[48]

A core reservation for HRW is the difficulty in adequately establishing proper accountability if things go wrong. Charles Raab calls for a refocus on the importance of principles when attempting to regulate surveillance (Ball, 2012, p.377). Gillom and Monaham take this further and argue that "'everyday resistance' was an important and productive dimension of anti-surveillance politics" (quoted in Ball, 2012, p.408). Perhaps similar politics will play out in resisting the militarisation of climate change? By such small steps can wider humanity play its role in reframing the proffered solutions to the costs and benefits of achieving a decarbonised future?

References

Alexander, J.B. (1999) *Future War: Non-lethal Weapons in Twentieth Century Warfare*. New York: St. Martin's Press.

Altmann, J. (2008) *Millimetre Waves, Lasers, Acoustics for Non-lethal Weapons – Analyses and Inferences*. Osnabrück, Germany: Deutsche Stiftung Friedensforschung. Available from: https://www.ssoar.info/ssoar/handle/document/26039

47 Editor's note: Original link defunct, see https://bbm.de/aktuelle-ausstellungen

48 http://news.cnet.com/8301-17938_105-57586858-1/killer-robots-may-wage-mechanical-slaughter-u.n-warns/

Amnesty International. (2002) *Terror Trade Times.* Issue No.3, June. Available from: http://www.amnesty.org/en/library/info/ACT31/001/2002/en

Amnesty International. (2003) *The Pain Merchants- Security Equipment and Its Use in Torture and Other ill treatment.* London: Amnesty International. Available from: https://policehumanrightsresources.org/pain-merchants-security-equipment-use-torture-ill-treatment

Arthur C., and Wright, S. (2006) Targeting the Pain Business. *The Guardian.* 5 October. Available from: http://www.theguardian.com/technology/2006/oct/05/guardianweeklytechnologysection

Asaro, P. (2012) On banning autonomous weapon systems: human rights, automation, and the dehumanization of lethal decision-making. *International Review of the Red Cross.* 94(886), June, pp. 687-709.

Asian Development Bank. (2012) *Addressing Climate Change and Migration in Asia and the Pacific.* Philippines: Asian Development Bank. Available from: https://www.adb.org/sites/default/files/publication/29662/addressing-climate-change-migration.pdf

Baker, J., Ehrhart, C., and Stone, D. (2008) Hotspots – predictions and action. *Forced Migration Review.* 31, pp. 44 – 45.

Ball, K., Haggerty, K.D., and Lyon, D. (ed's). (2012) *Routledge Surveillance Studies Handbook.* Abingdon: Routledge.

BBC. (2011) Greece plans Turkey border fence to tackle migration. *BBC News.* 4 January. Available from: http://www.bbc.co.uk/news/world-europe-12109595

Biermann, F., and Boas, I. (2008) Protecting Climate Refugees: The Case for a Global Protocol. *Environment- Science and Policy For Sustainable Development*, 50(6), pp. 8-16. Available from: https://www.tandfonline.com/doi/abs/10.3200/ENVT.50.6.8-17

Bigo, D. (2012) Security, Surveillance and democracy. In Ball, K., Haggerty, K.D., and Lyon, D. (ed's). (2012) *Routledge Surveillance Studies Handbook.* Abingdon: Routledge, pp. 277-284.

Bolton, M. (2015) From Minefields to Minespace: An Archeology of the Changing Architecture of Autonomous Killing in US Army Field Manuals. *Political Geography.* 46, pp. 41-53.

Brown, O. (2007) *Climate Change and Forced Migration: Observavtions, projections and implications. Human Development Report 2007/08.* Geneva: United Nations Development Program.

Brown, O. (2008) The numbers game. *Forced Migration Review.* 31, pp. 8-9.

Brauch, H. G. (2005) Threats, Challenges, Vulnerabilities and Risks in Environmental and Human Security. *Studies of the University: Research, Counsel, Education* (1) Bonn, UNU-EHS SOURCE Publication.

Brzoska, M. (2012) Climate Change as a driver of Security Policy. In Scheffran, J., Brzoska, M., Brauch, H.G., Link, P.M., and Schilling, J. (ed's). (2012) *Climate Change, Human Security and Violent Conflict – Challenges for Societal Stability.* Germany: Springer-Verlag, pp. 165-184.

British Medical Association. (2007) *The use of drugs as weapons: the concerns and responsibilities of healthcare professionals.* London: BMA. 24 May. https://wellcomecollection.org/works/axh7rs2q

Castles, S. (2002) *Environmental change and forced migration: making sense of the debate.* University of Oxford, New Issues in Refugee Research - UNHCR Working Paper 70. Available from: http://www.unhcr.org/3de344fd9.html

Castles, S., and Miller, M. J. (2009) *The age of migration: international population movements in the modern world.* 4th ed. Basingstoke: Palgrave Macmillan.

Christian Aid. (2009) *Human Tide: The Real Migration Crisis.* London: Christian Aid.

Cromwell, D., and Levene, M. (ed's). (2007) *Surviving Climate Change- The Struggle to Avert Global Catastrophe*. London: Pluto Press.

Crowley, M. (2013) *Regulation of "wide area" riot control agent delivery mechanisms under the Chemical Weapons Convention.* Bradford Non-lethal Weapons Project & Omega Research Foundation. April. Available from: https://www.statewatch.org/media/documents/news/2013/jun/riot-control-agents-chemical-weapons-convention-report.pdf

Cutler, A. (2005) Security fences. *The Atlantic Magazine*. March. Available from: https://www.theatlantic.com/magazine/archive/2005/03/security-fences/303734/

Dando, M. (2001) Genomics, Bioregulators, Cell Receptors and Potential Biological Weapons. *Defense Analysis.* December (17), pp. 239-257.

Dando, M. (2002) Future Incapacitating chemical agents: the impact of genomics. in Lewer, N. (ed). (2002) *The Future of Non-Lethal Weapons: Technologies, Operations, Ethics and Law.* London: Frank Cass.

Davison, N. (2009) *'Non-Lethal' Weapons.* London: Palgrave.

Doucet, I., and Lloyd, R. (ed's) (2001) *Alternative anti-personnel mines – the next generations.* London: German Initiative to Ban Landmines, Berlin and Landmine Action.

Doyle, M. (2012). Obama's drone wars and the normalisation of extrajudicial murder. *The Guardian.* 11 June. Available from: https://www.theguardian.com/commentisfree/2012/jun/11/obama-drone-wars-normalisation-extrajudicial-killing

EU Business. (2012) EU refuses to fund 'pointless' Greece-Turkey border fence. *EU Business.* Available from https://www.eubusiness.com/news-eu/greece-immigration.f17/

European Commission. (2012) *European Neighbourhood Policy, EC.* Available from. http://www.ec.europa.eu/world/enp/index_en.htm

European Council. (2008) Joint Paper by the Commission and the Secretary General/High representative concerning, Climate Change and International Security, to European Council. 14 March. Available from: https://www.consilium.europa.eu/uedocs/cms_data/docs/pressdata/en/reports/99387.pdf

Evans, M. (2007) *City Without Joy: Urban Military Operations into the 21st Century.* Australian Defence College. Occasional Series no.2, Canberra, Australia. Available from https://smallwarsjournal.com/blog/city-without-joy

Farrell, N. (2010) *All you need is a (separation barrier).* Third Coast Audio International Festival 2010. Available from: https://www.thirdcoastfestival.org/feature/all-you-need-is-a-separation-barrier

Foresight: Migration and Global Environmental Change. (2011*) Final Project Report.* London: The Government Office for Science.

Fiske, P. (2000) Border patrol with Iran's drugbusters. *BBC News.* 19 May. Available from: http://news.bbc.co.uk/1/hi/programmes/from_our_own_correspondent/755532.stm

Geddes, A. (2003) *Still Beyond Fortress Europe? Patterns and Pathways in EU Migration Policy.* Liverpool: University of Liverpool.

Global Humanitarian Forum. (2009) *Human Impact Report: Climate Change - The Anatomy of a Silent Crisis.* Geneva: Global Humanitarian Forum.

Gold, D. (2008) The Golan Heights and the Syrian-Israeli Negotiations. *Jerusalem Centre for Public Affairs.* 8(1). Available from: https://jcpa.org/the-golan-heights-and-the-syrian-israeli-negotiations/

Graham, S. (2009) The Urban 'Battlespace.' *Theory, Culture & Society.* 26(7-8), pp. 278-288.

Graham, S. (2010) *Cities Under Siege: The New Military Urbanism.* Verso: London.

Guild, E. (2009) *Security and Migration in the 21st Century*. Polity Press: Cambridge.

Haggerty, K., and Trottier, D. (2013) Surveillance of/and Beyond Nature: Monitoring Beyond the Human. *Society & Animals.* Available from: http://www.academia.edu/3727857/Surveillance_and_of_nature_monitoring_beyond_the_human

Halpin, E., Trevorrow, P., Webb, D., and Wright, S. (2006) *Cyberwar, Netwar and the Revolution in Military Affairs.* New York: Palgrave.

Hambling, D. (2002) Star Wars hits the streets. *New Scientist.* (176) 12 October, pp. 42-45. Updated in Hambling, D. (2004) Stun Weapons to target crowds. *New Scientist.* (182), 19 June, p. 24.

Hambling, D. (2011) Riot Shields could scatter crowds With Wall of sound. *New Scientist.* 14 December. Available from: http://www.newscientist.com/article/mg21228425.300-riot-shields-could-scatter-crowds-with-wall-of-sound.html

Hambling, D. (2013) Tagging by drones could replace lethal strikes. *New Scientist*. 219(2931), pp. 5-57.

Hayes, B. (2006) *Arming Big Brother: The EU's Security Research Programme*. Amsterdam: Transnational Institute (TNI)/Statewatch.

Hayes, B. (2009) *NeoConOpticon – The EU Security Complex*. Amsterdam: Transnational Institute(TNI)/Statewatch. Available from: http://www.statewatch.org/analyses/neoconopticon-report.pdf

Hayes, B. (2012) The surveillance – industrial complex. In Ball, K., Haggerty, K.D., and Lyon, D. (ed's). (2012) *Routledge Surveillance Studies Handbook.* Abingdon: Routledge, pp. 167-175.

Hobbing, P. (2010) *The Management of the EU's External Borders from the Customs Union to FRONTEX and E-Borders*. Brussels: Belgium Centre for European Policy Studies (CEPS), pp. 63-72.

Hornqvist, M. (2004) The Birth of Public Order Policy. *Race & Class.* 46(1), pp. 30-52.

Human Rights Watch (HRW). (2012) *Losing Humanity – The Case Against Killer Robots.* Washington: Human Rights Watch. Available from: https://www.hrw.org/report/2012/11/19/losing-humanity/case-against-killer-robots]

Humble, T. (2011) *Pressure at the Levees – Exploring the Growth of Border Securitisation and its Impact on Climate Induced Migration.* Unpublished thesis submitted in part fulfilment of BA in Peace Studies and International Relations, Leeds Metropolitan University.

Intergovernmental Panel on Climate Change (IPCC). (2007) *Intergovernmental Panel on Climate Change. Fourth Assessment Report. Working Group II: Impacts, Adaption and Vulnerability.* Geneva: Intergovernmental Panel on Climate Change. Available from: https://www.ipcc.ch/report/ar4/wg2/

Jakobeit, C., and Methmann, C. (2012) Climate refugees as Dawning Catastrophe? A Critique of the Dominant Quest For Numbers. In Scheffran, J., Brzoska, M., Brauch, H.G., Link, P.M., & Schilling, J. (ed's). (2012) *Climate Change, Human Security and Violent Conflict – Challenges for Societal Stability,* Hexagon Series on Human & Environmental Security and Peace, Vol. 8, Springer-Verlag, Germany.

Jones, R. (2011) Border Security, 9/11 and the enclosure of civilisation. *The Geographical Journal.* 177(3), pp. 213-217.

Klein, N. (2007) *The Shock Doctrine.* London: Penguin.

Kington, T. (2009) Finmeccanica Expands Middle East Land Border Business. *Defense News.* 12 October.

Klotz, L., Furmanski, M., and Wheelis, M. (2003) *Beware the Siren's Song: Why 'Non-Lethal' Incapacitating Chemical Agents are Lethal.* Washington: Federation of American Scientists.

Lavenex, S., and Wichmann, N. (2009) The External Governance of EU Internal Policy. *European Integration.* 31(1), pp. 83-102.

Lewer, N. (ed). (2002) *The Future of Non-Lethal Weapons: Technologies, Operations, Ethics and Law.* London: Frank Cass.

Martin, B., and Wright, S. (2006) Looming struggles over technology for border control. *Journal of Organisational Transformation and Social Change.* 3(1), pp. 95-107. Available from: http://www.bmartin.cc/pubs/06jotsc.html

Mathiesen, T. (1999) *On Globalisation Of Control: Towards an Integrated Surveillance system in Europe.* London: Statewatch.

Modise, S. (2009) South Africa-Zimbabwe border fences disappear: opposition expresses fears. *Afrik News.* 27 July.
Available from: https://www.afrik-news.com/article15970.html

Moore, H. (2000) *Laser technology Update: Pulsed Impulsive Kill Laser (PILKL).* Paper presented to NDIA (2000), Joint Services Small Arms

Symposium. 29 August. Editor's note: original link defunct, but see: https://apps.dtic.mil/sti/pdfs/ADA393603.pdf

Myers, N. (2002) Environmental refugees: a growing phenomenon of the 21st century. *Philosophical Transactions of The Royal Society Biological Sciences*. 357(1420), pp. 609-618. Available from: http://rstb.royalsocietypublishing.org/content/357/1420/609.full.pdf+html

Nation. (2011) Pakistan to mine, fence Afghan border. *Nation.*

Omega Foundation. (2000) *Crowd Control Technologies – A report prepared for the STOA Panel of the European Parliament*. Available from: http://www.yumpu.com/en/document/view/11273571/crowd-control-technologies-omega-research-foundation

Pécoud, A., and Guchteneire, P. (2006) International Migration, Border Controls and Human Rights: Assessing the Relevance of a Right to Mobility. *Journal of Borderlands Studies*. 21(1), pp. 69-86.

Pilisuk, M. (2008) *Who Benefits From Global Violence and War?* Westwood CT: Greenwood/Praeger.

Renton, A. (2009) *Suffering the Science: Climate change, people, and poverty.* Oxfam Briefing Paper, Oxfam. 6 July. Available from: https://policy-practice.oxfam.org/resources/suffering-the-science-climate-change-people-and-poverty-114606/

Salter, M.B. (2005) At the Threshold of Security: A theory of International Borders. In:

Zureik, E., and Salter, M.B. (ed's). (2005) *Global Surveillance and Policing: Border, Security and Identity.* Devon: Willian Publishing.

Scheffran, J., Brzoska, M., Brauch, H.G., Link, P.M., and Schilling, J. (ed's). (2012) *Climate Change, Human Security and Violent Conflict – Challenges for Societal Stability,* Hexagon Series on Human & Environmental Security and Peace, Vol. 8. Germany: Springer-Verlag.

Schwartz, P., and Randall, D. (2004) An Abrupt Climate Change Scenario and Its Implications for United States National Security, Contract Study for the U.S. Defense. Washington DC: DoD. Available from: https://www.iatp.org/documents/abrupt-climate-change-scenario-and-its-implications-united-states-national-security

Smith, P.J. (2007) Climate Change, Mass Migration and the Military Response. *Orbis.* 51(4), pp. 617-633.

Statewatch. (2006) EU: border control for the 21st Century-automated passenger processing. *Statewatch.* 16(1), pp.1-2.

Toffler, A., and Toffler, H. (1993) *War & Anti-War: Survival at the Dawn of the 21st Century.* USA: Little Brown and Co.

United Nations. (2007) *Security Council Holds First Ever Debate on Impact of Climate Change on Peace, Security, Hearing over 50 Speakers, UN Security Council 5663 Meeting.* 17 April. New York: United Nations.

United Nations. (2009) *Climate Change and Its Possible Security Implications.* Report of the Secretary-General, A/64/350. 11 September. New York: United Nations.

UNU-EHS (United Nations University). (2005) As ranks of 'Environmental refugees' Swell Worldwide, Calls grow for Better Definition, Recognition, Support. *United Nations University.* Available from: https://www.eurekalert.org/news-releases/746072

United States Space Command. (1997) *Vision for 2020.* Colorado Springs: Peterson Airforce Base. Available from: https://thecommunity.com/wp-content/uploads/2018/08/Vision2020.pdf

Vandystadt, J. (2012) 'Greek problem' at heart of debates on migration. *Europolitics: The European Affairs Daily.* 7 March.

Warner, K., Olivia, D., and Stal, S. (2008) Field observations and empirical research. *Forced Migration Review.* October (31), pp. 13-15.

Webb, D.C. (2007) Thinking the Worst: The Pentagon Report. in Cromwell, D., and Levene, M. (ed's). (2007) *Surviving Climate Change- The Struggle to Avert Global Catastrophe.* London: Pluto Press.

Wheelis, M., and Dando, M. (2005) Neurobiology: A Case Study of the Imminent Militarization of Biology. *International Review of the Red Cross.* 87(859). Available from: www.ikrk.org/eng/assets/files/other/irrc_859_whelis_dando.pdf

White, G. (2011) *Climate Change and Migration: Security and Borders in a Warming World.* New York: Oxford University Press.

World Bank. (2009) *World Development Report 2010: Development and Climate Change.* Washington: World Bank.

Wright, S. (1998) *An Appraisal of the Technologies of Political Control.* STOA Panel, European Parliament. DG Research, 6 January. Available from: http://cryptome.org/stoa-atpc.htm

Wright, S. (2006) Sub-Lethal Vision: varieties of military surveillance technology. *Surveillance & Society.* 4(1/2), pp. 136-153.

Wright, S., and Martin, B. (2006) Looming Struggles Over Technology For Border Control. *Journal of Organisational Transformation and Social Change.* 3(1), pp. 95-107.

Wright, S. (2007a) When Drugs become Weapons. *The Guardian.* 24 May. Available from: https://www.theguardian.com/technology/2007/may/24/guardianweeklytechnologysection.weaponstechnology

Wright, S. (2007b) Preparing For Mass Refugee Flows - The Corporate Military Sector. In Cromwell, D., and Levene, M. (ed's). (2007) *Surviving Climate Change - The Struggle to Avert Global Catastrophe.* London: Pluto Press, pp. 82-101.

Wright, S. (2012) Policing Borders in A Time Of Rapid Climate Change. In Scheffran, J., Brzoska, M., Brauch, H.G., Link, P.M., and Schilling, J. (ed's). (2012) *Climate Change, Human Security and Violent Conflict – Challenges for Societal Stability,* Hexagon Series on Human & Environmental Security and Peace, Vol. 8. Germany: Springer-Verlag, pp. 351-370.

Zetter, R. (2008) Legal and Normative Frameworks. *Forced Migration Review.* 31, pp. 62-63.

Zhi, C. (2012) Israel to build wall along Jordanian border: Netanyahu. *Xinhua News Agency.* 1 January. Available from: https://en.trend.az/world/israel/1975942.html

Looming struggles over technology for border control

Brian Martin and Steve Wright[1]

Abstract

New technologies under development, capable of inflicting pain on masses of people, could be used for border control against asylum seekers. Implementation might be rationalized by the threat of mass migration due to climate change, nuclear disaster or exaggerated fears of refugees created by governments. We focus on taser anti-personnel mines, suggesting both technological countermeasures and ways of making the use of such technology politically counterproductive. We also outline several other types of 'non-lethal' technology that could be used for border control and raise human rights concerns: high-powered microwaves; armed robots; wireless tasers; acoustic devices/vortex rings; ionizing and pulsed energy lasers; chemical calmatives, convulsants, bioregulators and malodurants. Whether all these possible border technologies will be implemented is a matter for speculation, but their serious human rights implications warrant advance scrutiny.

Keywords: border control; non-lethal weapons; human rights; backfire; asylum seekers; taser mines

Introduction

There are millions of refugees in the world, many of them fleeing war and persecution. Although most of these people have found asylum - sometimes only temporary - elsewhere in their own countries or in nearby countries, the refugee 'problem' has caused the governments of many rich countries to develop ever more drastic measures to prevent unauthorized entry. At the same time they have mobilized public opinion against refugees.

Corporate globalization is breaking down traditional societies, opening economies to foreign investment. But the free flow of capital is not matched by

1 The version of this article is adapted from https://www.bmartin.cc/pubs/06jotsc.html It appears in print in the *Journal of Organisational Transformation and Social Change*, 3(1), 2006, pp. 95-107

an equivalent free flow of labour. Global mass media present unrealistic visions of western affluence while governments tighten entry requirements.

As refugees have been demonized by western governments and mass media, supporters of human rights have been put on the defensive. Yet things could become much worse.

A new era of sub-state warfare emerged after 11 September 2001, in which all refugees are viewed as suspect and new measures are considered to hold refugees outside of the borders of rich countries whilst their applications are processed (Statewatch 2003), or to biometrically track 'asylum seekers' once they are inside their chosen state of refuge.

According to Article 33 of the 1951 Geneva Refugee Convention, 'No Contracting State shall expel or return ("refouler") a refugee in any manner whatsoever to the frontiers of territories where his life or freedom would be threatened on account of his race, religion, nationality, membership of a particular social group or political opinion.' However, within Europe, huge 'Eurodac' databases have been set up to fingerprint every refugee to use this convention so that attempts to enter one EU country are prevented when another EU country previously refused permission (SEMDOC 2002). Rapid advances in computation technologies using eye and face recognition will enable such tracking to become algorithmic and 'official non-residents' could be effectively barcoded and electronically branded when passing through external and internal gateways.

A new state security context

Such migrations are not happening in a vacuum. Affluent countries are creating advanced weapons technologies that are used in wars frequently leading to the displacement of civilians. Energy-intensive affluence is contributing to climate change that is already being seen in security terms because of its potential to rapidly generate huge numbers of refugees. Human-induced climate change could lead to sea level rises of several metres. Most of the world's key centres of population are on seaboards and highly vulnerable to the negative impacts of flooding.

From 1995, the EU has conceptualized the securitizing of the environment whilst lacking any influence to strategically integrate member states' military forces. A European Parliament resolution in 1999 noted that 'the number of "environmental refugees" now exceeds the number of "traditional refugees" (25 million compared with 22 million)' (EU 1999: 93). Analysts such as Vogler

(2002) have noted that whilst the EU has stopped short of characterizing refugees as a security threat, it has perceived the flow of refugees as putting 'direct pressure on EU immigration and justice policies.'

Advisors to the US military have been more forthright. A secret report prepared for the Pentagon in 2003 and obtained by the media warns of catastrophic climate change leading to future wars being fought over the issue of survival rather than religion, ideology or national honour (Schwartz and Randall 2003). The report predicts that rich areas such as the US and Europe would become virtual fortresses to prevent millions of migrants from entering after being forced from land drowned by sea level rise or no longer able to grow crops, with more than 400 million people in sub-tropical regions at risk. They predict massive numbers of migrants arriving at Southern European shores from hard-hit Africa and mega-droughts affecting the world's major bread baskets, including America's midwest, where strong winds cause soil loss. Different regions would suffer disproportionately; for example, China's huge population makes it especially vulnerable and Bangladesh is predicted to become virtually uninhabitable because of rising sea levels.

Another source of mass human flows is political crisis or disaster. The explosion of just a single nuclear weapon in a city - for example in the Middle East or South Asia - could trigger an avalanche of refugees fleeing the actual explosion, fallout or the risk of future attacks. A serious accident at a nuclear power plant could have similar consequences. Such possibilities could lead some states to seal their borders and to deploy technologies to prevent crossings by civilians.

We do not make predictions but rather suggest that there are several contingencies - climate change, war, terrorist attack, political emergency - that could lead large numbers of people to flee their homes and for states to seek to seal their borders against masses of people seeking asylum. Furthermore, even without a massive increase in human migration, it is possible for governments to create fears about such an occurrence that could be used to politically justify border policing. In other words, the refugee 'threat' is socially constructed: there doesn't need to be a real issue for technology to be deployed (Pickering 2004). Furthermore, the very deployment of such measures creates an assumption that there is a security crisis and helps to legitimate further developments.

Reframing human displacement strategies and options

Schwartz and Randall (2003) concede that it may already be too late to prevent a disaster that becomes a unique national security threat because there is no obvious enemy to attack. However, that has not stopped US military planners treating the threat as deserving of a technological treatment.

For several decades, militaries have been pouring funds into developing so-called non-lethal weapons, such as plastic bullets, electroshock batons and pepper spray. Some of these have already been adopted by police, military and state security forces. In addition to physical equipment, the category of non-lethal weapons includes techniques of human tracking, area denial, and advanced techniques of intimidation and interrogation, such as sensory deprivation - so-called 'torture-lite'. These tools are already being used on an everyday basis to quash dissent and to restrict access (Omega 2000). Another generation of sub-lethal incapacitating weaponry lies in the wings waiting new applications. In conference proceedings of specialist security seminars, refugee issues are reframed from a matter of humanitarian assistance into a new technopolitics of exclusion. (For detailed discussions of advances in so-called non-lethal weaponry and possible future capabilities and options, see the Janes seminars on non-lethal weapons and the non-lethal weapons symposia at Ettlingen, Germany hosted by Fraunhofer ICT.)

The intersection of the growing refugee 'problem' and futuristic techniques of technological control gives rise to some frightening possibilities in the next decade or two. New technologies give the capacity to inflict pain on whole groups of people. For example, in addition to electroshock batons that are used against individuals, weapons are being developed by governments and corporations to incapacitate entire crowds, based on chemical, biological, neurological and directed-energy mechanisms. Such weapons have been designed with mass incapacitation in mind and could have a tactical role when used for border protection against refugees, protesters at rallies, and any massed assembly. Some of these are aimed at area denial and use a targeting method that is both indiscriminate and victim-activated.

Our aim here is to explain some of the new technologies for social control and to give ideas about how they might be opposed. Because few of these technologies have been implemented, with some scarcely past the drawing board, our assessments are inevitably preliminary and speculative. Our aim here is not to predict the future but rather to warn about current trends and to suggest ways of carrying out technical and social analyses that can help those opposed to technological assault. We also want to draw attention to the ethics of some of the possible countermeasures to such technologies, when attempting to advance social justice in a time of terror.

Arsenals and scenarios

The term 'non-lethal weapon' is often a misnomer, because people can be killed as well as permanently disabled by these weapons. This can occur when weapons are used contrary to specifications, such as plastic bullets fired at close range, or when the target is vulnerable, such as electroshock used against a person with a weak heart. Sometimes 'less-lethal weapon' or 'sub-lethal weapon' is used to indicate the ambiguity. However, because of their nature, many of these weapons can be deliberately abused to inflict torture or force compliance via pain (Amnesty 2003). Many of the technologies being developed for area denial or exclusion purposes have never been subjected to independent medical evaluation. It is worth mentioning some of the varieties of weapons to illustrate the medical uncertainties surrounding their alleged harmlessness (Wright 2002).

There are a number of new mechanisms for such weapons currently being explored, including taser anti-personnel mines; high-powered microwaves; armed robots; wireless tasers; acoustic devices/vortex rings; ionizing and pulsed energy lasers; chemical calmatives, convulsants, bioregulators and malodurants.

Some of this technology is so alien that the best way to imagine how it will be used is via imaginative devices such as science fiction stories or possible-use scenarios. In the future, science fiction and Hollywood can probably provide some of the most powerful warnings about the need for adequate social impact or technology assessment of such devices.

With a much more modest budget it is more appropriate for us to provide illustrative technological scenarios. We use taser landmines as our primary example, giving an overview of the technology and its likely applications and then suggesting some possible technical countermeasures, namely ways that targets of the weapons might avoid or neutralize them. We then suggest some more generally applicable political countermeasures, namely ways for targets or opponents of the weapons to challenge taser landmines, at the point of use or earlier during production, sale or implementation. We are also mindful of the potential future role of support networks that may be better equipped than the immediate targets, lending their energy and external resources to providing bridges out from areas otherwise technologically denied. In a later section we introduce a number of other scenarios and possible technical countermeasures.

Taser landmines

A taser is an electroshock weapon. It delivers a high voltage, typically 50,000 volts, to the target, resulting in excruciating pain and a shutdown of major muscle groups, causing physical collapse. A typical weapon used in policing fires two darts at the target, with trailing wires. Once an electrical connection is made, the voltage is turned on, disabling the target even through clothing.

The taser is supposed to be non-lethal, causing no permanent damage, but there have been reported cases of deaths and miscarriages linked to taser use, though causation has been contested by police. A recent report by Amnesty International alleges that there have been over 70 deaths attributable to taser use in the US and Canada (Amnesty 2004). What is undoubted is the extreme pain caused by tasers. When a group of volunteers experienced the effect of a taser, only one was willing to accept exposure for the full five seconds before the voltage was automatically cut off, and not a single one volunteered for a second shock (Rappert 2003).

The idea of the taser landmine is to arm a landmine not with an explosive but with a taser. A person triggering the mine would be hit by the taser darts and immobilized. The taser would give regular shocks over an extended period, up to an hour.

A field of taser landmines could serve as a form of non-lethal border protection. An area would be mined; a few guards would be available to arrest or release victims of the mines.

Given the high level of pain caused by even a few seconds of taser shocks, the consequences of many minutes of shock are truly horrific, and would likely result in post-traumatic stress disorder if not worse.

Technological countermeasures

As with any minefield, an obvious countermeasure is avoidance, namely getting through the field without triggering any mines. But the risks are so great that this seems unwise. Another option is triggering mines by tossing objects into the field, by using long non-conducting probes (such as wooden poles), or by sending an automatic vehicle into the area. Another approach is protection, for example a large shield surrounding the body, separated by insulation. Riding in a car would easily provide protection - but not in difficult terrain. It is also possible to imagine electromagnetic countermeasures designed to disrupt taser electronics. These are likely to be far too advanced for most refugees to contemplate initially. But there will be a learning curve as refugees find out about the technology and try out crude measures to resist or avoid it. Later, sympathetic NGOs might be able to provide both information and practical assistance in creating mechanisms to disable the mines or to drive vehicles into the mined areas that can produce safe bridges once all the existing ordnance has been triggered. Testing might indicate for example that devices as simple as a pulsed water pistol are sufficient to trigger the device; modern toys have quite high ranges and include substantial reservoirs. Or more simply, a large sports utility vehicle (SUV) or landrover could be driven from the other side and spray paint used on the ground to mark a safe route. Even relatively simple devices such as a lawn mower with fixed wheels could be adapted and let loose if the terrain was smooth. Another option is the use of animals, such as sheep or goats, that could be herded through a minefield to create a safe path for humans, though at the cost of hurting the animals.

Political countermeasures

One of the attractions of non-lethal weapons, from the point of view of their promoters, is that they have a more benign appearance and are thus less likely to cause concern than old-fashioned lethal weapons such as guns. If refugees were shot down in cold blood at borders, this could cause outrage, but if they were deterred by chemical or electrical techniques, outrage might be reduced.

Torture is almost always carried out in secret, because it is widely seen as reprehensible. However, torture carried out using sensory deprivation may be presented as not quite so bad as a brutal beating, though it can be just as damaging. We therefore are interested in ways that defenders of human rights can ensure that appropriate outrage results from illegal use of non-lethal weapons. To provide a framework for analysing political countermeasures, we use the theory of backfire dynamics (Jansen and Martin 2003, 2004; Martin 2004, 2005; Martin and Wright 2003).

If an action is perceived as unjust and information about it is communicated to receptive audiences, it has the capacity to backfire against those held responsible. For example, a cold-blooded massacre of peaceful protesters can backfire against the killers or the government held responsible (Sharp 1973). Prominent examples include the 1960 Sharpeville massacre in South Africa, which greatly stimulated international opposition to apartheid, and the 1991 Dili massacre in East Timor, which led to a huge increase in international support for East Timorese independence.

Attackers have several ways to inhibit this backfire process: (1) cover-up; (2) devaluation of the targets; (3) reinterpretation of what is happening; (4) use of official processes to give the appearance of justice; and (5) intimidation and bribery.

These five methods are commonly used when asylum seekers are held in detention camps, in order to prevent outrage from this inhumane treatment. For example, in Australia (Callaghan and Martin 2004), (1) many detention camps are far from population centres and kept off limits to the media, to prevent the general public knowing the damage caused to inmates. (2) Refugees are demonized as threats to the integrity of the nation, as self-seeking, as inferior, and as terrorists. (3) Use of detention camps is said to be about border protection, not about denial of human rights. (4) Appeal procedures for refugees give the appearance of justice and thereby reduce immediate outrage, but in practice, due to cost, slowness and procedural complexity, perpetuate the detention process. (5) Detention itself is a form of intimidation. Protest against detention can be met by deportation or by bureaucratic reprisals such as denial of family reunions.

To oppose injustice, each of these five methods needs to be countered. (1) The obvious way to counter cover-up is through exposure, for example through films of conditions in detention camps. (2) The best way to counter devaluation is to humanize refugees, for example through personal profiles of individuals. (3) To counter official defences of refugee policy, the significance of human rights needs to be continually emphasized. (4) For opponents of refugee policies, it is tempting to pursue legal or procedural paths such as court challenges to the treatment of individual refugees. The danger is that this may chew up large amounts of money and energy and take a very long time while policies create ever more victims. Procedural routes, if pursued, need to be combined with publicity in order to maximize public outrage. (5) There are two main ways to counter intimidation. One is to refuse to be intimidated. The other is to expose the intimidation itself. This applies not just to refugees but also to others. For example, journalists and editors can go ahead and publish stories despite legal threats, and expose the threats in order to discredit them.

International solidarity movements are also important in reminding perpetrators of human rights violations that they can and will be held accountable for their actions. Persistence is crucial though often difficult. In 2004, something occurred that previously would have hardly seemed believable: 27,000 Chilean victims of torture during the dirty wars from 1973-1992 (under the internationally supported Pinochet regime) were granted lifetime pensions (Gallardo 2004).

To illustrate how the backfire approach can be used, we examine the scenario of taser landmines, looking in turn at each of the five methods of amplifying outrage.

1. The horrifying consequences of taser landmines need to be exposed, if possible well in advance by explaining the human effects of long-term exposure to tasers. Should an actual taser minefield be constructed, the visual effect is not likely to be striking: photos would not be dramatic, even of a person trapped by a taser. More useful would be confidential reports of the effects of long-term taser exposure or personal testimony of these effects.
2. Before venturing into a field of taser landmines, it would be useful to carry out personal interviews with refugees, combined with photos. With computers and digital cameras, this could be carried out on the spot and communicated to wider audiences. This would bring refugees to life as 'real people' rather than faceless intruders.
3. Proponents will paint taser landmines as a legitimate, non-lethal technique to prevent unauthorized border crossings. Opponents need to present counterarguments, including the extremely damaging effects of long-term exposure to tasers, as well as more general arguments about human rights.
4. Legal or procedural paths, such as seeking a legal ban on the technology or on sales to particular regimes, can be useful especially if used as a tool to create awareness and concern. It would be unwise to rely entirely on formal channels, because laws and regulations are too easily delayed, eviscerated, circumvented or overturned. For example, the taser mine itself is cynically designed to be compliant with the Ottawa Treaty against landmines. Future campaigners need to continue to examine the way these mines are actually used, because they may actually violate the treaty once deployed.
5. Those seeking to expose the inhumane nature of the mines, by collecting and publishing information, need to stand up to threats and legal actions and not succumb to the temptation of accepting funding from organizations that expect recipients not to rock the boat.

It is important to remember that backfire only occurs when there is a perceived injustice, often linked to unfairness, disproportionality or norm violation. When peaceful protesters are violently attacked, this is commonly perceived as unjust because the protesters did nothing to deserve the severity of the attack. But if even a few protesters fight back, this can change the situation to one perceived as a confrontation with violence on both sides, and for many observers outrage is likely to be reduced even though there is still a disproportionality in the use of violence.

Similarly, if refugees are seen as victims of a brutal technology - taser landmines in this case - then they are likely to be viewed sympathetically. But if the refugees or their supporters are seen as being aggressive, for example by blowing up landmines, then some of this sympathy may be lost. Therefore, in looking at technological countermeasures, it is important to keep in mind the image presented to observers. Nonthreatening, defensive methods are likely to be viewed more favourably than violent aggressive ones.

Other area denial scenarios

High-powered microwaves

This device enables a pencil beam of microwave radiation to be focused on a human body at some distance. The result is near instant pain that can only be alleviated by moving out of the beam's path. Such weapons pose all the hazards associated with microwave radiation, with the eyes being particularly vulnerable to a cooking effect. The pain induced is meant to make the dose self-limiting but much higher exposure would become likely if lethal force or barriers blocked off escape routes. The official line is that the devices are safe, though no official technical data has been released. A November 2004 conference at Bradford University on non-lethal weapons questioned the assumption of safety. A participant observed that a natural response to intense eye pain is to shut the eyes - hence making targets effectively blind so that they could no longer navigate a safe way out. Another expert said as far as he knew there was no automatic cut-off on the device which would close it down once a human reached a disabling temperature. Such blind targets would microwave cook en masse. An effective challenge to the apologists for such weapons is to advocate transparency and legal accountability. We will need to establish ways to control or oppose such innovations or face the prospect of successive generations of refugees and activists being the guinea pigs for each successive newcomer to the growing arsenal of unconventional disabling weapons.

At the time of writing this device is a mobile platform but it is not difficult to imagine such technologies being deployed at borders in roving beam fashion. It has been reported that these devices would be deployed in 2005, probably in Iraq (Lococo 2004).

The obvious countermeasures include either physical destruction of the device via some form of disruption, including rocks, or to mirror the beam back to source. The danger of such resistance is that it is likely to provoke the deployment of more lethal technology. A more defensive technology might be to set up a water curtain spray (if water is readily available), because this would dissipate the directed energy into the water as heat. For individuals, aluminium foil blankets and mirror sunglasses afford some protection and could be used on vehicles too. A high-tech form of countermeasure might be the use of 'microwave bridges' to redirect the radiation back to source. However whilst such techno-jiu-jitsu devices are appealing in principle, without the ability for proper field-testing they are likely to remain the domain of government-funded countermeasure programmes that are already investigating how to overcome such border control devices.

Armed robots

Armed robots are algorithmic self-deciding intelligent mobile devices armed with either lethal or sub-lethal weapons and capable of operating as border patrol agents. What was once science fiction is now a reality. Robots bearing incapacitating technologies are now marketed as programmable sentinels of organized violence that will work without respite. The potential hazards are those associated with weapons operating without finer points of discrimination or being deliberately deployed in an abusive configuration especially when on automatic mode and hunting in packs.

Isaac Asimov's science fiction was predicated on rules that no robot should ever be programmed to harm a human being. That design criterion remains fictional: these devices have the potential to be a form of ruthless border patrol that can make rottweilers passé. Unlike rottweilers, such 'self-deciding vehicles' will not be able to be lured off with a juicy piece of steak. However, all such devices must be mobile and their patrol route governed by terrain. Like fictional Daleks, old robots could not go upstairs or negotiate steep hills or holes, so setting up suitable obstacles would enable robot-free bridges to be temporarily secured. New robots, such as the Foster-Miller armed military robots, planned for deployment in Iraq in 2005, can walk upstairs (Anon 2005). (Foster-Miller is a subsidiary of QinetiQ, a company in the Carlisle group, which is heavily involved in oil exploration.) Unlike humans, such robots generate neither letters of condolence to grieving parents nor are they ever likely to be court-martialled for killing an unarmed civilian.

To deal with armed robots, opponents can use tools to tip them over. Most such devices are vulnerable to fire: already the web provides instructions on using mixtures of petrol, soap flakes and polystyrene that would be sufficient to napalm them out of kilter but it is likely that other members of the robot gang will be pre-programmed to report such attacks and request reinforcements. Less violent approaches involving minimum equipment include netting to immobilize robots and black spray paint if a robot is dependent on electronic camera vision for orientation. However, aerial robots may be harder to resist, especially if they are designed to spray calmatives or project other paralysing and incapacitating systems on to crowds. As yet UAVs - unmanned aerial vehicles - are very expensive but that may change. In such circumstances, their Achilles heel is the telecommunications link, which could be targeted with a simple microwave weapon based on a car-battery powered device using a microwave oven and satellite dish.

Wireless tasers

These devices work by spraying plasma from a water cannon device: in essence, conductive liquid spray allows electrical-energy-inducing equipment to transfer the shock to the crowd. This technology is being actively researched in Germany and Russia and depends on relatively calm conditions (Fortov et al. 2003; Meisterhans 2003). Countermeasures could be focussed at either diverting the stream of plasma or earthing the flow of electricity with a physical metal-covered barrier. If it was a static location then using a car-battery-powered set of fans might be sufficient to divert the flow off target. Physical pre-assembled foil-covered shields might be just as useful in cutting off the flow.

Alternatively, if any mains source is available, a counterblast could be attempted by rubber-gloved activists since the plasma will conduct power both ways and it seems unlikely that the device would be built to run on other than grid electricity. A more daring way of achieving this aim would be rocket powered hooks with metal lines used as marine life saving equipment but, if such devices are in short supply, other earthing devices using coiled wire might be attempted. Indeed, hundreds of commercially available helium-filled foil balloons might serve admirably or, if helium was unavailable, the more flammable natural gas could be used.

Acoustic devices/Vortex ring

Acoustic devices can cause disorientation by producing very loud noises. Infra-sound can be created using two ultrasound beams. Pyrotechnically generated sound rings can create either knock-down effects at a distance or carry other incapacitating agents. However, critics doubt the viability of some acoustic weapons, since permanent damage to the ear is possible. Vortex ring technology is still at the prototype stage but blunt trauma injuries are likely to be similar to those associated with water cannon (Deiming et al. 2001).

Ionizing and pulsed energy lasers

Laser light in the UV spectrum can ionize the air sufficiently for it to conduct high voltage electricity, thus making possible directed energy weapons. Their hazards are essentially those associated with electroshocking a diverse population including susceptibility to stress-induced heart attacks, pacemaker failure and induction of post traumatic stress. A new variant has recently been reported from the US Joint Non Lethal Weapons Directorate, namely the pulsed energy projectile that is scheduled to hit the streets by 2006. It started life as the 'Pulsed Impulsive Kill Laser' but has been retuned to create a shock wave by vapourizing the first thing it hits (Hambling 2002, 2004). Its technical specifications have been well guarded but some superfluous injury and traumatic shock induction seem likely. At this stage, the most effective countermeasures revolve around challenging the inhumane nature of using a weapon whose physiological effects on a mixed audience cannot be known in advance.

Chemical calmatives, convulsants, bio-regulators and malodurants

A wide range of chemicals that create a paralyzing effect can be delivered to targets by existing mechanisms for delivering chemical or malodorous agents. Bioregulators would be targeted at interfering with body functions that maintain steady body temperature, heart rate, breathing and heart rates, etc. However, one person's tranquillization is another's lethal dose. In field circumstances, it is impossible to guarantee a uniform effect. Further advances in molecular biology are being directed at specific receptor sites in the human brain that can induce fear and anxiety. These breakthroughs create capacities that no government has ever been shown to use responsibly. The developments pose a huge challenge to NGOs wishing to avoid an arms race in the life sciences (Dando and Nathanson 2004). Yet the strongest objection to their future development remains the fact that they are illegal in most plausible scenarios of future use; this offers a strong campaigning platform.

Conclusion

The introduction of border control using methods such as taser landmines, armed robots or high-powered microwaves is a frightful prospect, given the physical, emotional and social damage that would ensue. We hope that none of these scenarios is actually played out, but feel it necessary to explore the possibility in order to raise concern. We assume that refugees, activists and others will continue to face new technologies in the arsenals of states determined to go beyond the limits of morality and the law. The ethical question for activists during such times, as ever, is what choices should be made if we are to sustain a role as human rights defenders?

In outlining scenarios, we have mentioned some technological countermeasures. We also outlined political countermeasures to taser landmines, noting that similar political countermeasures would apply to the other scenarios. We know that some of these activities will in themselves invite legal and possibly police and military challenge. Our assessments are intended to stimulate thinking about possibilities rather than provide definitive answers.

The nightmare scenario is that such area denial technologies are imposed in a mechanistic manner that isolates large numbers of people desperately fleeing disaster and conflict. The dilemma then for those determined to engage in humanitarian action is what can and should be done to counter such technologies. Much depends on how much preparation time there is and what values are being defended. We believe that activists need to address the unpalatable truth of the emergence of technologies specifically designed to undermine current nonviolent strategies. Technological countermeasures are only part of the solution to human rights abuses due to border control technologies. The challenge is to design effective and humane countermeasures that do not invite a more violent response. We encourage others to replicate and innovate means of technological and political resistance and maintain a focus on the central issues of human rights.

Acknowledgements

We thank Sharon Callaghan, Truda Gray and Andrew Herd for helpful comments on drafts of this paper. This work is supported by the Australian Research Council and by the Social Science Research Council in Washington, DC.

References

Amnesty International (2003) *The Pain Merchants: Security Equipment and its Use in Torture and Other Ill-Treatment,* 2 December, http://web.amnesty.org/library/Index/ENGACT400082003. Accessed 27 November 2005. [Location in 2019: https://www.amnesty.org/en/documents/ACT40/008/2003/en/]

Amnesty International USA (2004) 'Excessive and Lethal Force? Amnesty International's Concerns about Deaths and Ill-Treatment involving Police Use of Tasers', 30 November, http://web.amnesty.org/library/index/engamr511392004. Accessed 27 November 2005. [Location in 2019: https://www.amnestyusa.org/reports/usa-excessive-and-lethal-force-amnesty-internationals-concerns-about-deaths-and-ill-treatment-involving-police-use-of-tasers/]

Anon (2005) 'US Plans "Robot Troops" for Iraq', *BBC News,* 23 January.

Callaghan, S. and Martin, B. (2004) 'Igniting Concern about Refugee Injustice', *Education and Social Action Conference 2004* (ed. Rick Flowers), Sydney: Centre for Popular Education, University of Technology, Sydney, pp. 299-303.

Dando, M. and Nathanson, V. (2004) *Biotechnology, Weapons and Humanity II,* London: British Medical Association, Board of Science and Education.

Deiming, L. et al. (2001) 'Infrapulse Generator: An Effective Non-lethal Weapon', Conference on Non-Lethal Weapons: New Options Facing the Future, Ettligen, Germany: Fraunhofer, Institut Chemische Technologie, 25-26 September.

EU (1999) 'Resolution on the Environment, Security and Foreign Policy,' Official Journal of the European Communities, C128, A4-0005/99 (7 May), pp. 92-96.

Fortov, V. et al. (2003) 'Remote Operation Electroshocking Devices', Non-Lethal Capabilities Facing Emerging Threats, 2nd European Symposium on Non-Lethal Weapons, Ettligen, Germany: Fraunhofer, Institut Chemische Technologie, 13-14 May.

Gallardo, E. (2004) 'Chilean Victims to Get Payments', *Miami Herald,* 30 November.

Hambling, D. (2002) 'Star Wars Hits the Streets', *New Scientist,* 176 (12 October), pp. 42-45.

Hambling, D. (2004) 'Stun Weapons to Target Crowds', *New Scientist,* 182 (19 June), p. 24.

Jansen, S. C. and Martin, B. (2003) 'Making Censorship Backfire', *Counterpoise,* 7, pp. 5-15.

Jansen, S. C. and Martin, B. (2004) 'Exposing and Opposing Censorship: Backfire Dynamics in Freedom-of-Speech Struggles', *Pacific Journalism Review,* 10 (1), pp. 29-45.

Lococo, E. (2004) 'Raytheon Takes Aim with Heat Ray', *Bloomberg News,* 2 December.

Martin, B. (2004) 'Iraq Attack Backfire', *Economic and Political Weekly,* 39 (17 April), pp. 1577-1583.

Martin, B. (2005) 'The Beating of Rodney King: The Dynamics of Backfire', *Critical Criminology,* 13, pp. 307-326.

Martin, B. and Wright, S. (2003) 'Countershock: Mobilizing Resistance to Electroshock Weapons', *Medicine, Conflict and Survival,* 19, pp. 205-222.

Meisterhans D. (2003) 'Non-Lethal Capabilities: Stand-off Electrical Incapacitation (Plasma-Taser)', Non-Lethal Capabilities Facing Emerging Threats, 2nd European Symposium on Non-Lethal Weapons, Ettligen, Germany: Fraunhofer, Institut Chemische Technologie, 13-14 May.

Omega Foundation (2000) Crowd Control Technologies (An Appraisal of Technologies for Political Control). Report to the Scientific and Technological Options Assessment (STOA) Panel of the European Parliament, June, http://www.europarl.eu.int/stoa/publi/pdf/99-14-01-a_en.pdf. Accessed 27 November 2005. [Location in 2019: http://www.europarl.europa.eu/thinktank/en/document.html?reference=DG-4-JOIN_ET(2000)168394]

Pickering, S. (2004) 'Border Terror: Policing, Forced Migration and Terrorism', *Global Change, Peace & Security,* 16, pp. 211-226.

Rappert, B. (2003) 'Shock Tactics', *New Scientist,* 177 (15 February), pp. 34-37.

Schwartz, P. and Randall, D. (2003) 'An Abrupt Climate Change Scenario and its Implications for United States National Security,' October.

SEMDOC (Statewatch European Monitoring and Documentation Centre) (2002) 'Statewatch Comments for House of Lords Select Committee on the European Union, sub-committee "F": Commission Communication on Illegal Immigration', 24 April, http://www.statewatch.org/docbin/evidence/immig2002.html. Accessed 27 November 2005.

Sharp, G. (1973) *The Politics of Nonviolent Action,* Boston: Porter Sargent.

Statewatch (2003) 'EU Buffer States and UNHCR "Processing" Centres and "Safe Havens"', http://www.statewatch.org/news/2003/jun/07eubuffer.htm. Accessed 27 November 2005.

Vogler, J. (2002) 'The European Union and the "Securitisation" of the Environment', Human *Security and the Environment: International Comparisons* (eds. E. A. Page and M. Redclift), UK: Edward Elgar.

Wright, S. (2002) 'Future Sub-lethal, Incapacitating and Paralysing Technologies - Their Coming Role in the Mass Production of Torture, Cruel, Inhumane & Degrading Treatment', *Statewatch News,* November 2002, http://www.statewatch.org/news/2002/nov/torture.pdf. Accessed 27 November 2005.

Japan's hidden arms trade

Robin Ballantyne[1]

The 2004 government announcement that it was considering joining the US in the production of a missile defence system was deeply troubling to Japanese and Asians concerned about Japan's expansive military posture in tandem with the US. Over the years, Japan has created a high tech non-nuclear military force. But it has steadfastly maintained an official ban on weapons exports. Many feared that the move heralded the end of Japan's nearly 40-year-old ban on arms exports.

Since 1976, the Japanese government has proclaimed that "Japan shall not promote 'arms' exports, regardless of the destinations."[2] This stance has been advanced by ministers and officials in the domestic and international arena, who stress that Japan does not participate in the global arms trade. For example, in 2000 Sugiura Seiken, the Senior Vice Minister for Foreign Affairs informed a UN conference that: "Japan has been actively pursuing arms control and disarmament. We do not permit the export of arms to any country."[3]

However, in December of 2004 it became clear that Japan's position as a weapons manufacturer and weapons exporter were under review. Not only was the Japanese Government considering taking part in the Missile Defence Programme, but the Chief Cabinet Secretary also announced that Japan may consider other opportunities for joint development and production with the US, as well as projects with other countries "related to support of counter-terrorism and counterpiracy."[4] In addition, Prime Minister Koizumi confirmed the possibility that Japan may sell arms to Southeast Asian nations to fight piracy.[5]

These statements, and particularly the Missile Defence project, are being undertaken both in response to rising Japan-North Korea tensions, and in the

1 The Asia-Pacific Journal, 3(1). 2005. With gratitude to Mark Selden, editor.

2 Japan's Policies on the Control of Arms Exports http://www.mofa.go.jp/policy/un/disarmament/policy/ accessed 22 November 2005.

3 Sugiura Seikin, Senior Vice Minister for Foreign Affairs of Japan Speech to the UN Conference on the Illicit Trade in Small Arms and Light Weapons in All Its Aspects. 9 July 200

4 Statement (https://japan.kantei.go.jp/tyokan/2004/1210statement_e.html) by the Chief Cabinet Secretary. 10 December 2004.

5 Japan Signals Key Military Shift http://news.bbc.co.uk/1/hi/world/asia-pacific/4084249.stm 11 December 2004

wish to strengthen the capacity of Southeast Asian countries to protect Japanese shipping through the Malacca straits.

However, the truth of the matter is that these plans do not indicate a dramatic change in policy. Far from having a record of no arms transfers, Japan has been and continues to be, actively involved in the sale of small arms and dual-use goods to other nations. Due to a lack of transparency in the reporting system, however, important questions remain concerning the precise nature of various military exports.

Small arms

Japan has been one of the lead actors in the 2001 UN Programme of Action to Prevent, Combat and Eradicate the Illicit Trade in Small Arms and Light Weapons in All Its Aspects (PoA). It has donated substantial sums of money for various weapons collection programmes worldwide, most notably, over $10 million for programmes in Sri Lanka, Cambodia and Sierra Leone.[6] Furthermore, Japan continues to campaign for the establishment of an international system to mark and trace small arms.[7]

As the former Japanese ambassador to the Conference on Disarmament stated, Japan has assumed this lead role on the PoA because "many countries felt that Japan is the standard-bearer of multilateral disarmament affairs because Japan enjoys the high moral ground of not exporting small arms."[8] However the fact is that Japan actually conducts a thriving small arms export trade. The international annual publication, the Small Arms Survey, for example, reported that in 2002 Japan exported $65 million worth of small arms which, in monetary terms, ranks Japan amongst the top eight exporters of small arms world-wide for that year.[9]

---

6 Japan to enforce arms reduction policy (http://web.amnesty.org/web/web.nsf/pages/ttt3_japan) accessed 7 March 2005. And Government of Japan's National Report (http://www.mofa.go.jp/policy/un/disarmament/weapon/report0306.html) on the Implementation of Programme of Action (PoA) to Prevent, Combat and Eradicate the Illicit Trade in Small Arms and Light Weapons in All Its Aspects accessed 17 July 2003

7 Speech (http://www.mofa.go.jp/policy/un/disarmament/weapon/speech0307.html) by Ambassador Amano Yukiya, Director-General for Arms Control and Scientific Affairs. Accessed 17 July 2003.

8 Inoguchi Kuniko, former Japanese ambassador to the Conference on Disarmament, Asahi Shimbun, 20 September 2004.

9 Weapons at War: Small Arms Survey. 2005 (Oxford, Oxford University Press, 2005), p.102-105.

The Japanese government evades this issue by contending that "hunting guns and sport guns are not regarded as 'arms'"[10] and therefore the self-imposed ban on arms exports only applies to guns of a military specification. This raises the question of what differentiates a military specification gun from a sporting or hunting weapon. However, the Japanese Ministry for Export, Trade and Industry (METI) provides no comprehensive definition. Instead it decides on a case-by-case basis whether or not a weapon should be defined as being of military specification.

The finessing of the definition of "arms" to exclude sporting and hunting weapons may ensure that Japan adheres to its ban on arms in the eyes of the policy makers but in reality this is a cynical interpretation. While METI claims that there is a distinction between a sporting weapon and a military weapon, the fact of the matter is that almost all tactical shotguns—the type of weapon used by military and police forces throughout the world—are modified civilian guns.[11]

Each year small arms kill approximately 500,000 people around the world. So great is their impact on human security that Kofi Annan observed: "In terms of the carnage they cause, small arms, indeed, could well be described as 'weapons of mass destruction'."[12] The small arms used in these deaths are not restricted to those of a military specification. In armed conflicts around the world hunting and sporting weapons are routinely used to commit violent acts and abuse human rights. In recent years Amnesty International has reported the use of such weapons by death squads in Algeria and armed political groups in the Solomon Islands.[13] Clearly, when one is looking down the barrel of a gun it matters little whether the weapon in question is deemed to be of the sporting or hunting, or military variety.

Questionable exports

Further questions about Japan's dedication to a ban on arms exports are raised by an examination of data submitted to the UN Commodity Trade Statistics

10 National Report (http://www.mofa.go.jp/policy/un/disarmament/weapon/report0306.html) on the Implementation of Programme of Action (PoA) to Prevent, Combat and Eradicate the Illicit Trade in Small Arms and Light Weapons in All Its Aspects. 22 November 2005.

11 Information from article Kalashnikov Saiga-12S shotgun is tailored for tactical requirements, Jane's International Defence Review. 1 May 2002.

12 War on Terror Fuels Small Arms Trade, The Guardian, 10 October 2003.

13 A Catalogue of Failures: G8 Arms Exports and Human Rights Violations. (https://www.amnesty.org/en/documents/ior30/003/2003/en/)

database (Comtrade) which records the import and export details voluntarily submitted by the customs departments of countries worldwide.[14] According to information submitted by the Japanese customs department to this database, in 2001 Japan exported US$55.7 million worth of "Bombs, Grenades, Ammunition, Mines, & Others." The vast majority of this total went to the US. However, according to the import data submitted by other countries, other recipients of this equipment from Japan included Denmark, Germany, South Korea, Malaysia and Thailand.

Furthermore, according to information that Japan submitted to the Comtrade database in 1999, Japan exported "Military Weapons" to Indonesia and Malaysia and in 2000, Japan exported "Military Weapons" to Israel. Also according to the data submitted by Japan, it has exported "Parts & accessories of Military Weapons" to a large number of countries over several years. And in 2003 Japan reported that it had exported "military rifles, machine guns and other" to the Philippines.

Japanese Customs use the same system of classification for registering exports as does the UN. This means that the Japanese definition of an export will be consistent with the UN definition. So when, for example, Japanese Customs report that "military rifles, machine guns and other" have been exported, according to the UN definition that means that the export must have contained one of the following: Self-propelled Artillery weapons; Rocket launchers; Flame-throwers; Grenade launchers; Torpedo; Torpedo tubes and similar or Other. Of course a note of caution must be added in that the "other" at the end of the list may refer to a number of different items ranging from military rifles to optical devices for use on firearms. Although the Japanese Customs choose to sub-divide the categories when they submit information to Comtrade, thus providing a greater level of detail, even this information does not give a sufficiently detailed breakdown of exactly what items were in the export.

Since there is no domestic report of arms exports, and the information submitted to Comtrade is sufficiently vague as to prevent any meaningful analysis, it is impossible to verify the exact nature of the equipment in these transfers. Until the Japanese government reveals details of these exports, questions will remain as to whether they complied with the "no arms trade" policy.

---

14 Figures used in this article all come from the Comtrade data (http://www.nisat.org/) available on the website of the Norwegian Initiative on Small Arms Transfers (NISAT)

Dual-use goods

A bright light is shone on Japan's involvement in the arms trade when one examines exports of defence electronics and dual-use equipment. Ever since its inception, a gaping hole has existed in the ban on arms exports, specifically products that have both military and civilian applications may escape the ban on military exports. In the 1980s Japanese companies began taking advantage of this loophole by making inroads mainly into the U.S. defence market, providing semiconductor chips for guided missiles and camera lenses used in reconnaissance systems. Since then Japanese components have found their way into a large number of security and defence products across the globe, such as silicon sensors, which are at the core of BAE Systems Inertial Measurement Units used for missile guidance systems,[15] or the Sony Exwave-HAD 800 Line TV camera incorporated in the Denel military and paramilitary turrets.[16]

It seems that even certain vehicles used by the military are able to evade the export ban by using the dual-use window of opportunity. Military forces throughout the world can be seen riding Toyotas, Suzukis and Mitsubishis. In March of this year the Omani Engine Engineering Company announced that it would be basing its Nimer 1 light armoured personnel carrier on a Toyota Land Cruiser 4x4 chassis.[17] The vehicle, which will have firing ports and the possibility of mounted machine guns, is clearly for military use, yet because the Land Cruiser chassis can also be exported for civilian use, it escapes the ban on arms exports. In August 2004 ShinMaywa promoted its US-1A amphibious aircraft designed for search and rescue but also for maritime patrol and antisubmarine warfare roles. While the assistant manager of defence systems at the company acknowledged that Japan is prohibited from exporting defence systems he insisted that the craft was available for purchase and could be used for "multipurpose missions."[18]

Transparency and truth

The essential problem when analysing Japan's adherence to its "no arms trade" policy is the lack of transparency in the reporting of the export licences that have

15 Saab Bofors to lead NLAW Jane's Defence Industry, 1 July 2002.

16 The ever-clearer view from above International Defense Review 1 September 2004.

17 The ever-clearer view from above International Defense Review 1 September 2004

18 Assistant Manager, Godo Tadoroko quoted in Jane's Defence Weekly, 25 August 2004.

been granted for goods used in the defence industry. Although Japan makes annual submissions to UN databases regarding its exports, these submissions are voluntary and, as can be seen from the Comtrade data above, do not always tally with what other countries claim to be receiving from Japan. More importantly, unlike many other countries such as Germany, Finland, UK or USA the Japanese government provides no annual report detailing the licences that it has granted for arms or goods used in the defence industry. This means that the Japanese public and press has no access to information concerning what defence goods may have been exported and whether these exports comply with the spirit or the letter of a policy banning arms exports.

It is nevertheless clear from the number of small arms and dual-use goods openly exported, that Japan has, for a number of years, had a fairly active arms trade, despite its declaration to the contrary. Japan's claim that it has no arms trade leaves it open to the charge of duplicity and deceit.

With the Japanese government proposing major changes related to weapons production and exports, now would surely be a time to provide an open and honest account of the nation's actual involvement in the arms trade, and to establish a formal system of reporting that lays to rest doubts about the military content of exports. Such information would end the hypocrisy and denial that currently reigns.

The work of Fethullah Gülen and the role of non-violence in a time of terror[1]

Steve Wright

Peace by peace

The notion of peace by peace has a rich Western tradition from Tolstoy to Martin Luther King. In the East, the non-violent tradition is much more ancient. Emperor Asoka, presiding over India in the third century BCE slaughtered more than a hundred thousand before experiencing a Buddhist conversion which led him to proselytizing for non-violence, from a distinctly spiritual and pragmatic perspective (Seneviratana, 1994).

Middle Eastern spiritual leaders teaching non-violence have had an enormous significance in the West, but it is a truism that there has been much less of a 'connect' between spiritual theory and earthly praxis. Two thousand years of Christianity has not led to a reduction of violence – far from it since Christians have slaughtered each other for much of that period and most other faiths as well. And yet the diversity and complexity of the Christian community cannot be so easily dismissed in terms of their differing dimensions of tradition, time and space.

We know that many Christian communities, inspired by their faith, have successfully attempted to translate their spiritual ethics and a belief in non-violence into a practical set of transformative actions. For example, Pax Christi and the Quakers teach peace through service at community, national and international levels. It is not an exaggeration to say, for example in the UK, that nearly all the most significant groupings for social change and peace have benefited from the funding of Quaker groups like the Joseph Rowntree

1 This work originally appeared as a chapter in Paul Weller and Ihsan Yilmaz's edited volume, 'European Muslims, Civility and Public Life: Perspectives On and From the Gülen Movement', published in 2012 by Continuum Publishing, an imprint of Bloomsbury Publishing Plc. The chapter is republished with gracious permission from Claire Weatherhead at Bloomsbury.

Charitable Trust, without which a tremendous set of changes for the good would simply not have happened.

However, at a state level, despite the non-violent message of Christianity's founding figure, the practical messages have been much more mixed. Indeed within living memory we have witnessed military chaplains blessing nuclear missiles and a genocide against Jewish people being rationalized on ideological and utilitarian grounds by a self-defined Christian Hitler (Steigmann-Gall, 2003). During the Second World War, the head of the Catholic Church, Pope Pius XII, refused to speak out in opposition to Nazi crimes against the Jewish peoples and, while the Vatican has since apologized for this silence, it is a permanent stain on its ethics.

What is of most significance in these debates is the integrity of spiritual teaching about peace and non-violence and the processes by which such beliefs are made manifest in practice. An absence of integrity in such processes suggests either impotence or hypocrisy. But it could also be read as confusion. Just because the Nazis said they were Christians did not mean they were and there is much other evidence that Nazism as a movement was strongly anti-Christian, and strongly influenced by pagan, occultist and similar beliefs (Pauwels and Bergier, 2007; and Poewe, 2006). Nevertheless, despite the content of Christianity's teaching, the so-called 'German Christian Movement' tried to enlist them into the service of National Socialist approaches to the Volk.

And this is my point: believability is the extent to which teaching and practice are one. This is what is so attractive about the Gülen movement to external observers since, even to an outsider, the motivation is to unify outward behaviour with spiritual credo. Peace is, of course, central to Islamic teaching. The Qur'an (59:23) refers to it being one of God's names. Islamic scholars have cogently argued that the Sunnah or Prophet's way, can be understood as a deliberate choosing of the path of non-violence – a distinctly Islamic approach to non-violence based on *dawah* or peaceful struggle for the propagation of Islam.

It is in this sense that Fethullah Gülen's contribution might best be understood through the lens of Western practices of non-violent action for social change. This remains a slow process of recognition since it is only in recent years that the larger peace research networks have begun to recognize and assimilate the thoughts of Islamic scholars on non-violence and that this form of non-violence is active and transformative (Paige, Satha-Anand and Gilliat, 2001). Of course within Islam, Arab elders have used such principles for centuries to resolve family and community disputes and there is a continuum of practice for scholars willing to research it as such (Abu-Nimer, 2003).

Historically, the East has provided us with some of our most inspirational teachers, translating their spiritual beliefs into a philosophy of both peace cultures and peace through non-violent direct action. All of us active in peace movements today will acknowledge their debt to Mahatma Gandhi. His quest was seen as a process of transformation, of tackling the violent injustices of the largest empire ever assembled. He rejected violence as a tactic because in the long term it was counter-productive: 'I object to violence because when it appears to do good, the good is only temporary; the evil it does is permanent' (Gandhi, 1925: 178). For Gandhi, 'Victory attained by violence is tantamount to a defeat, for it is momentary' (Gandhi, 1919: Leaflet 13).

There are certain similarities between Gandhi's deeply practical spiritual teaching and sayings and those of Fethullah Gülen—for example, Gandhi's persistent concern with the world of inner spiritual responsibility, crystallized in his often-quoted remark: 'As human beings our greatness lies not so much in being able to remake the world ... as in being able to remake ourselves' (cited by Easwaran, n.d.). Yet for Western peace activists, the power of Gandhi's contribution is that it incorporates dimensions of technique which can be replicated elsewhere. This is the framework that pioneer peace researcher Theodore Lentz once called a 'Science and Technology of Peace' (Lentz, 1972, see also Eckhardt, 1971).

Both Gandhi and Gülen stress the importance of truthfulness and this is an important test for any movement towards peaceful change: does it work in practice? The quest for 'testing truth' occupied not only the earliest philosophers but also the earliest scientists. The seventeenth-century English natural philosopher, Francis Bacon, once said, 'Truth is so hard to tell, it sometimes needs fiction to make it plausible.' But he went on to conceptualize a founding notion of scientific practice, namely that of falsifiability. Bacon also said that: 'Truth emerges more readily from error than from confusion' (in Spedding et al., 1968: 210). In other words, all notions of truth should be open to question and testability.

This was an approach which put Copernicus and Galileo into conflict with the Church of Rome, because their astronomical observations and resultant hypotheses contradicted the then dominant doctrinal explanation of biblical doctrine. The result was a classic story of paradigm challenge and shift (Kuhn, 1962). Bacon himself was aware of the dangers of telling truth to power: 'Truth is a good dog; but always beware of barking too close to the heels of an error; lest you get your brains kicked out.' And yet Francis Bacon's abiding conclusion was that 'Truth is the daughter of time, not of authority' (in Spedding et al., 1968). Why is this relevant to any comparative discussion of modern notions of 'non-violence' especially in regard to Turkey?

Gülen's approach to non-violence is rooted in Anatolian Islamic belief systems which, to an outsider; are based on the timeless wisdom of the Qur'an which is viewed as immutable holy writ. However, a closer reading reveals that Gülen sees the inspiration of his faith as a work in progress rather than being 'set in concrete'. He values inter-faith dialogue and ongoing cultural exchange as evidenced by his role as Honorary President of the Journalists and Writers Foundation.

By contrast, alternative approaches to non-violence theory—such as Gene Sharp's tactics and theories of civil disobedience (Sharp, 1973), or Brian Martin's work on 'backfire techniques'—are essentially heuristic (Martin, 2007). They are about learning by doing. Sharp lists one hundred and ninety-eight methods of what are essentially techniques used as part of a political rather than a spiritual process of non-violent direct action. These include protest and persuasion; social, economic and political non-cooperation; and non-violent intervention.

Similarly, Brian Martin's work is a study of the dynamics of state power in facing down resistance and how certain tactics of non-violence can use Gene Sharp's techniques as a form of political jiu-jitsu which has the power to make the weak stronger by making repressive policies of the authorities 'backfire'. Does that mean Gülen's work on non-violence is ossified by comparison? No, on the contrary, he is open to the scientific process and sees science and religion as complementary as long as there is a social responsibility among the scientists.

What it does mean is that there may be limits on the extent to which the different processes of nonviolence in action can cross-fertilize. Is such a conclusion deterministic? Again the answer is no, since at the core of Gülen's teachings, is the importance of education. His perspectives on technological innovation are instructive since Gülen emphasizes the importance of society understanding what else is innovated when new technologies are constructed.

In coming to any conclusions about the relevance of such differing paradigms of non-violence in practice and in faith, it is worth being humble. Most authors in this field have to admit to some level of ignorance of one path, or the other or both. The current author is no exception. I am sure that I have only a crude grasp of the writings of Fethullah Gülen; neither may I do justice to key non-violence theorists such as Gandhi or Sharp. Nevertheless, I think the exercise of comparison is worthwhile.

Western voices have stereotyped Islam to a dangerous extent as a violent, backward system of beliefs which breed a medieval approach to justice and a terrorist approach to world politics. Gülen is aware of these stereotypes which he has addressed in his typically thoughtful way. In the sense that he offers a powerful approach to spiritual change in Turkey and the wider world which is based on a non-violent understanding of core Islamic values, the non-Islamic world should listen.

Gülen has written widely on the Sufi notion of *Safa'* (purity) and the challenge of ridding the human heart of the things that contaminate it: jealousy, hatred, feelings of vengeance and suspicion. His antidote from the Qur'an is mercy, tolerance and forgiveness. Gülen's philosophy is beginning to be understood by non-Islamic scholars as offering a bridge between worlds. It is an inspirational philosophy whose essence is education in action, teaching love, tolerance and mutual cultural respect.

In many senses the Gülen movement is a practical global effort for peace and understanding. And yet paradoxically in Turkey is where its essence has been most widely understood and misunderstood. On the one hand by all accounts the moral teaching in Gülen schools offer an exemplary moral and practical training for young people. And yet there are sectors in the military that distrust any pro-Islamic movement of whatever description because of the threat they perceive to Turkey's avowed secular identity. Fethullah Gülen himself has made it clear that the movement has no interest in seizing economic, political or cultural power either inside or outside of the country. In an interview with Turkish newspaper *Zaman*, he has reiterated his spiritual credo of serving humankind by self-sacrifice:

> *As in the past, I am currently maintaining the same distance to all political parties. Even if power, not only in Turkey, but that of the entire world, were to be presented to me as a gift, I have been long determined to reject it with contempt (Tekalan, 2005).*

Although we might take this at face value, perceptions are often just or even more important than realities. And this is possibly the missing link between our different cultural perspectives on non-violence. It is not enough simply to withdraw from future political challenges to a spiritual movement towards peace. Even though that might be necessary, it is not sufficient.

Gülen's expressed philosophy does not falter when it comes to characterizing the unacceptability of terrorism. For him, terrorism is against the very fabric of Islam. On the basis of his erudite understanding of the Qur'an: no Muslim can be a terrorist and no terrorist a Muslim. Western commentators lack the scholarly authority within Muslim communities that Gülen brings when he concludes that suicide bombing, whatever, wherever, whenever is absolutely forbidden in Islam and for those that commit such crimes, the logical prospect is eternal banishment. It is important that such debates over interpretation are had within the Muslim community and that powerful voices are heard that can, with full knowledge, declare and make an extremely articulate attack on those who would attempt to use religious justification to commit atrocities: 'Islam never approves of any kind of terrorism' (Gülen, n.d.).

There is no ambiguity there. And yet there is a need for caution. It is possible that a willingness clearly to define a position according to faith, while absolutely necessary, may still be insufficient. Those building new communities in turbulent times also need to better understand the dynamics of non-violent action in order to preserve their integrity, even in the face of those who seek to either undermine or destroy it. Other key figures have subsequently reinforced these messages, including Dr Muhammad Tahir-ul-Qadri's (2011) *fatwa* announcing that 'suicide bombings and attacks against civilian targets are not only condemned by Islam but render the perpetrators totally out of the fold of Islam, in other words to be unbelievers'.

Equally important in avoiding further polarization is the Western response. It is of historic significance that the newly elected US President, Barack Obama, chose (in April 2009) Istanbul to make a pivotal speech addressing the Arab world with the bridging message: 'The United States is not and will never be at war with Islam.'

Cultures of peace

Under the auspices of the International Peace Research Association (IPRA), considerable analytical work has been done on what constitutes a true culture of peace. It is worth reflecting on these elements before moving to the specific question of comparative approaches to non-violence. One of the foremost minds conceptualizing the nature of cultures of peace is former IPRA Director Professor Paul Smoker who, together with his wife Dr Linda Groff, articulated the necessary steps for creating such cultures (Smoker and Groff, 1995).

The approach of Smoker and Groff towards cultures of peace is unusual, comprehensive and apt since they are explicitly identifying dimensions that

Gülen's teaching identifies as important: namely relationships with others, relationships with nature and relationships with God. Their view is holistic and assumes an inner-outer world relationship towards peace. They explore different levels of the evolution of the peace concept in the West. First of all, there is *peace as an absence of war*—in other words, peace as a precursor for making progress on the other dimensions of non-violent peace.

Then there is peace as '*negative peace*' (in other words no war) and peace as '*positive peace*' (in other words, no structural violence). This summarizes the position of the Norwegian Peace Researcher, Professor Johan Galtung (1969). That is, even when there is an absence of overt conflict the system is still structurally violent if people starve when there is food available; people do not receive medical treatment when the society has hospitals to treat them; women and men of equal rank do not enjoy promotion because of gender or ethnic prejudices; and so on. '*Negative peace*' is when there is still structural violence: positive peace is the absence of both overt and structural violence. Such notions may have particular bearing within an Islamic context if matters of faith preclude equal opportunities. There is also '*feminist peace*' (referring to the macro and micro levels of peace). To quote Smoker and Groff (1995):

> *During the 1970s and 80s, a fourth perspective was ushered in by feminist peace researchers, who extended both negative peace and positive peace to include violence and structural violence down to the individual level. The new definition of peace then included not only the abolition of macro level organized violence, such as war, but also doing away with micro level unorganized violence, such as rape in war or in the home. In addition, the concept of structural violence was similarly expanded to include personal, micro and macro-level structures that harm or discriminate against particular individuals or groups.*

Such an approach is also related to what might be called '*Gaia-peace*' (peace with the environment) and finally, also, '*holistic peace*' (inner and outer peace). Smoker and Groff (1995) emphasize the importance of this last dimension, arguing that both outer peace-making (more emphasized in the West) has to be complemented by holistic inner peace (more practiced in the East). For them 'the achievement of either inner or outer peace helps create the conditions necessary for the creation of the other type of peace'. This is a crucial part of Gülen's teaching. Smoker and Groff suggest that multicultural visions of peace are required and formally made such an analysis to the UN over a decade ago (Smoker and Groff, 1995).

Sharp's tactics and politics of non-violence

Vision is one aspect; transformation is another. This author's concern is about how different approaches to non-violence can be operationalized at a rate that can make a difference and in a way that is self-reflexive so that new, more effective, ways of non-violent change can evolve. Gandhi's work on civil disobedience has been a magisterial influence on what has so far emerged in the West and probably the key exponent of tactics of non-violent action is the American Gene Sharp. In his first volume on non-violent action Sharp (1973) questions why there is such an inertia among populations who put up with cultures of violence and repression when they could enjoy a vastly different system if only they could collectively engage? He identifies habit behaviour; fear of sanctions; the inner constraining power of moral obligation; self-interest; psychological identification with the ruler; zones of indifference and an absence of self-confidence as key factors (Sharp, 1973).

Some of these lessons are pertinent to the Gülen movement as are the lessons Sharp elaborated about why a non-violent approach has not been recognized in the mainstream as a legitimate means of struggle for justice and a better world. Sharp concluded that there is, in fact, an invisible history and there are a number of reasons why such non-violent philosophies have failed to enter the national psyche. They include an absence of romanticized non-violent heroes given that historians have accepted the dominant culture's view that violence is the only legitimate form of combat. Sharp criticizes Western historians for their bias towards violence, viewing this as a conspiracy of the ruling class to keep the people ignorant of their own power. For him (Sharp 1973: 73), non-violence requires a 'new way of viewing the world'. It is a paradigm whose time has not yet come. Non-violence has never been seen as a coherent conceptual system. Consequently, historical examples of nonviolent action are viewed as isolated events rather than as different aspects of the same technique of struggle. For Sharp:

> *Non-violence is unfairly compared to violence. Nonviolence is often used when violence has no chance of success. When nonviolence fails, the method is condemned. But when violence fails, the strategies or tactics are blamed—not violence itself as a method. Nonviolence successes are written off as flukes. Partial successes are seen as total failures (Sharp, 1973: 16-20).*

Brian Martin and the dynamics of backfire

In the third volume of Sharp's first book, he examines the dynamics of non-violent action as a means of understanding what works and why. Such analyses are crucial if non-violent processes are to become living heuristic realities rather than dry scholastic or monastic theories. Sharp teaches how the power imbalance between groups can be used to the advantage of the weak by a process of political jiu-jitsu and how these tactics can succeed even in the face of quite brutal repression. This was one of the first efforts to understand how non-violence can disperse power through communities, bringing increased self-esteem and personal development—phenomena that are also being reported in the emergent Gülen-inspired communities. Such healing and empowering processes lie in sharp distinction to the use of violence, which creates feelings of callousness and dehumanization which affect victims and victors alike.

The Australian researcher Professor Brian Martin has taken some of these analyses and techniques further in a theory which he calls 'backfire' (Martin, 2007). Typically, non-violent activists exposing injustices by the authorities against a weaker group, can precipitate righteous indignation or outrage. Martin examines the dynamics of these processes in order to empower those who would use non-violent action but then face official retribution. He concludes that perpetrators typically use five main methods to inhibit outrage and prevent backfires—namely, covering up the event; devaluing the target; reinterpreting what happened; using official channels to give the appearance of justice; and intimidating and bribing the people involved (Martin, 2007: 118-43). Martin also examines the propaganda and 'black' or 'grey' media operations which typically accompany any official cover-up. These have the aim of creating public outrage against the target of the operation, and can be analysed using the same framework. To be effective, a 'black' operation uses deception to foster an interpretation that the victim was actually responsible. The ('black') attack is not covered up—it has to be open in order to backfire—but responsibility for it is hidden.

He provides invaluable information for countering such attacks, including exposing those really responsible for the event; validating the target of the operation (the falsely alleged perpetrator); interpreting the official operation as unfair and underhanded; avoiding or discrediting official investigations, at least when they seem likely to dampen public outrage; and resisting intimidation and bribery. Such behaviour has spontaneously been evolved by many non-violent groups wishing to sustain behaviour consistent with their beliefs. In fact

I would argue that the behaviour of Bediuzzaman Said Nursi is a case in point. Nursi used his spiritual insights to follow similar tactics albeit at a substantial personal cost to his health (Markham and Ozdemir, 2005). These responses and counter responses can become quite complex. According to Martin and Gray (2007: 16):

> *In a conflict between a powerful and a weak side—for example between a group of police and a single suspect, or between a government and a small group of opponents—the powerful side holds many advantages. If the weak side mounts an attack, this can provide the pretext for the powerful group to use its superior resources. The exception is when the powerful side is exposed in a gross abuse, for example when police seriously assault a suspect or troops gun down protesters and this abuse is exposed to a wide audience, leading to a change in public opinion.*

Despite the fact that Fethullah Gülen has adopted an inspirational spiritual rather than a politically instrumental approach towards implementing non-violent pathways to peace, many of these negative techniques have been used against both him and his followers. This has been so much so that Gülen now lives in exile in the United States of America. In the sections that follow, the question is put about the extent to which the non-violent philosophies of Gülen resonate with the more 'Western' implementation and instrumentalist strategies outlined earlier and whether useful bridges be built between these two worlds.

Gülen's non-violent spiritual paths and practices

Attempting any reasoned comparison of Gülen's non-violent philosophy with those of more Western practitioners is fraught with difficulties, not least because of the way that Gülen's life and work has been moulded by the very specific cultural roots of Anatolian Islam and the specific writings of Said Nursi, though it would be a mistake to think that Gülen's approach is merely a next generation of Nursi's approaches. A more accurate description of the relationship would be that of mentor (see Leaman, 2007). And yet there are some interesting overlaps. Nursi used the tactic of silent withdrawal and non-cooperation in many of his struggles towards resolving conflict without bloodshed. In many ways the maltreatment and imprisonment of Nursi is a classic case of backfire, since his repeated representation of the evidence to different tribunals and his unjust punishment actually served as a recruitment engine for his movement and brought about exactly the opposite outcome of that desired by the authorities.

From an outsider's perspective, the Gülen movement can be considered to have an explicit ambition of eroding structural violence—for example, through providing education and shelter to youngsters. But any Western non-violence theorist, taking a purist approach, would find elements within the movement's organizations that do not square with classic non-hierarchic theories of peaceful cultures. Such criticisms could be seen as invalid by the Gülen community. Yet from a Western point of view, the centralization of power via the *buyuk abiler* (literally 'elder brothers') might be seen as evidence of hierarchy and an unequal distribution of power.

These 'elder brothers' are former students of Gülen who can talk informally about the movement and about their activities and how they are implementing its teachings on social responsibility. But insiders would say this is simply not true, and that it is merely an accusation without any evidence, since the movement is decentralized and only loosely connected, with *Abiler* acting only in an advisory capacity.

Many of these confusions will be influenced by cultural differences especially in regard to the traditional role of women in Turkish society and the central and unquestionable bedrock of the Qur'an which cannot be questioned in any way, without attracting counter-criticism. Western peace movements adopting non-violent strategies regard them all as a work in progress and not very much is so sacrosanct that it is beyond review. And yet this would be to miss or misinterpret another vital cultural ingredient—the remarkable generosity of Turkish people which in this author's experience is unfettered.

There are also difficulties in wedding all the prescriptions of the Sharia to a philosophy of complete non-violence. This is a contradiction which is not unique to Islam—Christian and Jewish views on punishment, turn the other cheek versus an eye for an eye are cases in point— but again such a black and white interpretation can miss the core point, which is that justice should be proportional to the crime. Even the great Emperor Asoka, whose life's work became the promulgation of Buddhist scripture, refused to revoke the death penalty for reason of public order, despite this view being an outright contradiction of Buddhist teachings (Seneviratana, 1994).

In many senses, Gülen is following the holistic, spiritual and cultural approaches to peace identified earlier by Smoker and Groff. The movement inspired by him is now a global faith-based movement with schools in more than 100 countries, including Kazakhstan, Kenya, Bangladesh, Pakistan, Indonesia, Brazil and Bosnia.

Why should this matter? Gülen's teaching gives effect to the teaching of the Qur'an realizing it by performing daily acts of service based on peaceful social change. Such an approach in a time of terror can make a difference through inter-faith dialogue. To my mind, the Gülen-inspired Abant platform for dialogue is akin to the Pugwash movement when it first began its work to prevent nuclear war in the 1950s. Pugwash allowed a backchannel for diplomats and scientists to keep talking even during the difficult days of the Cold War and led to the processes which not only ended the Vietnam War but also the Cold War too.

Such inter-faith dialogue is more important now than ever. The simplistic negative Western stereotypes of Islam need to be constructively challenged by Muslims as well as academics, media and politicians in the West. Gülen's active compassion for peaceful change based on a precise reading of the Qur'an, can act as a powerful antidote to those who would smear Islam with the label of terrorism. Such work can only be achieved through creating a critical mass of thinkers and doers who will engage in peace in the wider world and that characterizes the movement today.

Conclusions

It is wise to be cautious given the turbulent political changes occurring both within Turkey and on its borders with Kurdistan, Iran, Bulgaria, Georgia, Greece, Armenia, Azerbaijan, Iraq and Syria, and now, through a series of contagious spasm wars, the whole of the Middle East. It could be argued that the Gülen approach to peaceful change from a truly enlightened Islamic perspective is necessary, but not yet truly sufficient. It continues to be a work in progress.

During this time of rapid change and potential instability the very success of the Gülen movement could be misinterpreted by those with alternative agendas and alliances in the Middle East. In some senses the conference at which the paper was first given on which this chapter was based was an act of wisdom by the Gülen community in taking the initiative to broaden the worldwide base of those who are sympathetic to the credos of the movement and wish its work well. The challenge to us all is to find ways of future collaboration that do not undermine our strengths and differences but complement projects and processes with which we are broadly in tune.

As in previous times, wise authorities make provision for famine and flood when there are no signs that these are inevitable. So in this time, it is wise to think through future peaceful responses to challenges that may or may not come. For example, the extent to which the 'dialogue movement' can once again respond to state repression using non-violent means may become the test of the integrity of the movement. Many techniques evolved by non-violent activists elsewhere in the world could then come to be of use and significance for the Gülen movement. This is especially important given the current across the Middle East: the only way these new societies can grow free and survive the peace is through mutual tolerance, education and the eradication of overt and structural violence.

In all his writings, Gülen's answer to human conflict is love, mutual understanding, tolerance, dialogue and education. Again and again, Gülen draws these themes to the fore. For him they are fundamental and he says 'other things are accidental' (Gülen, 2004e). Of particular significance is Gülen's adherence to a philosophical position of non-violence when confronted with opposition, both tactical and moral. In his book, *Towards a Global Civilization of Love and Tolerance,* he cautions that we must be:

> *As if without hands against those who strike us and without speech against those who curse us. If they try to fracture us into pieces even fifty times, we still will remain unbroken and embrace everyone with love and compassion. And with love toward one another, we will walk toward tomorrow (Gülen, 2004e: 50).*

Many commentators on Gülen's teachings also underline his emphasis on tolerance as a precursor for peaceful co-existence. Yilmaz (2007: 25) stresses Gülen's role in 'social-cultural activism' because of his exemplary role of establishing dialogue and building peace between Muslims and non-Muslims. For Yilmaz, here we have peace being built up at a micro-level. Gülen, like Rumi before him, both made inter-cultural dialogue 'their main tool of social innovation and conflict resolution for social inclusion, coherence and peaceful co-existence' (Yilmaz, 2007: 25). But Yilmaz (2007: 38-9) also recognizes that such an approach does not receive universal recognition with, for example, many Muslim opponents seeing Gülen's rapprochement with the Catholic Church as traitorous. Handling such wilful misinterpretations of Gülen's thought will be a future challenge for the movement both within and without Turkey.

Writers such as Richard Penaskovic (2010: 147) see Gülen as a bridge between Islam and the West, while others such as Klas Grinell (2010: 85) see him as transcending such divisions; for him, Gülen goes beyond boundaries and is a 'border transgressor'. For Karina Korostelina (2010: 123), Gülen takes this further by using dialogue as a source for peaceful co-existence between Muslims and Christians in a secular state. Here Gülen's approach is about heuristic process. Even though there are differences between East and West, dialogue can create the capacity to find 'relatedness' in people who are vastly different from us.

Others such as Robert Hunt have highlighted the need to more fully explore Gülen's contribution to the dialogue of religion and science, while recognizing key issues about relative legitimacy: 'Closely related to this must be an exploration of Gülen's teachings to post-modernity' (Hunt and Aslandoğan, 2006: 6). Hunt goes to the nub of the problem when he discusses the challenges of placing the movement in context, especially given the proven commitment of movement participants to engage with the multi-religious dimension of globalization through inter-faith dialogue. Hunt cogently argues the problem of competing meta-narratives and identifies the pitfall in the face of such meta-narrative claims, that all dialogue can cease because 'from within a meta-narrative there is no need to listen to the other' (Hunt and Aslandoğan, 2006: 9). The paradox for Hunt is that:

> *[A]t the same time, globalization is rapidly making dialogue between holders of meta-narrative claims a near existential necessity. Western scholars have been working diligently on this problem for some decades. A distinctly Islamic contribution would be of great value in understanding how Muslims can fruitfully relate to globalization (Hunt and Aslandoğan, 2006: 6).*

The truth 'that is' and the truth 'that should be' are two very different worlds. Gülen's favoured approach has involved reform through education. If, as Victoria Levinskaya (2007: 333) tells us, the acquisition of modern knowledge is mandated by Islam itself, then holistic education has been Gülen's way.

Is there any evidence of success? The short answers is yes; the evidence is both magnificent in its level of individual achievement by both pupils and teachers in Gülen inspired schools, but also filled with promise for the potential it holds for transforming civil societies. But it has to be said that potential will remain only as a potential without a very clear set of policy initiatives to use such education and its positive effects. However, that education has a remarkable potential to unleash the social changes that will lead societies in transition away from division and the Janus-faced threats of terrorism and authoritarianism, to truly sustainable peaceful futures.

References

Abu-Nimer, Mohammed. (2003) *Nonviolence and Peace Building in Islam: Theory and Practice.* Gainesville: University Press of Florida.

Spedding, James, Robert Leslie Ellis, and Douglas Denon Heath. (1968) *The Works of Francis Bacon.* New York: Garrett Press.

Easwaran, Eknath. (n.d.) *Gandhi the Man: How one man changed himself to change the world.* Tomales, CA: Nilgiri Press.

Eckhardt, W. (1971) "Symbiosis between Peace Research and Peace Action". *Journal of Peace Research.* 8(1), pp. 67-70.

Galtung, Johan. (1969) "Violence, Peace and Peace Research". *Journal of Peace Research.* 6(3), pp.167-191.

Gandhi, Mohandas K. (1919) "Satyagraha Leaflet No.13: Satyagraha Movement". *In* Mohandas K. Gandhi. *The Collected Works of Mahatma Gandhi. Vol. 17: 1 May, 1919 – 28 September 1919.*

Gandhi, Mohandas K. (1925) *Young India.* 21st May, p.178.

Gülen, Fethullah. (n.d.) Fethullah Gulen's Response to the Sept. 11 Terrorist Attacks. *Gulenmovement.com* Available from: https://www.gulenmovement.com/fethullah-gulens-response-to-the-sept-11-terrorist-attacks.html

Gülen, Fethullah. (2004) *Toward a Global Civilization of Love and Tolerance.* Clifton, NJ: Tughra Books.

Hunt, Robert A., and Yüksel A. Aslandoğan (ed's). (2006) *Muslim citizens of the globalized world: contributions of the Gülen movement.* Clifton, NJ: The Light.

Kuhn Thomas S. (1962) *The Structure of Scientific Revolutions.* Chicago: University of Chicago Press.

Leaman, Oliver. (2007) "Nursi's Place in the Ihya' Tradition". *The Muslim World.* 89(3), pp.314-324.

Lentz, Theodore F. (1972) *Towards a Technology of Peace.* St. Louis: Lentz Peace Research Laboratory.

Levinskaya, Victoria. (2007) "Resemblance of Fethullah Gulen's Ideas and Current Political Developments in Uzbekistan". *In* Conference Proceedings *Peaceful Coexistence: Fethullah Gulen's Initiatives for Peace in the Contemporary World.* Erasmus University, Rotterdam, 22-23rd November 2007.

Markham, Ian, and Ibrahim Ozdemir (ed's). (2005) *Globalization, Ethics and Islam: The Case of Bediuzzaman Said Nursi.* Farnham: Ashgate.

Martin, Brian. (2007) *Justice Ignited: The Dynamics of Backfire.* Lanham, MD: Rowman & Littlefield.

Martin, Brian, and Truda Gray. (2007) "Backfires: White, Black and Grey". *Journal of Information Warfare.* 7(1), pp.7-16.

Paige, Glenn D., Chaiwat Satha-Anand, and Sarah Gilliatt. (2001) *Islam and Nonviolence.* Honolulu, Hawai'i: Centre for Global Nonviolence.

Pauwels, Louis, and Jacques Bergier. (2007) *The Morning of the Magicians: Secret Societies, Conspiracies, and Vanished Civilizations.* New Edition.

Pensakovic, Richard. (2010) "Gülen on Healing the Rift between Islam and the West". *In* John L. Esposito, and İhsan Yılmaz (ed's). *Islam and Peacebuilding: Gülen Movement Initiatives.* New York: Blue Dome, pp.123-143.

Poewe, Karla. (2006) *New Religions and the Nazis.* New York: Routledge.

Seneviratana, Anuradha. (ed.) (1994) *King Asoka and Buddhism – Historical and Literary Studies.* Kandy, Sri Lanka: Buddhist Publication Society.

Sharp, Gene. (1973) *The Politics of Non-Violent Action.* Boston, MA: Sargent.

Smoker, Paul, and Linda Groff. (1995) "Spirituality, Religion, and Peace: Exploring the Foundations for Inner-Outer Peace in the 21st Century". *In* Conference Proceedings *Second UNESCO Conference on "Contributions of Religions to a Culture of Peace".* Barcelona, December 1994.

Steigmann-Gall, Richard. (2003) *The Holy Reich: Nazi Conceptions of Christianity, 1919-1945.* Cambridge: Cambridge University Press.

Tahir-ul-Qadri, Muhammad. 2011. *Fatwa on Terrorism and Suicide Bombings.* London: Minhaj-ul-Quran International.

Tekalan, Serif Ali. (2005) A Movement of Volunteers. Fgulen.com Available from: http://fgulen.com/en/conference-papers-en/the-fethullah-gulen-movement-i/a-movement-of-volunteers

Yılmaz, İhsan. (2007) *Peaceful Coexistence: Fethullah Gülen's initiatives in the contemporary world.* London: Leeds Metropolitan Press.

The ECHELON trail: An illegal vision

Steve Wright[1]

Abstract

This article tells the story behind the uncovering of the US operated global telecommunications interceptions system now known as ECHELON. It begins with the use of fieldwork techniques in the early 1970's exploring the configuration of Britain's Post Office Towers—these were ostensibly the microwave links through which Britain's long distance telephone calls were made. This modelling process revealed a system within the system of microwave towers linked to the American Base of Menwith Hill in the North York Moors. All the key researchers were then promptly arrested, a raid by Special Branch on the author's university at Lancaster ensued and later a show trail for the other main researchers, most notably Duncan Campbell. Eventually in 1988, Duncan wrote up the ECHELON story, which for its time was an incredible piece of detective work using materials lifted from waste bins by the women activists campaigning around the Menwith Hill Base. Little notice was taken until 1997 when an obscure book by Nicky Hager, Secret Power explained the role and function of ECHELON in more depth. The author represented these findings in a policy report to the European Parliament on the technology of political control that led to a process of political debate and disagreement of the ethics of such a system which continues even today.

Introduction

Studies of surveillance are challenging, and often demand a sustained research commitment. It is no coincidence that many of the key British researchers active in this field in the early 1970's remain so today. I am currently still working on issues of what are essentially tools of social and political control—both professionally as an Associate Reader at Leeds Metropolitan University in the Praxis Centre, ethically as a lecturer in the School of Applied Global Ethics and politically as chair of the Board of Trustees of Privacy International.

1 (2005) Surveillance and Society, 3(2/3), pp.198-215. With gratitude to the editor, Torin Monahan, for republication permission.

This article describes how I became engrossed in studying 'technologies of political control', and tracked the members of the security industrial complex, responsible for proliferating it to some of the world's most unsavoury regimes. More specifically, it relates how a lowly postgraduate researcher stumbled across the entrails of a global telecommunications interception system; precipitated the first Special Branch police raid on a British University; provoked the first ever parliamentary debate on the British secret police; and accidentally detonated a worldwide political and ethical debate on the existence of a futuristic global electronic spying network, now known as 'ECHELON'. In relating my personal experience of researching the ECHELON trail, I hope to illustrate how many of the challenges facing surveillance scholars during critical periods of their work can be faced and eventually overcome without the researcher becoming part of the food chain of the process they are watching.

ECHELON is a (now out-of-date) code name given to the US National Security Agency's worldwide facility for the mass interception of electronic telecommunications including, phone, fax and email using key words and context. It works on the basis that other telecommunication links can be used to siphon off messages travelling by satellite, microwave relay link or fibre optic cable, if they intercept such streams at a key node, and can work at a prodigious rate of more than 2 million intercepts per hour. Essentially, the system can work because for some of its journey, telecommunications traffic is travelling as an electronic stream that can be intercepted if the appropriate infrastructure is in place. However, the current wisdom is that ECHELON does not exist in the way it was originally construed but is now thought to be a collection of subsets of interception capabilities using a range of code names of which we remain ignorant. Nevertheless, for the sake of simplicity, it makes sense to continue to use the generic label 'ECHELON' whilst recognizing that new surveillance algorithms have evolved since the early researchers built their crude paradigms.

My interest in surveillance studies began over three decades ago when no such field existed. I was a student at Manchester University on an unusual course, entitled 'Liberal Studies in Science'. The course attempted to bridge the communication gap between science and the humanities, and create 'literate scientists' (in the wake of C.P Snow's famous critique of the 'two cultures'). The training given by the course certainly paid off in the years which followed, since it enabled its students to look at specific technical problems with perspectives from many different disciplines.

I became fascinated by the process of technology assessment: the attempt to examine unforeseen impacts of technological innovation. For example, the course examined nuclear arms races, and the parallels with arms races emerging in counter-insurgency conflicts, which were then in the news, fired my imagination. The course's coverage of the Vietnam War highlighted a new generation of military systems which had potential domestic uses such as helicopter-mounted flight stabilized CCTV night vision cameras, already beginning to find a market in policing the U.S. home front.

At the same time on the UK home front, the British Society for Social Responsibility in Science (BSSRS) was just beginning to examine the deployment of new weapons and technologies in the burgeoning 'troubles' in Northern Ireland: a province that was about to become the most surveilled zone in Europe. BSSRS conceptualized this new equipment as a 'technology of political control'. According to BSSRS, this technology encompassed new crowd control technologies designed to appear safe (rather than be safe), new torture technologies designed to induce psychological breakdown; and new surveillance and telecommunication systems that provided a powerful nervous system for 'the strong state'.

A fledgling researcher

Managing the transition from being someone who is broadly interested in social and political matters to a so-called 'surveillance scholar' is not a simple matter. It's hardly a direct process, and the zigzags require a talent for organising adequate time, resources and relationship issues that can potentially blight the career of any fledgling researcher.

More important than any of these practical difficulties is the matter of personal determination which, in any new field, hovers precariously close to obsession if the contribution is to sustain. In the case of the field research on ECHELON, which, in the early days, was largely to do with the orientation of aerials, this obsession risks being classified as Asperger's syndrome of which collecting images of antennae can, in some cases, be symptomatic! The syndrome is worth looking up to see if you have these symptoms—but essentially the complaint involves an inward obsession, some impairments in social interaction and repetitive behaviour patterns—named after Hans Asperger (1906–1980), an Austrian paediatrician.

Nevertheless, whatever leads to the strong motivation to study a particular strand of surveillance must be more powerful than the inevitable setbacks that will emerge along the way, including no money, no recognition, no job and no progress. This has probably changed somewhat today since surveillance studies have become more mainstream. Yet it is still reasonable to suggest that for the new or less established scholar, the more controversial the study, the more likelihood there is of roadblocks and the higher the need for networks and support. However, some of the most cutting-edge conceptualization is always done alone. Indian philosophers have a term for it—Tapasia—or straightening by fire.

I can trace my own motivation back to the summer of 1973, when I experienced in India what in retrospect I can only describe as epiphany (see below). It was an intense time. I was travelling East through Afghanistan during the summer holidays and there was a coup d'etat on my 21st birthday. I was out on the streets of Kabul and managed to snatch a picture of the new President Muhammad Daoud. If I could have got across the Khyber Pass and delivered the picture to Reuters, it would have paid for the entire trip. Alas my film was taken at gun point a few minutes later by one of his armed guards, which was an early lesson in the power and politics of stolen images in a time of revolution. My later work was to focus on obtaining good evidence of the deployment of certain technologies, an activity that depends, paradoxically, on the use of surveillance technology to contradict more official claims of what was going on.

Today I see all politics as flows of information, management, manipulation and paradigm change: in my view those who control information control the physical world too. Back then it emerged into my thinking in an almost mystical way, in one of the most sacred Hindu towns of India, Benares. I was watching a never-ending stream of bodies being brought on to the burning grounds for incineration. It was a smoking vision of Hell with semi-naked figures turning over the corpses to burn them more effectively. What was once a human face was cleanly lifted off the skull - the mask of life was now rendered into fried meat. We all end up as ashes but even here, the ashes were being eaten by pyre dogs feeding on bits of backbone with loose remnants of human flesh hanging off.

I had a semi-visionary experience of witnessing a scene from Bosch. 'The Garden of Earthly Delights' had turned sour and I was left wondering whether any of us could ever make a difference to such a revolting production line. It became a metaphor. My meditation turned to war and the accelerating, endless, disgusting waste of it all. I felt I wanted to make a stand against a technological determinism that turned us into helpless watchers or worse, collaborators. With just £20 in my pocket, I made the long journey home and a determination never to give up.

Within two years I had focussed my research on new social control and death technologies. New weapons for internal control were emerging for sub-state conflict control during counter revolutionary operations whilst to me unbelievably hideous fragmentation weapons containing thousands of razorblade-like flechettes were being evolved for more conventional warfare—with civilians being the inevitable consumers.

I was convinced that much of the crowd control and 'torture lite' technology I had begun to research in Northern Ireland would be adapted` and adopted eventually by all states wishing to technically fix their social and political problems. (This has indeed been the case and much of the technology used in Northern Ireland now forms part of the burgeoning crowd control and internal security sales market. The sensory deprivation based 'torture lite' techniques developed in Northern Ireland have most recently found their way into the US Guantanamo Bay internment camps in Cuba and to Abu Ghraib Prison in Iraq.

None of this early research exploration could be followed very adequately at the undergraduate level of degree I was then pursuing in the UK. Determined to find a new niche, I decided to follow a course of postgraduate study. Unfortunately, my degree level was insufficient to justify finance. My thesis was so difficult to assess by conventional criteria, after debate amongst the examiners, it was upgraded from a poor level pass, to what was essentially a distinction grade. This was largely because of the sheer vision of political control technologies it had sought to encompass. The British degree system uses face to face meetings with external examiners in cases where there is any doubt. I had such an interview in 1975 where alas, I had a technical argument with my external examiner, Brian Flowers, who was later to become Chancellor of Manchester University. So that was that. I was out in the cold and had to find less academic work. However, Flowers did suggest that even though I was a hot-headed young man I should find a way of pursuing my research. Just weeks later, I was employed by the University's Gardening Centre and as luck would have it ended up sweeping the roads just outside my old department in the Maths Tower. One day, the Head of the Department, Professor Michael Gibbons walked by, and seeing my lowly station remarked, "that'll teach you to argue with Brian Flowers!"

But serendipity can play a fateful role in any researcher's life: they key lesson is to accept the blows but never give up. Fortunately, I had found a place where I could do the research work I wanted and was accepted at Lancaster University's Programme of Peace and Conflict Research. In the meantime, I'd noticed an article in the Guardian that said that Brian Flowers was being considered to be the next scientific advisor to the government.

I wrote to Brian Flowers saying I had followed his advice, had found a suitable course to continue my research and perhaps he could suggest where I might find the resources to follow it through? Lesser men in authority would have dismissed such a cheeky request from an eccentric student determined to follow an unusual research topic: 'Social Control and Death Technologies.' To his credit, and my everlasting gratitude, the now Lord Sir Brian Flowers found a way of assisting the funding of my studies in that crucial first year, through a grant from the Society for Education in the Applications of Science. Without that essential first funding, I would have lost so much impetus. Timing is often everything but I've never lost that early lesson in the vital skill of fund raising, that every critical researcher must learn.

The programme of peace and conflict research

By October 1976 I was ready to travel to Lancaster University. It had been an eventful year. I had married in the 1975, a son had been born the following spring, but I had secured a place, finance, a house and a creative supervisor, Dr. Paul Smoker. Yet the single-minded need to relentlessly pursue the research took its toll on the time I devoted to my family. From my perspective, a year would soon go and only solid research progress would yield any chance of future funding from the SSRC. I didn't realize how important family support is during any period of active interference by state agencies in the research process, nor did I comprehend the realities of family members being a vulnerable flank through which any research activist can be attacked.

In times of political turbulence like now, it is especially important that researchers discuss such personal security matters with their families and agree their limits, fears and expectations. If I'd known what was in store, I would have remained a temporary assistant gardener but during those early days I enjoyed a sweet freedom to follow my research. I soon built a useful network of key individual researchers and NGO's, many of whom I am still working with to this day.

The Director of the Programme of Peace and Conflict Research, Dr. Paul Smoker was one of the founding fathers of modern peace research. Indeed he set up the first UK based peace research centre at Langthwaite House on the back road between Galgate and Caton in the early Sixties. I had cause to pass the old buildings of this first centre as I bicycled my way home from the university to the small village of Brookhouse where I then lived. What caught my attention was that Langthwaite was now surrounded by antennae and in an adjacent field there was a larger radio mast with a dish and a horn, which the locals believed was a colour TV relay station: it wasn't. The route towards challenging that local piece of folklore would involve rethinking technical capacity available for telecommunications interception, and the way that technological creep broke the boundaries of authorised tapping, checks and balances into something completely new.

Truth lies open to all?

Lancaster University's motto—'Omnibus Patet Veritas' very much appealed to me. It means 'truth lies open to all'. I was fascinated by the contradictions between this ideal and the hidden dimensions of political control—especially in the UK where civil servants were required to sign the Official Secrets Act.

I was working on a range of different techniques for assessing new technologies of political control. This included an examination of the growth of surveillance in the UK, which had significantly changed over the last two decades. It is useful to look at the context in which this research was taking place. For example in 1957 when Lord Birkett produced the official report on telephone interception in the UK, telephone tapping was very much a cottage industry. Since then telephone interception has grown into today's hi-tech networks.

Nevertheless when figures were officially updated in 1980, many MP's were surprised by the relatively modest official increase over the intervening 23 years: from 129 warrants in 1958 to 411 in 1979 for England and Wales. However the 1980 paper on the Interception of Communications did admit that one warrant could cover multiple intercepts on an entire organisation and its members e.g. CND. It was also revealed that the Secretary of State 'may delegate' to the civil service the power to amend a warrant. Thus the total number of lines monitored was going to be substantially more than the number of warrants issued.

Another anomaly was revealed when MP Clement Freud asked whether the number of interception orders currently in force was cumulative or whether the number given simply indicated how many new orders had been published. The then Home Secretary, William Whitelaw, refused to answer leaving open the possibility that key permanent warrants for MI5 and Special Branch were only issued once. It might also have been supposed that the development of international terrorism in the early Seventies had further fuelled the growth of telephone surveillance. However the public record showed a different story. The sharp boom in UK telephone tapping came immediately after Birkett, who recommended that in future official figures on tapping should not be made public.

Thus the main growth period in telecommunications surveillance occurred in the Sixties before international terrorism—the ostensible reason for official surveillance in the Eighties - had become a major problem. If anything, the official record shows that the growth rate slackened in 1970, just as terrorism, particularly in Northern Ireland, had intensified. It could not be the full story. In this respect the White Paper gave a clue. It did not cover telephone tapping in the Province, nor did it cover warrants signed by the Foreign Secretary for the Government Communications Headquarters (GCHQ)[2] and the Secret Intelligence Services, nor tapping warrants signed by the Prime Minister.

These were particularly significant omissions, given that just one permanent warrant signed in 1967 authorized GCHQ to intercept all overseas telegrams. Indeed the sudden drop in Home Secretary warrants after 1975 can be partially explained by this transfer of the surveillance workload from MI5 to GCHQ in conjunction with the US National Security Agency (NSA) and without reference to parliament.

Bypassing formal democratic authorisation and transparency of interceptions thus became a state norm—but how could surveillance researchers ever hope to get evidence of such a top secret network—especially since the penalties under the Official Secrets Act were draconian—up to 14 years in jail? The short answer, as is often the case, was by accident.

Whilst researching another issue of state security structures, a journalist, Peter Laurie, was updating his book, 'Beneath The City Streets' and was seeking the assistance of knowledgeable researchers such as Duncan Campbell. Duncan Campbell even then, was probably the foremost telecommunications researcher of his generation—a journalist who went on to play a pivotal role in exposing ECHELON and identifying the policy grounds needed to bring it back under some semblance of democratic control. Laurie was looking at the emergence of Emergency centres of Government being prepared for World War III, which would create secret citadels to facilitate post nuclear holocaust communication command and control.

Laurie's thesis was that many of these secret centres were beneath the key nodes in the array of new post office microwave towers, which were springing up around the UK. For Non-British readers it is worth explaining that whilst we have local cable and fibre-optic for our urban telecommunications links, once these leave cities it proved cheaper to send them longer distances by a

2 GCHQ is the British node of ECHELON – a telecommunications interceptions sub-network very much dependent on the superior technology and logistics of its bigger American Brother, the NSA

network of microwave towers or antennae spaced at distances of approximately twenty miles. Such microwave beams are relatively accessible to interception by another microwave beam crossing their path.

Laurie had published some pictures of some of these towers in the Sunday Times and in 1977 the time was ripe to update his book and publish a full map of where the towers were located. The assumptions were completely fallacious but it led a small group of researchers to model the UK entrails of ECHELON without realizing the true significance of their activities until the state severely overreacted.

I unwittingly got caught up in the dragnet following a request from Duncan Campbell to take some pictures of my local telephone microwave node—an aerial or antennae located near a moor named the Quernmore—and also the designation of the larger antennae by Langthwaite House. What happened next proved to be a major turning point in the confidence of surveillance scholars to research state structures. Apart from David Wood's (2001) excellent thesis, little has been written about the personal side of getting caught up in such an enterprise. This was my experience of mapping what turned out to be an illegal paradigm.

Mapping an illegal paradigm

I had been asked to conduct field research in its most literal sense. I was to go out into a field, take an image of a construct, note its configuration and share that information with a network which would use the data to affect political change. This was a perspective consistent with my overall drive. I remain uncomfortable with research which can be deemed to be 'social astronomy' or what less generous colleagues characterise as 'academic masturbation.' In my view the whole point of doing such work is to be applied, and that means directing surveillance studies to policy change. Such 'research activism' is easier said than done—although the first steps, in this case, are relatively simple.

In theory, the practical research steps required to uncover any such secret surveillance links were a technically straightforward, albeit arduous undertaking. A map of the legitimate telephone network was compiled on the basis of telephone directories and associated exchanges. This pattern of links, which are officially in place to relay calls, can then be compared with a map of relays actually found from field research. Microwaves travel in straight lines over relatively short distances so it is simply a question of using compass map and ruler to find the next relay in the grid[3]. The 'field map' is then simply subtracted

3 A brief summary of all these trials is provided in Newsday, Nov. 10, 1981.

from the official map using what are, in methodological terms, essentially Mills' methods of addition and subtraction.[4] The anomalous system came to light. (See Figure 1).

Figure 1: UK Phone Tap System

4 This is a classical methodology for identifying logical arguments of induction and deduction.

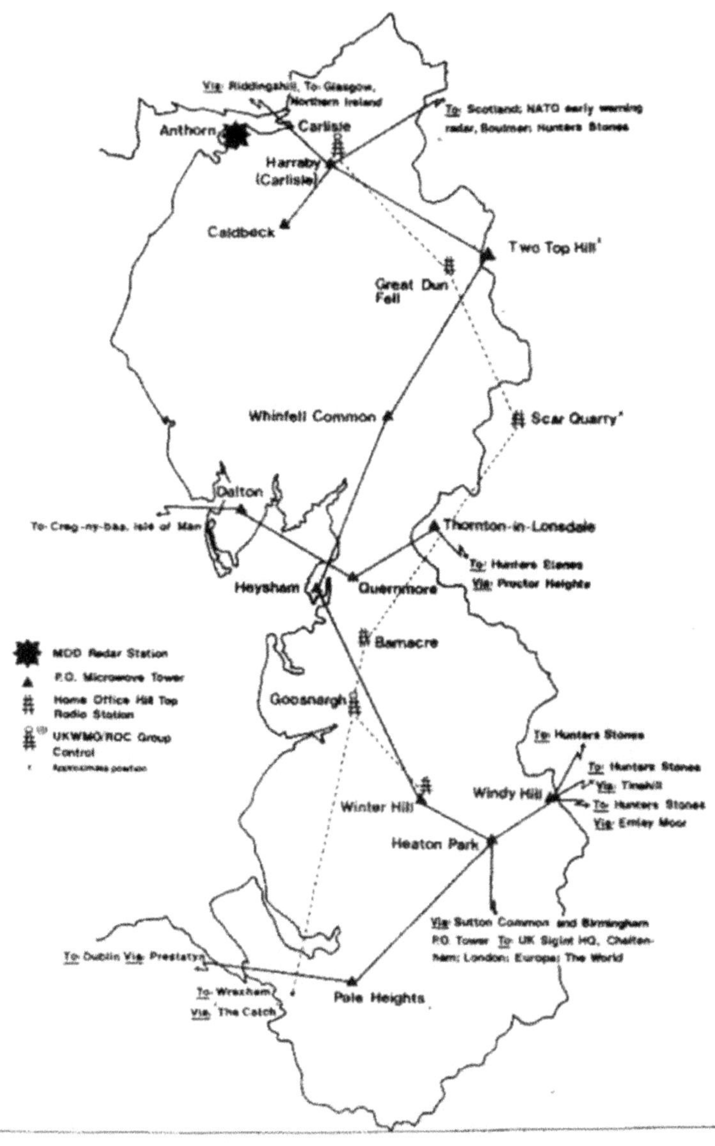

*From Poole & Wright, Target NorthWest, 1982.

Figure 2: the location of the Quernmore Aerial

I took the original pictures during the Winter of 1977 using a simple instamatic camera, it even had shots of Damon, my baby boy, on the reel. I sent it off to Duncan Campbell, together with a map explaining that a dish faced in the direction of Northern Ireland and a horn was pointing in the direction of the Yorkshire Moors and Menwith Hill. The significance of the orientation of specific horns and dishes is that they provide a precise direction of the next link in the chain.

In fact the Quernmore aerial (Figure 2), was connected by a series of other relays such as Thornton in Lonsdale (Figure 3) and Hunters Stones via Proctor Heights before being physically linked to the NSA site (Figure 4). A short time later on February 18 1977, Duncan Campbell was arrested under section 2 of the Official Secrets Act, because he and a fellow journalist met with a soldier to discuss questions of signals intelligence. Nothing much of significance was exchanged that night but because Campbell's telephone was bugged, police knew of the meeting which was a technical breach of the British Official Secrets Act which all members of Her Majesty's Forces sign. Once Duncan was arrested, his correspondence addresses provided the target list for further arrests—including one chap who sent him a Christmas card, and in the end, me.

Figure 3: The Thornton Relay

Figure 4: The terminal at NSA Menwith Hill

Researching such systems was previously thought to be legal, if only open sources were used. How can a secret be a secret if it isn't really secret? After all, the Sunday Times had already published a compendium of such aerial photographs. The mistake in this assumption was that research on intelligence could easily be re-designated by the authorities as intelligence itself. The added value of what could be seen as 'mere' academic modelling was that an analysis of classified data would have yielded the same results. The research paradigm was then tantamount to an illegal vision and although the logic seems very 'Alice in Wonderland', the same tactics to challenge researchers were used repeatedly during that period. There were several testing trials of researchers attempting to understand the role and function of arrays of various antennae in those days using just open sources. The ABC trial in England (essentially the Duncan Campbell case), the Rabbit Trial in Oslo which centred on peace researchers who were examining secret configurations of such antennae in Norway, the Wilkes Trial in Sweden which used various open lists to model military activities and the Christensen trial in Denmark. The military authorities in all these cases attempted to legally restrict empirical research on state surveillance structures.[5]

The special branch raid on Lancaster university

Not all knowledge is from rational sources. Even the term paranoia literally means 'beyond knowledge (para: beyond; noia: knowledge). On the night of 5th April 1977 I had a stormy, seemingly pointless argument with my wife. In frustration I declared that my wife didn't understand the work in which I was engaged and 'one day my work would walk through the front door.' The instant response, quite deservedly, was 'you're being melodramatic – I'm going to bed!' I reflected on this afterwards thinking it was a bit melodramatic and that I was making needless emotional waves.

A few hours later loud knocks on the door heralded the arrival of 6 Special branch officers who make it clear that they wanted co-operation otherwise they will use 'blatant search techniques'. This implied that not only would they turn the place over but that the search would become very obvious to the neighbours. Without the argument of the night before, I might have caved in. Because of it and a silly sense of 'I told you so' I calmly suggested that what they were doing infringed academic freedom and was unprecedented. This episode of déjà vu was so well documented in the light of subsequent events, Brian Inglis used it in his book, the Hidden Power. The lesson here is whilst one should never give way to paranoia, it is useful to develop and trust your intuition. Our minds are capable of intuitive leaps which are ours to use even if we can not necessarily rationally explain them and the history of science is full of such episodes. Our challenge is to use hunches as a methodology to conjecture with or refute.

In fact my then neighbours were so alarmed by the presence of six burly strangers strolling around our house they called the local police! The officer knocked on our door and was given short shrift by Detective Chief Inspector Moffat of Scotland Yard, who told him, 'It's official so piss off'. I queried what it was that I was alleged to have done and the Kafkaesque atmosphere was

5 A brief summary of all these trials is provided in Newsday, Nov. 10, 1981

heightened by the response that it is an official secret and I cannot be told. In the meantime, my diaries and entire research correspondence were removed. I discovered later that the police don't steal, the technical term is detinue—i.e. they hold on to items longer than they should, a matter which can be devastating if a researcher is working to pre-set deadlines.

In this heavy atmosphere of confrontation with secret police officers, it would have been easy to roll over but I felt it was important to stand up to their infringement of my rights to research. How was another matter. I could easily see how my academic future could be blown out of the water if a full secrets trial resulted from what was to all intents and purposes a fishing expedition.

I was taken by car to Lancaster University. It was the Easter holiday period and the special branch officers expected 'that a bit of arm twisting' would give them easy access to my offices in an otherwise empty campus. But the politics department was crawling with academics who were demanding proper procedures be followed. After some delay, I thanked the officers for their lift to campus and announced that I had work to do and proceeded to exit the car. This forced their hand and I was arrested under the official secrets legislation and taken to meet with Professor Phillip Reynolds the Pro-Vice Chancellor, together with various university and college officials who had assembled: Dr Roxbee Cox, Fylde principal and Mr. Forrester, Academic Registrar.

The atmosphere was tense. Special Branch demanded access to my room and I pointed out that principles of academic freedom were involved. After all I had only ever used open sources, had simply followed the university motto and no one had explained the nature of any charges laid against me. Detective Chief Inspector Moffat replied that 'this was an issue of national security' and told me that they had a warrant. Professor Reynolds demanded that they go through the proper channels, to which Moffat replied that he had six men present and would start breaking down doors in the department if access was denied. People began sweating—it was an unforgettable moment. I broke it by emphasizing that I had nothing to hide and suggested that they could search to their hearts' content.[6] The atmosphere was thankfully lightened a bit later with the arrival of my supervisor, Dr Paul Smoker, who amidst the hub bub in the corridors managed to give me a burst of the Beatles hit, 'Listen Do You Want To Know A Secret – Do you Promise Not to Tell?' Perfect: but I was later held in Lancaster Police Station for several hours, refused a solicitor and when finally released was told, sometimes you fellows are too clever for your own good.'

6 For a contemporary account of this episode see Lawrence, B. (1977) 'Nasty Branch hit Bailrigg, Scan, Edition 1, 26 Aprll, page 1.

The raid turned my research plans upside down not to mention the impact it had on my personal life. However it was many times worse for the main researchers, Crispin Aubrey, John Berry and Duncan Campbell (now deemed the ABC defendants), who were facing the full rigours of an official secrets act trial. And yet there was a puzzle: why had Special Branch undertaken such a foolhardy exercise as to raid a British University—how come I'd touched on a raw nerve? It quickly dawned on me that I had inadvertently stumbled on a network connected with the configuration of the antennae I had photographed on the Quenmore Moor, which the authorities were desperate to keep secret. It seemed incomprehensible. I knew that Menwith Hill was a US base, but what was the link with UK phone lines, and especially the link to Northern Ireland? Just where were the results being transmitted—to the US, but how—by satellite? The system must be huge. It felt like a science fiction movie.

We now know that most US intelligence is gathered by signals intelligence using huge computers to trawl through the worlds' telecommunications looking for selected key words using a complicated algorithm and dictionary system of key words and operated by the NSA (the National Security Agency). At that time hardly anyone had heard of the NSA despite the fact that it was the largest purchaser of computers on the planet. The days of intelligence gathered by James Bond characters or Human Intelligence (Humint) are long gone. What we didn't know was that the US Base at Menwith Hill, with its field of radomes, was the largest NSA base on earth with many roles and function of which ECHELON was just one. It was and is involved in missile monitoring and guidance as well as satellite monitoring and control. But at that juncture all we had were jigsaw puzzle pieces and we had begun to build a model of a futuristic system of interceptions—the bulk of which as we know now, is in space. The fuller model could only be developed later as further jigsaw pieces fell into place.

However, the pragmatics of defending my position became all consuming. The university provided me with a Lancaster lawyer. He advised me that he had been told by the Special Branch officers that the researchers I have been co-operating with are extremely dangerous people and that I should cut off all contact with them. I developed the strong impression that this fellow was more used to matrimonials and conveyancing. Worse—I was paying for this disinformation. In such circumstances, one has to experience a rather steep learning curve. I sacked my solicitor and found a much more expensive firm from Liverpool: Bremner, Sons and Corlett, who were more used to dealing with Special Branch and who took a tad more professional approach in following their client's wishes. I was advised that if I wished to take legal action to regain my papers it must go through a higher legal authority and I would have to meet with a barrister in Chambers. As a very poor student, the financial implications were horrendous and I could see a significant chunk of my terms grant disappear in legal fees.

I was told that the lawyers for the ABC defendants had been faced with considerable official paranoia over the case and that they were not being allowed to receive the trail committal papers unless their offices were equipped with high security safes. The succinct legal advice I was given was that if I continued in the task of trying to get my research papers back, 'my future research, career and even my life would be in danger.' I clearly needed a stiff drink after that and some further moral and political support. I went to see the then VC, a wise Quaker, Sir Charles Carter who had been influential in setting up the first Programme of Peace research in the University.

After our meeting, on the 5th May 1977, he released the following statement:

> *Those who work in universities cannot expect to be exempt from the application of the law, but they can reasonably ask for sympathetic understanding of their duty to seek access to all evidence relevant to their studies. Truth is not something to be determined by the state.*

This was an important intervention which received national publicity. By coincidence, the Student Union had invited Duncan Campbell up to Lancaster from the ABC solidarity committee. He was able to take a copy of the statement to Robin Cook MP (Cook who died earlier this year, went on to become British Foreign Secretary and eventually father of the House of Commons). Cook opened the first ever British parliamentary debate on the Special Branch and defended my right to research without political interference.[7]

There was certainly political interference. We started to receive odd threatening phone calls at home, finance was desperate and I had just weeks to bid for continuing grants. My marriage could no longer take the strain and we separated on 7 June 1977 as the rest of the people in our street celebrated the Queens Silver Jubilee. A few weeks later, my wife's father had a heart attack and died and in deep grief she had a breakdown which eventually involved me in extracting her from the hospital and attempting to heal her troubled heart. But it was too late, the damage had been done and I had to go to ground. I got a job digging fields for £1 an hour, just within sight of the shadow of the Thornton in Lonsdale microwave tower. It was a completely desolate time but I vowed

7 Hansard 5 May 1977, col 806.

that one day I would get justice for the injustice that I had endured. It was a powerful mantra but there was no guide book as to how such a lofty goal could be achieved: just patient persistence. Twenty years would pass before I would get my chance. In the meantime, my lawyers obtained copies of my research correspondence, I was released from police bail, the ABC defendants fought and won their freedom in one of the most dramatic political trials of the 1970's and I got back to the business of completing my PhD. All the surveillance researchers of that era had quickly realised just how important it was to join together to research state structures, if they are not to be picked off one by one when a particular security alert gets out of hand. From that crucible, the first regular journal monitoring state surveillance was born—State Research (now Statewatch) which continues its excellent ground breaking work to this day.

The Omega Foundation

It was a long time before I could create the requisite networks of solidarity and understanding, moving to Manchester in 1981 to return to my roots after the riots of the summer when I published a full page article in *the Guardian* about the hard military policing style which was on the horizon. Oftentimes I felt like a sorcerer's apprentice but in 1984 I succeeded in my application to become Head of Manchester City Council's Police Monitoring Unit. This provided a firm grounding in politics as 'the art of the possible' as well as providing ample opportunities to re-examine police accountability. It also brought me back into contact with Tony Bunyan who had been a central figure in the ABC Defence Committee and a solid source of insight and support during those difficult times. Tony was now the head of London's Police Monitoring Committee with an awesome remit. He was and is a great teacher on how even a small group in civil society can make a political change.

In 1989, after the demise of the Police monitoring initiatives in the UK as the leftwing Labour City Hall Councils which had originally financed them lost ground to the Labour political right, I went on to work with a trusted friend to set up the Omega Foundation, to track the proliferation of military, police and security equipment to the torturing states.

Scientific and technological options assessment (Stoa) and an appraisal of the technology of political control

In 1996, the Omega Foundation was commissioned by the European Parliament to write 'An Appraisal of the Technologies of Political Control.' Late in the day, I decided that maybe the time was right to raise the issue of the interception of communications. Duncan Campbell had returned to the subject in 1988[8] and recently that work had been extended by the New Zealander Nicky Hager in his book 'Secret Power.'[9] It was complete serendipity since I accidentally came across adverts for the book in Washington whilst visiting Terry Allen, then editor of Covert Action Quarterly.

It raised important issues about political control of a system which could technologically bypass any constitutional guarantees any state had protecting citizens from illegal surveillance. Its existence went beyond just privacy, a global network of surveillance which could target financial and political institutions was an instrument for political management: ubiquitous but invisible.

I also wanted to include new work on the FBI's collusion with EC authorities to get more intimate access to European telecommunications for policing purposes. Tony Bunyan had hundreds of documents on this but in the winter of 1996 had yet to write them up. I inadvertently gate crashed the Statewatch staff Christmas party and in an expansive mood, Tony Bunyan agreed to publish his findings in the next issue of Statewatch. I could then quote his report as an authoritative source in the report I was writing for the European parliament's Science & Technological Options Panel, which was deadlined for March 1997. However, it did not go to committee until December 1997 and would have been largely ignored had it not been for a Daily Telegraph article by Simon Davies which alerted the international media.

ECHELON exposed

The section dealing with ECHELON in the STOA report only ran to a few pages. The paragraph which drew most attention concluded:

> *Within Europe, all email, telephone and fax communications are routinely intercepted by the United States National Security Agency, transferring all target information from the European mainland via the strategic hub of London, then by satellite to Fort Meade in Maryland via the crucial hub at Menwith Hill in the North York Moors of the UK. Unlike many of the electronic spy systems developed during the Cold War, ECHELON is designed for primarily non-military targets: governments, organisations and businesses in virtually every country. The ECHELON system works by indiscriminately intercepting very large*

8 Campbell, D. 1988 They've got it taped, *New Statesman*, 12 August.

9 Hager, N. (1996) *Secret Power: New Zealand's Role in the International Spy Network*, Craig Potton Publishing, PO Box 555, Nelson, New Zealand.

quantities of communications then siphoning out what is valuable using artificial intelligence aids like Memex to find key words. Whilst there is much information gathered about potential terrorists, there is a lot of economic intelligence, notably intensive monitoring of all the countries participating in the GATT negotiations. With no system of accountability, it is difficult to discover what criteria determine who is not a target.

Nothing in the STOA report was new but its packaging in a formal report for the European Parliament led to a 'tipping point'. Interest in ECHELON mushroomed and all the European Member States had parliamentary debates about it. In September 1998, I was asked to produce an edited study updating the earlier report and included calls for a series of new studies to determine the level and extent of ECHELON's activities. Of these, Duncan Campbell's Interception Capabilities 2000 was the most informative and helped to redefine our knowledge of the role, function and activities of ECHELON.[10]

These reports laid the foundation of the European Parliament's temporary ECHELON Committee, which created some of the best most informed organised knowledge on the existence of ECHELON, its activities and limitations.[11] Almost every serious newspaper in the world has now covered ECHELON. Why? Because one package of organised knowledge, put together in a serious format was able to catalyse subsequent interest. Nevertheless, that package in itself was the fruit of scores of other researchers' activities, not least, the courageous Menwith Hill Women's camp activists who gleaned much of the secret documentation on which Duncan Campbell based his studies. The documents were 'liberated' via the time honoured research methodology of 'bin-ology'—the illegal raiding of bins and plastic rubbish bags inside the base.

Conclusion

The moral of the ECHELON story is that a network of researchers can both model, reinterpret, understand and politically challenge even awesomely funded and politically sensitive surveillance organisations such as the NSA (although I might admit to having second thoughts if I had seen the Gene Hackman movie 'Enemy of the State' before I wrote the STOA report.) Even at that juncture,

10 See http://www.iptvreports.mcmail.com/ic2kreport.htm accessed December 2005. [Editor's note: this URL is now defunct; Campbell's report can be found at: https://fas.org/irp/eprint/ic2000/ic2000.htm].

11 For the final report see http://cryptome.org/ECHELON-ep-fin.htm accessed December 2005. [Editor's note: this URL is now defunct; the final report can be found at: https://www.duncancampbell.org/menu/surveillance/echelon/IC2001-Paper1.pdf.

the early reception of the European Parliament was hostile in some quarters with questions about whether ECHELON even existed.

However, the STOA report contained detailed recommendations for further work on understanding new surveillance technologies and their political impact including the commissioning of new work on ECHELON. It was no coincidence that on my recommendation, the author of the key final document proving ECHELON's role was Duncan Campbell, the original ECHELON researcher and ABC defendant. His report to STOA, Interception Capabilities 2000, remains one of the clearest expositions on the way that ECHELON works as well as a healthy self-critique of some of the assumptions made including the capacity of the NSA to do continuous real time speech recognition, authentication and direct printout. There were limits but these were burgeoning new research areas too. These reports provoked an intense debate in the European Parliament and the setting up of a Temporary ECHELON Committee. There is now a rich literature on ECHELON which stretches way beyond what any one researcher could have accomplished. The more important sites are available via Surveillance and Society home pages. How was that paradigm shift achieved? Essentially by a network of researchers working on a variety of different jigsaw puzzle pieces - with one researcher injecting these findings into an appropriate political arena, at the right time.

Has the debate continued? Well yes and no. Immediately after the terrorist attacks on New York in 2001, I requested the STOA committee investigate the political implications of the failure of ECHELON to pre-empt the attack on the basis that such a highly invasive intelligence set up could only justify its existence if it was a prophylactic entity preventing such atrocities before they happened. STOA did commission the report but to its own chosen think-tank. There was not going to be any deeply critical NGO questioning of the role and functioning of sensitive intelligence agencies this time.

After 9/11, the debate rumbles on and many are beginning to fear that in the future such collaborative research will be thwarted by bogus security requirements and restrictions. Research scholars have to take the long view, assemble their findings and grow the supportive networks necessary for sustaining their effective work in the future. To quote my former supervisor, Paul Smoker—every major change requires a happener—and if it has happened—it's possible! It would be good to see these pages being used to explore the new role of ECHELON post 9/11. At a time when the newly joined former Eastern European states are being used for 'rendering' a.k.a. torturing political detainees, we might anticipate that ECHELON is being offered to many more policing and foreign intelligence agencies in the so called 'War Against Terror'. It is fairly probable that new algorithms for tracking down friendship networks and associates have emerged, based on what could well be dodgy social science assumptions of 'proximity equals collusion'. How can we locate the new ECHELON in the new world order? In the surveillance world, ECHELON and the NSA are the equivalent of the 900 lb gorilla. It is a challenge that future surveillance scholars will have to face.

References

Campbell, D. (1988) They've got it taped, *New Statesman*, 12 August.

Hager, N. (1996) *Secret Power: New Zealand's Role in the International Spy Network Nelson*, New Zealand: Craig Potton Publishing

Inglis, B. (1986) *The Hidden Power* London: Jonathon Cape

Laurie, P. (1970) *Beneath the City Streets*, Harmondsworth: Penguin

Lawrence, B. (1977) Nasty Branch hit Bailrigg, *Scan 1*, 26 April: 1

Snow, C.P. (1959) *The Two Cultures and the Scientific Revolution*, Cambridge: Cambridge University Press

Wood, D. (2001) *The Hidden Geography of Transnational Surveillance*, Unpublished PhD thesis, University of Newcastle upon Tyne, UK. http://www.staff.ncl.ac.uk/d.f.j.wood/thesis.htm [Accessed 01/12/05]

[Editor's note: the thesis can be accessed from this new URL: https://theses.ncl.ac.uk/jspui/handle/10443/3614]

A systems approach to analysing sub-state conflicts

Steve Wright[1]

Abstract

Purpose – The purpose of this paper is to provide a more holistic approach to analysing the impact of all the behaviour of a conflict's participants its overall dynamics, using the example of the Northern Irish troubles.

Design/methodology/approach – A novel multivariate time series approach developed by Professor Paul Smoker is presented which can map the dynamics of this conflict and its causal inferences as a series or "systemograms".

Findings – The case example reveals high levels of autocorrelation in the variety of techniques used by the state security authorities to suppress terrorism, indicating their strong role in maintaining this conflict. When more than one party exhibits such behaviour, the conflict "locks in".

Research limitations/implications – The work remains preliminary and historical. Data was collected on a month-by-month basis which suggests associated rather than direct causal influence. It would be useful to further explore these findings using data from similar conflicts.

Practical implications – Suggests that some counter-terrorism approaches may be dysfunctional especially those adopting sub-lethal weapons. Provides some insight into behavioural changes required to prevent conflict destabilisation.

Originality/value – Provides a novel conflict research methodology which allows the strong structural dynamics of the conflict to be seen – much the way that elapsed time photography enables hidden processes to be revealed. The raw statistics are presented here.

Keywords Cybernetics, Time series analysis, Conflict management, Northern Ireland

1 This article originally appeared in Kybernetes, 35(1/2) 2006, pp.182-194. With gratitude to Becky Taylor at Emerald Publishing for permission for republication.

Introduction

This paper is essentially an introduction to a new methodology which uses multivariate time series analyses to examine some of the hidden dynamics of the Northern Irish conflict from1969 to 1981. It draws on the conceptual work of one of the pioneers of peace research, the late Professor Paul Smoker, to describe systemic conflict relationships between all the parties to this conflict. Using some of the most comprehensive statistical documentation ever compiled on an internal conflict, the methodology reveals the highly structured nature of this conflict over a sustained period of time. The paper and its ancillary web sites present not only the data archive, but also make public the univariate, bivariate and multivariate time series programmes used to make the analyses, for the first time. The outputs are presented in the form of descriptions of associated influence or "systemograms" which can describe the dynamic and changing conflict ecology where apparently disparate conflict behaviour such as house searches, plastic bullet firings and the killing of military personnel, are highly correlated.

Measures of autocorrelation are used to suggest a loss of freedom in the actions of particular conflict participants. Particular attention is given to the use of "less-lethal weapons" and their impact on overall conflict dynamics. What emerges is that sectarian killings form a distinct conflict subset, whereas the counter-insurgency behaviour of the state security forces act as a conflict driver, ratchetting up the conflict as each more severe phase of the counter-insurgency programme is introduced. The paper attempts to introduce a more holistic or whole systems conflict approach which is both dynamic and puzzling, since in many paradoxical respects, it indicates co-operation between the various participants to carry on the conflict at a systemic level. A further concept which remains under explored is that of time level. Like elapsed time photography using different speeds to enable hidden processes to be revealed, the multivariate time series approach allows the in connectivity of the conflict's participants to be studied at different time levels. In nature many processes can only be seen if that right time level is accessed. This technique permits further exploration of that concept in regard to conflict.

The provisional lessons of this study are that sub-state conflict control measures can prove dysfunctional, especially when new technologies are used to attack combatants and civilians alike. The author represents it at this time simply because it potentially opens up the prospect of repeating the research methodology in other sub-state conflicts such as Israel and Iraq, if reliable data were ever to become available. It is also timely because of a push by US military planners, to redefine international law—in such a way that it permits the application of sub-lethal weaponry during sub-state conflicts at a level and on a scale which we have never seen before.

Background

The roots of this paper lie in work first undertaken when the author was a postgraduate student at the Richardson Institute, at the University of Lancaster, nearly three decades ago. The early research originally reported in the Journal of Peace Research (JPR) in 1978 outlined a series of nine hypotheses on how sub-lethal acts by state security forces, might dysfunctionally alter a conflict's dynamics in ways which led to a loss of control (Wright, 1978).

The first challenge was to find sufficient and accurate data on a conflict to test the nine hypotheses outlined in the JPR report and then to design a methodology capable of describing inferred causal influences. Fortunately, the Director of the Richardson Institute during that time, the late Professor Paul Smoker, had pioneered the use of new methodologies to examine the ways in which conflict processes could lock in. His time series study of the Sino-Indian conflict during the 1960s (Smoker, 1969) is seminal. Also instructive was Smoker's creative approaches to locating suitable data. According to one surreal account, he found the raw statistics for his Sino-Indian Study in the bins outside the Indian embassy where the bound telex exchanges between China and India were waiting to be cast away. He used this unique treasure trove of statistics to show that it was possible to use time series analysis of just two variables (the frequency and length of these respective telex messages), to predict when this conflict would break down.

Smoker was a founding pioneer of quantitative and simulation approaches in peace and conflict research and he was willing to adapt his Sino-Indian work to the much more complex task of examining the interaction and associated influences of scores of variables over different time levels. Part of that work was written up as a PhD thesis (Wright, 1987); some of it found its way into one of the first volumes on quantitative perspectives on terrorism (Wright, 1981). However, apart from a passing reference to the work in a report for the European Parliament's Scientific and Technological Options Assessment Unit on approaches to testing and assessing the hidden social and political impacts of technologies of political control in 1998 (Wright, 1998), the work lay moribund and too complicated and problematic to excite peace researchers not enthused by mathematics. The author was working on proofs of the 1978 Journal of Peace Research article referred to above when the secret police carried out their first raid on a British University trying to root out anyone who knew about the then top secret echelon system of mass telecommunications interception. The time series research was the only documentation they left behind—perhaps a telling negative indicator of the political utility of quantitative methods?

But for 9/11, the work may have continued to gather dust. However, the new US strategies of ignoring international law, the emergence of new polices seeking to target civilians and combatants together with new weapons technology and the dysfunctional effects of the current military containment strategies in the Middle East including Iraq and Israel, provoked the author to re-understand the challenge of attempting to quantify or even accurately describe, implied causal inferences in complex conflict dynamics. The following presentation, data, programmes and analyses should not be viewed as finished piece of work but more as a demonstration or illustration of an approach to those whom we hope can reassess their implications and limitations from a deeper understanding of statistics than the author possesses. In many senses this is a tribute and a plea to continue the creative work of Paul Smoker, whose imagination created the methodologies which are applied to illustrate this study. It is, however, argued that a whole systems approach is essential if we are to understand why certain peacekeeping functions and approaches do not work.

Testing hypotheses on destabilizing conflict processes in Northern Ireland

The hypotheses outlined in Wright (1978) were originally designed to examine the hidden and longer-term impacts of so-called "less-lethal weapons" such as plastic bullets—an area of armaments which has subsequently become much more significant as the US and other states develop new technologies for fighting asymmetric warfare after 9/11.

In short, the theory went like this: "In certain circumstances, the use of less-lethal weapons may be considered as an over corrective response." Through a cybernetic process of destabilizing feedback, over corrective responses can bring about an opposite effect to the one intended. Instead of containment, an over corrective response would lead towards an induction of uncontrollable conflict and further polarization. Thus attempts to control a situation with over corrective responses are thwarted because in effect the resulting system works against itself. This early study argued that the impact effectiveness of such technological\fixes would decline over time so that increasing amounts would be required to obtain the same powers of control. If powers of control were lost in this way, then a resurgence of the phenomena under control might develop as the fix lost potency. If the underlying dynamics were not realized, reliance on ever more powerful fixes would prove counterproductive as such cycles of destabilization would repeat themselves.

The paper argued that even if these hypotheses were true, it was likely that in the short term such weapons would appear to be an effective means of crowd control:

> *The possibility that they constitute a destabilizing factor in a conflict might only be revealed by a study which correlated their effects on a range of indicators for longer periods of time.*

One methodological challenge was that an input of aggression into a conflict by one party during one point in time which results in an output of retaliatory aggression at another period of time, the form in which this output manifests itself might be quite different from the form of input.

The British Army in Northern Ireland had adopted strategies from their Land War Operations Volume 111 which were essentially "counter-revolutionary operations". A key concern here therefore was that if a successively more oppressive set of phased counter-insurgency strategies comprised the software which programmed the behaviour of the dominant system of socio political control, then a self generating conflict could ensue. Thus the introduction of the second most severe phase of the counter-insurgency techniques may be legitimated through the waves of violent retaliation amplified by the use of less-lethal weapons during the first phase. Subsequently, phase two is likely to generate further dissent, which if handled by even more severe riot weapon deployment, may destabilize the situation sufficiently to legitimate the introduction of phase three and so on. Of course there were other factors and approaches applied which also played a role such as the coercive mechanisms used to facilitate internment without trial and the high levels of abuse suffered by the detainees.

The parallels with the current conflict in Iraq and Israel reveal similar dynamics but with rather more lethal than less lethal force being deployed. The sickening images of Abu Ghraib remind us that the sensory deprivation techniques using hooding and violent softening up treatments have transformed into standard operating procedures. But the concerns here are similar in that if the authorities fail to realize the impacts of their chosen conflict containment approaches, they risk having to deploy the entire gamut of the counter-insurgency spectrum of operations, in a manner tantamount to self-fulfilment. For Northern Ireland, even a crude time point analysis of political killings graphed against changes in socio-political control tactics, appeared to support this thesis (Figure 1). Of course in the case of the Northern Ireland conflict, the authorities were willing to release detailed statistical data. In Iraq, the coalition forces merely count their own dead and have refused to do body counts on killed oppositional forces or civilians caught in the crossfire for fear of raising echoes of Vietnam. However, one study published in the *Lancet* in October 2004 suggests nearly 100,000 casualties.[2]

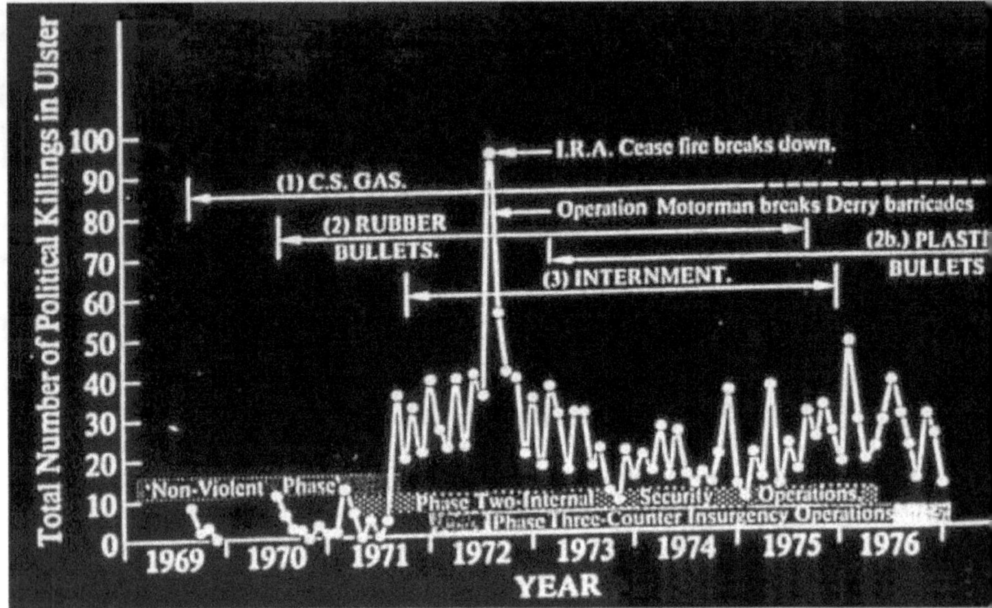

Figure 1. Military counterinsurgency phases and political killings in Northern Ireland

Data considerations

Clearly, establishing the statistics of any sub-state conflicts is always going to be problematic: Northern Ireland was no different, almost every provider of information might be accused of having a partisan view. The problem with the first crude model was that its description was based on the changes in only one empirical conflict indicator, namely the overall death count. It was, however, fruitful in suggesting that there were unforeseen relationships between state

2 Editor's note: this link has been updated, https://www.thelancet.com/journals/lancet/article/PIIS0140-6736(04)17441-2/fulltext

and non-state conflict activities which could be measured. It also provides a rudimentary framework to consider such changes. It also implied that the influence of a conflict action may persist within a conflict system, long after the event.

The challenge in attempting to develop even a basic holistic approach to just describing the Northern Irish conflict raised fundamental questions about how to select representative conflict indicators, how to find such data and how could substantial amounts of information on this conflict be presented in a meaningful way? The challenge was not just academic since any commentator on this conflict and others of its ilk is likely to draw fire because of inferred political bias. Paul Smoker saw a clear need for the process of interpretation to be clearly separated from the actual conflict description so that subjective bias could be eliminated as far as possible. We decided to pick variables that characterised incidents which most people would regard as being symptomatic of internal war. These included activities of state security personnel (such as house and vehicle searches, gas and plastic bullets fired, internment; paramilitary activists (shooting attacks, bomb explosions, Catholics assassinated, protestants assassinated, state security personnel (army, RUC and UDR) killed or wounded, kneecappings, etc.) and civilian victims of the conflict processes (e.g. civilians killed and wounded). Few other studies at the time had anything like this data—except perhaps for the Italian studies on terrorism published by Carlton and Scaherf (1981) but these had nothing like the level and frequency of events which characterised the Northern Irish troubles.

Taken together, these variables provide a significant measure of the Northern Ireland conflict's level and intensity. The data was collected from official sources such as the Northern Ireland Office, and the British Army and RUC Press Offices in the form of a monthly breakdown from 1969 to 1981. The full dataset and source references are provided here for the first time.[3]

Of course all such conflict data are problematic since each "event" is a summation of a much richer set of conflict processes and it is more usual for conflict participants to disagree on conflict statistics than agree (Omega Foundation, 2003) in regard to baton round figures, for example). However, it is arguable that this conflict is better documented than almost any other of its type and provides researchers with a unique framework to understand more about the conflict dynamics at work in what is now known as military operations other than war (MOUT).

3 Editor's note: The link provided by Steve is now defunct (www.imresearch.org/PraxisCentre/NIrelandStudy)

Some methodological considerations

Briefly, the univariate TSA enables a description of the level of influence which any variable's past behaviour exerts on that variables subsequent activity. This autocorrelation measure as it is termed provides an important indicator of emergent processes especially a loss of freedom. Highly auto-correlated behaviour is especially important since it is often associated with episodes where conflict participants lock in to their own conflict behaviour and become less responsive to actions of other conflict actors. In Figure 2, for example, a univariate time series analysis of riot munitions (CS gas cartridges, grenades and rubber bullets) shows not just highly predictable behaviour but also consistent mean level moving averages over considerable periods of time, as if the supply itself was the greatest determinant of the number of sub-lethal munitions fired.

The bivariate TSA enables a description to be made of the influence one variable's behaviour has on another, or more precisely, it provides a measure of the extent to which processes associated with the formation of variable A are implicated in the processes associated with the formation of variable B.

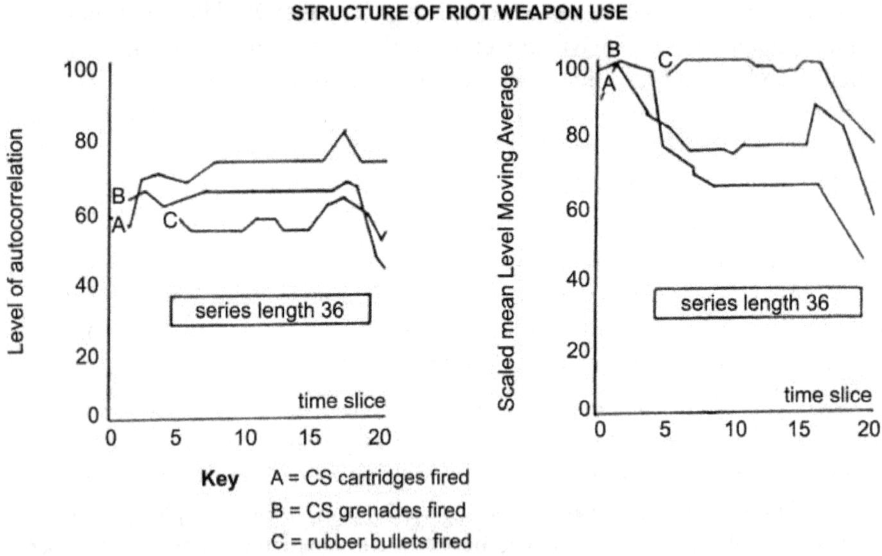

STRUCTURE OF RIOT WEAPON USE

Key A = CS cartridges fired
B = CS grenades fired
C = rubber bullets fired

Figure 2. High levels of autocorrelation and associated "Loss of Freedom" in riot weapon use

The multivariate TSA is a more complex technique, created to display the extent to which one variable's behaviour is implicated in the influences responsible for generating all the others, as it and they change over time. More precisely, it quantifies the overall connectivity of the influences generating all the variables; a measure of the strength of particular linkages together with an indication of the direction of any flows of associated influence which are revealed.

Smoker designed the technique as a multivariate cluster time series analysis, that is an amalgam of two different techniques, i.e. a clustering procedure and a time series analysis procedure. The clustering procedure is essentially a form of typal analysis derived from the work of McQuitty (1957). As a component of this methodology it is used to define each variable's time series as a member of a type, if its behaviour is more like the behaviour of other members of that type than it is like anything else. The time series components are derived from the works of Smoker (1969), Quenouille (1952) and Wold (1949).

The time series element serves to ascertain the direction and strength of any associated influences flowing within and between variables. The technical conventions, concepts and measures used to perform these measures together with the technical methodologies for interpreting the results are provided in our Praxis web site for those who wish to undertake a more detailed scrutiny.[4] The web site also provides detailed instruction on constructing a map of all these influences from the output of the multivariate TSA. This is an important element of this approach, since the descriptive systems map of flows of associated influences or "systemograms" can then be compared with other conflict data to make comparisons and evaluations of the impact of policies or any particular episode or activity on the overall conflict dynamics. The actual process of drawing out the "systemograms" is laboriously time consuming. However, in 1985, a research student at UMIST, Walker (1985) managed to semi-automate the process and this work is also available for anyone interested in taking such work further.

Mapping key participants' contributions to a conflict's dynamics

Mapping out the associated influence of key indicative variables of all the representative participants in a conflict, provides a more systemic picture of the conflict and enables us to at least describe the level and extent to which participants are actually cooperating to structure and maintain their conflict behaviour. It also enables us to identify the highly auto-correlated activities of any group which has in effect become autistic, being most influenced by their own behaviour rather than any of the other conflict participants. For the

4 Editor's note: The link provided by Steve is now defunct (www.imresearch.org/PraxisCentre/NIrelandStudy)

purpose of this study, a complete output of systemograms for time series 24, has been created on the associated url.[5] Here we will discuss only some of the structures and sub-systems emerging from a typical sequence and how this methodology could be applied to other conflicts experiencing similar forms of conflict behaviour.

In many ways, the multivariate systemogram approach enables a broad trawl of the data sets to actually identify highly structured behaviour. In practice, sub-systems emerge either between or within variable clusters as a consequence of undertaking this tracking exercise on the "systemograms". Variables within each sub-system develop certain patterns which sustain as typical features within each systemogram. These can be characterised as follows.

Active variables which have only strands of influence emanating out from them. They act on other variables rather than being significantly acted upon themselves; *reactive variables* have only strands of influence feeding into them; mixed variables both give and receive influence from other variables; *interactive variables* neither receive or give influence but correspond their influence with other variables to which they are linked; *highly auto-correlated variables* which feed a large part of their influence back into themselves indicating a pattern of self generation. Such variables are easy to spot in the systemograms since they are represented by conspicuous concentric circles or semi-circles. Eyeballing an illustrative systemogram sequence is perhaps the best way to understand this methodology.

An illustrative systemogram sequence

If the conflict time sequence contained in [the imresearch database][6] is examined systemogram by sytemogram, it is possible to discover whether the changing influence processes between different variables or within variable clusters are growing stronger or weaker. The change in the strength of the systemic process is revealed by the change in the level of correlation over selected time periods. Strengthening processes are associated with an increase in the level of correlation, whilst processes which are weakening, exhibit a decline in the level of correlation.

The systemograms used here (Figures 3 and 4) are provided simply to illustrate the methodological approach but a full analysis can potentially determine whether any political, military or NGO decision, policy or tactic is significant

5 Editor's note: The link provided by Steve is now defunct (www.imresearch.org/PraxisCentre/NIrelandStudy)

6 As above.

by empirically establishing when the particular "event" entered the sequence. If we define the influence horizon of an event as being the time period limit of the systemogram when its influence is first felt, the relevant systemogram TP $= t - n + L$.

Figure 3.Systemogram

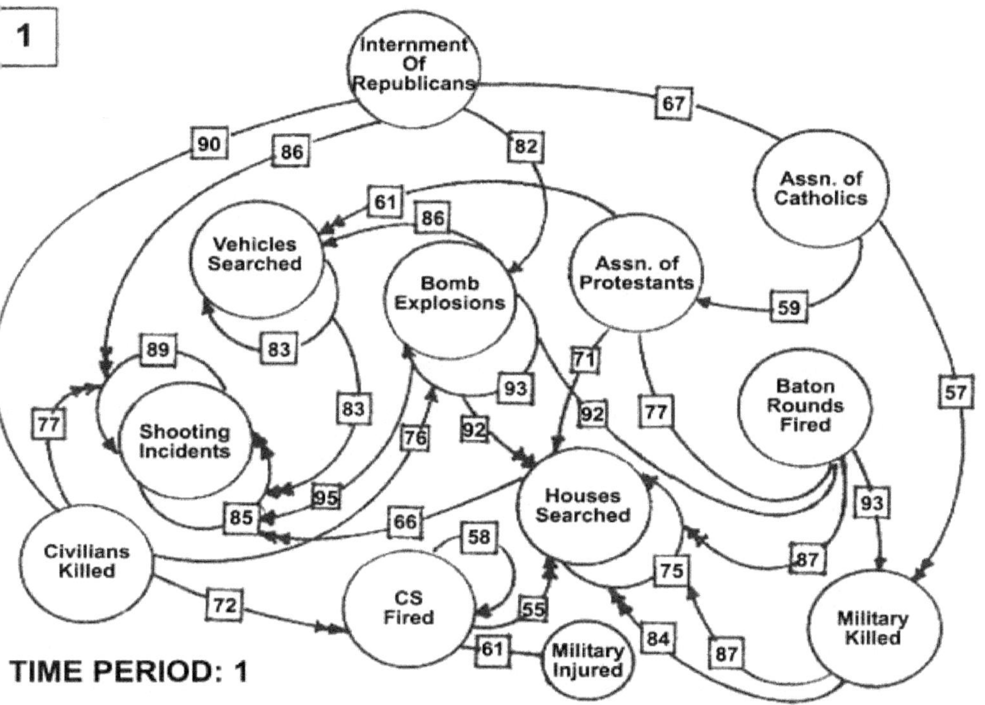

Figure 4. Systemogram 2

Where t = the chronological number of the appropriate month; n = the

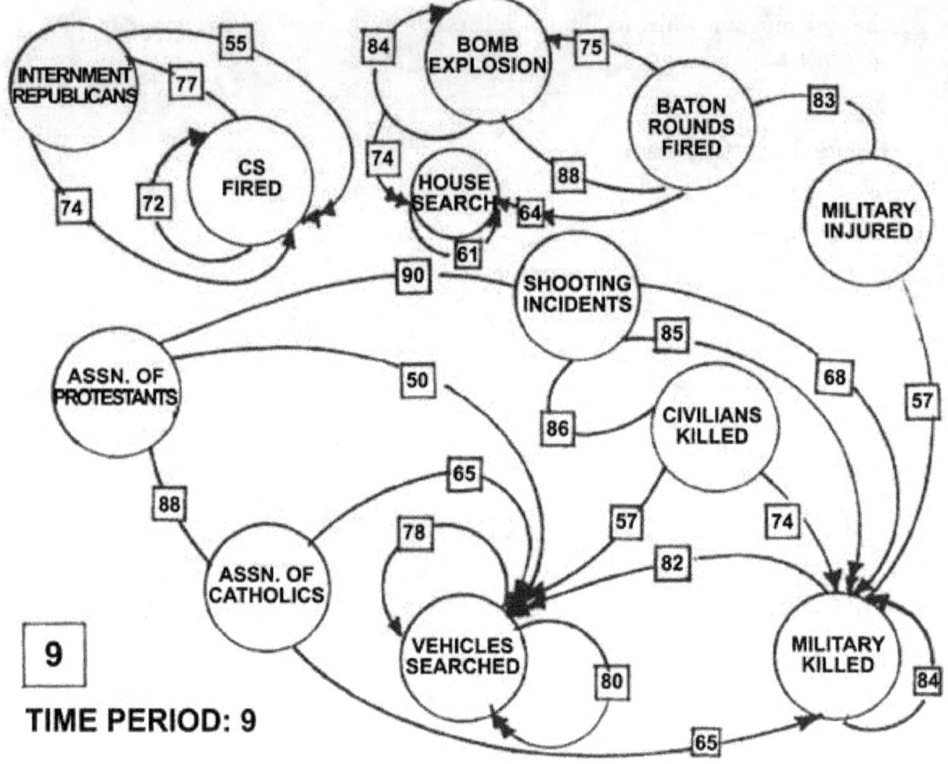

series length and L = the maximum time lag used.

For example, if we are interested in discovering whether or not the decision to introduce internment produced a measurable influence on the dynamics of the conflict, then we can find the first relevant systemogram if we know the following:

t = August 1971 (= 12 + 12 + 8) = 32

n = 24 (in this illustrative sequence)

L = 2 (in this particular study)

TP = 32 - 24 + 2 = systemogram 10

In systemogram 1, the most significant patterns of influence to emerge concern reactive variables, all of which are strongly auto-correlated. These include the process of vehicle searches (81); house searches (75) bomb explosions (93) and shooting incidents (89). By systemogram 5, these processes have structured with strong links between them. Bomb explosions and house searches are mutually influencing each other and bomb explosions are actively influencing vehicles searched (83). Some of these links confirm common sense—e.g. its natural to up searches of vehicles if bomb attacks are taking place but in systemogram 1 baton round firings are strongly acting on military killed (93). This is an interesting finding since traditionally any killing of military personnel is usually associated with punitive house searches, e.g. not just in Northern Ireland but in Iraq and Israel where the military action is so severe, that civilian houses are destroyed. In this first sytemogram, military killed is empirically described as actively influencing houses searched (87 + 84).

By systemogram 9, CS fired forms a separate cluster, reacting to the influence from Republican Internment (74 and 55); baton rounds are driving influence towards bomb explosions (75), which continues to drive influence into house searches. The assassination of Protestants and Catholics has become interactively linked (88) as military personnel killed continues to drive influence towards vehicles searched (82), as both variables yield high levels of autocorrelation (84 and 80, respectively), suggesting that these aspects of the conflict processes have become self organising structures (a full preliminary breakdown is provided in Wright, 1987).

If we tabulate the auto-correlated variables across the entire time sequence (Figure 5), we should expect a conflict "lock in" when several of the different conflict participant groups manifest some degree of autistic behaviour as measured by highly auto-correlated variables. In fact a series of "lock ins" emerges. At the beginning of the conflict, government searching and firing of CS was locked in with paramilitary bombings; shooting and killing of army personnel, until time period 25. A short phase of lock in emerges from the period 25 to 33 and then another from time period 33 to 44 and so on. According to Beer (1980):

> *This is a system in homeostatic equilibrium. Each part is structuring the other. So the structuring goes mutually on. If one part stops in this creative, evolutionary process, then the whole system breaks down. In Northern Ireland terms that is, the war is over.*

Exactly why so many of the British Army reactions developed such highly deterministic traits is a question which must be answered by future studies. Obviously military behaviour, by definition is variety reducing and incorporates standard operating procedures which can be systematically taught. The physical survival of urban guerrilla activists on the other hand, often literally depends on their unpredictability. The "variety increasing" aspects of their behaviour enables them to remain effective, alive and at large. The key issue here is of course the possibility that certain military doctrines are actually dysfunctional—in other words conflict exacerbating rather than conflict resolving.

Figure 5. "Lock In" profiles of Northern Ireland conflict participants 1969-1981

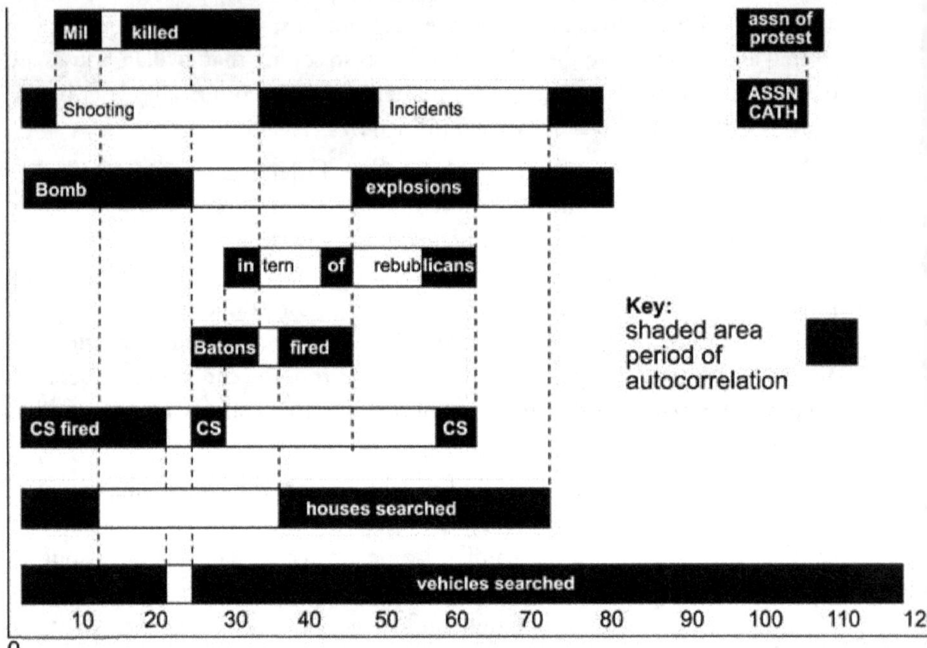

The presence of so much self-legitimating behaviour in the activities of military personnel should be of concern. Traditional counter-terrorist theories suggest such wars must be fought by taking out the hard men. Yet when freedom of decision is lost in the military group of participants on the level described above, the efficacy of such an approach to conflict resolution must be deeply questioned. The range of associated activities in this process appear to have just as much efficacy in evolving more hard men to get.

Conclusions

Having said that, it must be acknowledged that such quantitative approaches to whole systems conflict analysis are fraught with difficulties and their findings can seem opaque to non statisticians—including most policy makers. Anecdotal analyses is much easier to churn out and is far more accessible to sound-bite formation. Indeed any conference bringing the approaches of mathematical and conflict analyses together in systems terms is unusual. Richardson's conflict models are much less well known today than his weather forecasting equations—perhaps because with the advent of computers, his erstwhile laborious log calculations can now be instantly converted into understandable weather pictures that most of us can grasp (Richardson, 1960).

So few people work in these fields. A 1996 analysis of terrorism research in terms of the evolution of a body of knowledge, identified just 32 major members of the community (Reid, 1997). And the majority of these contributors make qualitative rather than quantitative contributions. Of course after 9/11, the media appetite for terrorist and conflict experts has been voracious but few new quantitative approaches are emerging except at the most basic death count level. Of course there has emerged a plethora of chronologies—many of which are open to challenge about objectivity and reliability. And even that is revealing since as was mentioned earlier in the ongoing Iraq conflict, the coalition partners would appear not to be as seriously documenting non coalition casualties, or at least not outside the prisons where different agendas for documenting conflict activities prevail.

A key question is utility. What can such studies tell us or reveal that is not more accessible from more anecdotal- or story-based analyses? The short answer is they can yield tremendous insight into the hidden structuring of conflict processes. This becomes increasingly important as the tactics and technologies being offered for asymmetrical warfare alter not only the casualty count but also the selection of who becomes a designated casualty. Nevertheless, such statistical studies need to be capable of showing a facility for generating testable hypotheses. A concern of this study has been to put reliable conflict data in the public domain for use by other researchers to do so. This sharing is slowly helping to birth new approaches.

For example, White and Falkenberg-White, in a ground breaking piece of research applied regression analysis to some of the data collated here and discovered that deaths caused by loyalist paramilitaries increased the number of persons killed by British soldiers. They concluded that one explanation for this curious finding given that most of those killed by the army were Catholics, might be evidence of "some kind of co-ordinated activity between Loyalist paramilitaries and members of the security services" (White and Falkenberg White, 1995). Whilst there is evidence now since 2002 to support such claims—especially in the light of the Stakeknife double agent fiasco, at other moments alternative agendas have emerged including protecting key members of Sein Fein to ensure the peace process was not derailed (Moloney, 2002).

A further possibility as yet not followed, is that other, ostensibly independent variables may be systematically linked to conflicts in ways which seem counter-intuitive. It is often remarked that more people have died in car accidents in Northern Ireland than in the troubles themselves, but no real research on possible hidden links has emerged yet. This methodology would enable other, less obvious conflict pathways to be measured and initially described and this would certainly be an area where even in conflict ridden countries such as Israel or Iraq, good data in principle may be sought.

Many of the counter-insurgency spasm wars which are characterising the early part of this century in Afghanistan, Israel and Iraq, are generating similar activities to the conflict in Northern Ireland: shooting incidents, car bombing episodes, civilians and military personnel killed, house and vehicle searches and internment, abuse and torture of suspected terrorists. If the authorities ever release their weekly or monthly statistical data on these wars, it would be worth establishing whether similar dysfunctional conflict structures and conflict "lock-ins" emerged.

In conclusion, we have entered a time when public presentation and information management are as much a part of conflict processing, as implementing military theories of peace keeping and conflict reconciliation. During periods of military intervention, the costs of following a misinformed policy are huge, yet the level of efforts and resources devoted to independent conflict assessment and monitoring activity are minuscule. During future periods of conflict, we need to find a way of more independently collecting the raw data of war if we are ever to effectively evaluate existing policies, especially the new "wars against terror". Without such objectivity we are all prey to propaganda. The important lesson from Northern Ireland is that if we are to truly understand future armed conflict dynamics, accurate data is paramount.

There needs to be much more pressure on governments to provide it and to set up structures which enable sufficient accountability for modern states to be legally challenged about the veracity of their statistical conflict data. The challenge to future researchers is to create descriptions and simulations of war which have sufficient truth content to challenge. One day we may even have an official operations research programme dedicated to sustaining peace.

References

Beer, S. (1980), Letter to S. Wright from Stafford Beer, 22 August.

Carlton, D. and Scaherf, C. (Eds) (1981), *Contemporary Terror: Studies in Sub-state Violence*, Macmillan, London.

McQuitty, L. (1957), "Elementary linkage analysis for isolating both orthogonal types & typal

relevancies", *Educational & Psychological Measurements*, Vol. 17, pp. 207-29.

Moloney, E. (2002), "Panorama missed the real story of collusion in Ulster", *Daily Telegraph*, 25 June.

Omega Foundation (2003), "Baton rounds: a review of the human rights implications of the introduction and use of the L2A1 baton", Round, Northern Ireland and Proposed Alternatives to the Baton Round, Northern Ireland Human Rights Commission, Belfast, April.

Quenouille, M.H. (1952), *Associated Measurements*, Academic Press, New York, NY.

Reid, E.O.F. (1997), "Evolution of a body of knowledge: an analysis of terrorism research", *Information Processing and Management*, Vol. 33 No. 1, pp. 91-106.

Richardson, L.F. (1960), *Statistics of Deadly Quarrels*, Quadrangle Books, Chicago, IL.

Smoker, P. (1969), "A time series analysis of Sino-Indian relations", *Journal of Conflict Research*, Vol. 13 No. 2, pp. 172-91.

Walker, T.J.V. (1985), "Automated plotting of complex multivariate time series analysis systemograms", dissertation BSc in Computation, UMIST, Manchester.

White, R.W. and Falkenberg White, T. (1995), "Repression and the liberal state: the case of Northern Ireland, 1969-1972", *Journal of Conflict Resolution*, Vol. 39 No. 2, pp. 330-52.

Wold, H. (1949), "On least squares regression with auto correlated variables & residuals", *Proceedings of the International Statistics Institute*, Berne, Switzerland.

Wright, S. (1978), "New police technologies: an exploration of the social implications and unforeseen impacts of some recent developments", *Journal of Peace Research*, Vol. 15 No. 4, pp. 305-22.

Wright, S. (1981), "A multivariate time series analysis of the Northern Irish conflict, 1969-1976", in Alexander, J. and Gleason, J.M. (Eds), *Behavioural and Quantitative Perspectives on Terrorism,* Permagon Press, New York, NY, pp. 283-328.

Wright, S. (1987), "New police technologies & sub-state conflict control", PhD thesis, Department of Politics, The Richardson Institute, University of Lancaster, Lancaster.

Wright, S. (1998), An Appraisal of the Technologies of Political Control: Interim STOA Report (PE 166.499), Luxembourg: European, available at: http://cryptome.org/stoa-atpc.htm accessed 31 March 2005).

Big brother is watching— and tapping your phone, searching your records on computers, identifying your voice, and getting ready to restrain and control you

Keith MacDonald[1]

The [Manchester] City Council's police monitoring unit staff are to be transferred to the Town Clerk's Department as research staff for police authority members—but the head of the unit until now, Dr Steve Wright, has spent 10 years in research on new police technologies. This is what he found.

Riot control spray more severe than CS gas, which causes temporary blindness, intense pain and hysteria, is "*as painful as being thrown naked into a bed of stinging nettles*", according to Dr Steve Wright, head of Manchester City Council's now-doomed police monitoring committee support unit.

The substance, known as CR, was discovered in all innocence by two scientists at Salford College of Technology in 1962. Suschitzky and Higginbottom,[2] who wrote it up in the Journal of the Chemical Society. The article set in motion a major new research programme at Porton Down, and some research was done at Manchester University medical school.

Splashed on the face, CR causes intense eye pain, "extremely painful" blepharospasm (involuntary blinking) which last 15-30 minutes, higher blood pressure, inner eye pressure and, in some people, hysteria.

Unlike CS gas, it dissolves in water so can be used in water cannon. It can also be used as a foam barrier.

These claims are made in Dr Wright's 700-page PhD thesis on New Police Technologies and Sub State Conflict Control, the result of 10 years' research. "*During the last few years*," he states, "*research and development work on CR has been stepped up in preparation for its future utilisation as a standard riot agent.*"

His thesis presents a nightmarish scenario of "state of the art" surveillance and control techniques, including:

1 This report by Keith Macdonald originally appeared in the Manchester Evening News, 2nd February 1988.

2 Editor's note: see https://pubs.rsc.org/en/content/articlelanding/1962/jr/jr9620002367/unauth

- Miniature TV cameras no bigger than the ballpoint of a Biro pen, which can be hidden in a tiny crack n the wall;
- Guns that fit into a cigarette case that fire poison darts to kill quietly;
- Phonetaps that identify individuals from voiceprints;
- Radar, developed in Vietnam, that can see through walls.

This is all part of what Dr Wright calls "*the UK policing revolution.*" He continues:

"An increasing common view is that there has been a movement from the friendly archetype of Dixon of Dock Green of the 60s and 70s to a more sinister 80s policing archetype—the menacing Star Wars' Darth Vader.

"During this transition period, senior police officers have agreed that it is the community which must decide the kind of police force it requires.

"Here lies the crux of the transformation in British policing: namely the extent to which the public have a say in police priorities and practices, and the level of democratic accountability within the system, which can permit local representatives to challenge a particular direction of policing policy."

He also states:

"New police technologies are becoming one of the most important factors in attempting sub-state conflict control. Such 'control' is more apparent than real, but serves the purpose of disguising the level of coercive repression being applied. An overall effect of this process is the para-militarisation of the police role."

Dr Wright's research was "*rudely interrupted,*" as he puts it, in 1977, when "*six Special Branch officers were despatched to seize material gathered from open sources.*" At the time he was doing research at Lancaster University. He had stumbled on a national phonetap network which, he says, fed information to American intelligence. The case was raised in Parliament, and after protests from his vice-chancellor, Sir Charles Carter, most of his papers were returned a year later.

"The episode dramatically illustrates the dilemma caused when academic research is deemed to be 'intelligence' by the state security structure under scrutiny," he writes.

Among the developments in advanced police technology, Dr Wright claims, are:

- Area denial systems, using at checkpoints extending scissors of spikes, such as "lazy tongs" used by the Army in Northern Ireland, or more formidable concertinas of razored barbed tape (a more active deterrent is the Prowler—the Programmable Robot Observer with Logical Enemy Response, literally an armed robot used for sentry or reconnaissance duty);

- In communications, "new systems now enable photographs, document copies, fingerprint and computer-stored intelligence files to be radioed into police vehicles on demand";
- Developments in computer programming for police purposes have advanced a system known as full text retrieval, which creates the basis for pre-emptive policing. Police computers programmed with multi-factor search routines can scan large collections of low grade information to infer links between individuals and "occurrences."

"Often the whole community, convicted and unconvicted alike, will find their way into the databases of such systems."

The thesis states: "*Multi-factor search systems allow searches for individuals based on extremely scanty informational sketches. For example, 'List all males with black curly hair, between 5ftt 8in and 5ft 10in, with a scar on the right cheek, frequenting pubs in the Croydon area.*"

Another observation: "*It is significant that a modern police operations room is becoming almost indistinguishable from its military counterpart.*"

- Identity recognition: As well as finger prints, the human voice can now become a unique, individual, identifying characteristic. In America, voice identification equipment is used commercially—for authenticating credit card customers on the phone, for instance—"but they can also prove extremely useful in the automatic eavesdropping of telephones on a large scale; an application which, it has been alleged, is now integral to both the work of GCHQ and the US National Security Agency."
- Surveillance: Electronic bugs can be hidden in rings, cigarette lighters, pens, ashtrays or candlesticks.
- An "infinity transmitter" fitted into a telephone mouthpiece means the targeted room can be eavesdropped at any time from any other phone in the world, simply by dialling the target number. The phone remains silent but all conversations in the room are accessible for the duration of the call.
- Ultra-miniature closed circuit TV systems smaller than the ballpoint of a Biro pen have been manufactured, which relay pictures via a fibre optic cable. These fibre optic cameras can be pushed through pin-sized

holes or cracks in walls and ceilings. Enlargement is possible with the latest systems, which are fitted with both zoom lenses and recording equipment.

- Radar surveillance is a development of the "foliage penetration system" used in Vietnam and originally designed for spotting guerrillas in thick jungle cover. The ZB 298 radar is capable of "seeing" through brick and cinderblock walls and can differentiate between people, vehicles and animals at distances up to 10,000 metres.

The thesis states: "*Secrecy surrounds the whole area of police surveillance, the new equipment they use and its capabilities: the operational units which deploy it, and the precise details of the rationale which decides who is targeted and why. Yet over the years a series of incidents have come to public notice which reveal an expanding role for political surveillance operations by the police special branch and the intelligence services within Britain.*"

These include, he alleges, the setting up of spy posts to watch gay pubs and black communities in Manchester.

"*Yet perhaps the most revealing incident in the North West*", Dr Wright states, "*concerned the activities of Mr Jim Anderton, the Chief Constable of Greater Manchester Police, who ordered the monitoring of personal police calls inside Chester House. If police themselves were not secure from covert police surveillance, can anyone be sure?*"

Dr Wright received his PhD from Princess Alexandra, Chancellor of Lancaster University, in December.

Dr Wright told me that the new forms of technology, which enhance the scope and power of policing, allow politicians and police "to technically fix social and political problems without resolving them."

"*The unforeseen consequences,*" he adds, "*are that if there's a technical fixing of these problems, they come back in a worse form.*"

Part of the thesis covers the export of new repressive technologies to third world fascists, now experiencing the world's worst social and economic problems, and there is a decision drifting towards creating new highly technological police states.

"*Britain is now becoming the second biggest exporter in the world in that policing revolution, and politicians in this country need to take decisive action to intervene in that unsavoury process.*"

Steve Wright Bibliography

Collaborative Works

Dastbaz, Mohammad, Edward Halpin, and Steve Wright. 2013. Emerging Technologies and the Human Rights Challenge of Rapidly Expanding State Surveillance Capacities. In Babak Akhgar, and Simeon Yates (ed's). *Strategic Intelligence Management: National Security Imperatives and Information and Communication Technologies.* Waltham, MA: Elsevier, pp. 108-118.

Halpin, Eddie, Philippa Trevorrow, Dave Webb, and Steve Wright (ed's). 2006. *Cyberwar, Netwar and the Revolution in Military Affairs.* London: Palgrave Macmillan.

Halpin, Eddie. F., and Steve Wright. 2013. The Hidden Dimensions of Global Information Networks What Price Privacy? In: *Proceedings of the Annual Conference of CAIS.* https://doi.org/10.29173/cais14

Hayes, Ben, April Humble, and Steve Wright. 2016. From Refugee Protection to Militarised Exclusion: What Future for 'Climate Refugees'? In: Buxton, Nick, and Ben Hayes (ed's). *The Secure and the Dispossessed.* London: Pluto Press, pp. 111-132.

Martin, Brian, and Steve Wright. 2003. Countershock: Mobilizing Resistance to Electroshock Weapons. *Medicine, Conflict and Survival.* **19**(3), pp. 205-222. https://doi.org/10.1080/13623690308409692
Also available from: https://www.bmartin.cc/pubs/03mcs.html

Martin, Brian, and Steve Wright. 2006. Looming Struggles over Technology for Border Control. *Journal of Organisational Transformation and Social Change.* **3**(1), pp. 95-107.

https://doi.org/10.1386/jots.3.1.95/1

Also available from: https://www.bmartin.cc/pubs/06jotsc.html

Martin, Brian, and Steve Wright. 2007. Countershock: Challenging Pushbutton Torture. In: Brian Martin (ed). *Justice Ignited.* Lanham, MD: Rowman & Littlefield, pp. 143-156.

Poole, Robert, and Steve Wright. 1987. *Target North-West: Civil Defence & Nuclear War in Cumbria, Lancashire, Manchester, Merseyside & Cheshire.* Lancaster: Civil Defence Study Group, Richardson Institute for Peace and Conflict Research, University of Lancaster.

Rappert, Brian, and Steve Wright. 2000. A Flexible Response? Assessing Non-Lethal Weapons. *Technology Analysis and Strategic Management.* **12**(4), pp. 477–492. https://doi.org/10.1080/713698500

Wood, David Murakami, and Steve Wright. 2015. Before and After Snowden: Editorial for the Surveillance and Security Intelligence after Snowden Issue (Part 1). *Surveillance & Society.* **13**(2), pp. 132-138. https://doi.org/10.24908/ss.v13i2.5710

Wright, Steve, and Tessie Humble. 2015. Techno-Politics of Exclusion. In: Cecilia Wee, Janneke Schönenbach, and Olaf Arndt (ed's). *Supramarkt.* Sparsnäs: Irene Publishing, pp. 233-269.

Wright, Steve, and Dave Webb. (n.d.) *Multivariate Time Series Approaches to Analysing the Northern Irish Conflict: Lessons for Future Sub-State Conflict Control.* Leeds: The Praxis Centre, Leeds Metropolitan University. Available from: https://eprints.leedsbeckett.ac.uk/id/eprint/2101/1/Timeseriespaper.doc

Policy

Ballantyne, Robin, and Noel Stott. 2011. *Submission on the Prevalence of Torture in Correctional Centres. Jointly Submitted to the Portfolio Committee on Correctional Services*

c/o Cindy Balie. Omega Research Foundation & Institute for Security Studies. Available from: https://static.pmg.org.za/docs/111130iss_0.pdf

Wright, Steve. 1987. Public Order Technology: 'Less-Lethal Weapons'. In: The European Group for the Study of Deviance and Social Control (ed's). *Civil Rights, Public Opinion and the State.* Florence, Italy: The European Group for the Study of Deviance and Social Control, pp. 70-96.

Wright, Steve. 1998. *An Appraisal of Technologies of Political Control.* Scientific and Technological Options Assessment (STOA) Working Document. 6 January. Luxembourg: European Parliament. Available from: https://cryptome.org/stoa-atpc.htm
[Link to the bibliography: https://cryptome.org/stoa-bib.htm]

Omega Foundation. 2000. *Crowd Control Technologies (An Appraisal of Technologies for Political Control): Final Study.* Scientific and Technological Options Assessment (STOA) Working Document. June. Luxembourg: European Parliament. Available from: https://www.europarl.europa.eu/RegData/etudes/etudes/stoa/2000/168394/DG-4-STOA_ET(2000)168394_EN(PAR02).pdf

Oxfam. 1998. *Small Arms, Wrong Hands – A Case for Government Control of the Small Arms Trade.* Oxford: Oxford.

Journal Articles

Ballantyne, Robin. 1998. The Technology of Political Control. *Covert Action Quarterly.* Spring, pp.17-23. Available from: https://covertactionmagazine.com/wp-content/uploads/2020/01/CAQ64-1998-1.pdf

Ballantyne, Robin. 2005. Japan's Hidden Arms Trade. *The Asia-Pacific Journal.* **3**(1).

Wright, Steve. 1977. An Assessment of the New Technologies of Repression. In: Marjo Hoefnagels (ed). *Repression and Repressive Violence Vol.7.* Amsterdam: Swets & Zeitlinger, pp. 133-165.

Wright, Steve. 1977. Technology and Politics. *Nature.* **267**(202). Available from: https://www.nature.com/articles/267202a0

Wright, Steve. 1978. New Police Technologies: An Exploration of the Social Implications and Unforeseen Impacts of Some Recent Developments. *Journal of Peace Research.* **15**(4), pp. 305-322. https://doi.org/10.1177/002234337801500402

Wright, Steve. 1991. The New Technologies of Political Repression: A New Case for Arms Control? *Philosophy and Social Action.* **17**(3-4), pp.31-54. Available from: https://core.ac.uk/download/pdf/46523072.pdf

Wright, Steve. 1992. Undermining Nonviolence: The Coming Role of New Police Technologies. *Gandhi Marg.* **14**(1), pp.157-165. Available from: http://nonviolence.rutgers.edu/document/IIP0153F04

Wright, Steve. 2001. Landmines: A Worse Fate Still to Come? *Review of African Political Economy.* **28**(90), pp. 649-650. https://doi.org/10.1080/03056240108704575

Wright, Steve. 2001. The Role of Sub-Lethal Weapons in Human Rights Abuse. *Medicine, Conflict and Survival.* **17**(3), pp. 221-233. https://doi.org/10.1080/13623690108409581

Wright, Steve. 2002. *Future Sub-Lethal, Incapacitating & Paralysing Technologies – Their Coming Role in the Mass Production of Torture, Cruel, Inhumane & Degrading Treatment.* A Draft Paper Presented to the Expert Seminar On Security Equipment & The Prevention of Torture. 25-26 October. London, UK. Available from: https://www.statewatch.org/media/documents/news/2002/nov/torture.pdf

Wright, Steve. 2004. Merchants of Repression. *Global Security and Cooperation Quarterly.* No.12, Spring.

Wright, Steve. 2005. The ECHELON Trail: An Illegal Vision. *Surveillance & Society.* **3**(2/3), pp.198-215. https://doi.org/10.24908/ss.v3i2/3.3501

Wright, Steve. 2006. A Systems Approach to Analysing Sub-State Conflicts. *Kybernetes.* **35**(1/2), pp.182-194. https://doi.org/10.1108/03684920610640308

Wright, Steve. 2006. Report. Sub-Lethal Vision: Varieties of Military Surveillance Technology. *Surveillance & Society.* **4**(1/2), pp.136-153. Available from: https://ojs.library.queensu.ca/index.php/surveillance-and-society/article/view/3459/3422

Wright, S. 2016, Watching Them Watching Us. *Ethical Space: The International Journal of Communication Ethics.* **12**(3/4), pp. 47-57.

Book Contributions

Ballantyne, Robin. 2010. Japan is Active in the Global Arms Trade. In: Christina Fisanick (ed). *Gun Control.* Farmington Hills, USA: Greenhaven Press.

Wright, S. 1981. A Multivariate Time Series Analysis of the Northern Irish Conflict 1969-76. In: Yonah Alexander, and J.M. Gleason (ed's). *Behavioural and Quantitative Perspectives on Terrorism.* Oxford: Pergamom, pp. 283-327.

Wright, Steve. 1983. The International Trade in the Technology of Repression. In: Sakamoto Y. and R. Klaassen (ed's). *Key Issues of Peace Research, Proceedings of the International Peace Research Association 9th General Conference, June 1981, Orillia Ontario.* IPRA.

Wrights, S. 1987. Public Order Technology: 'Less-Lethal Weapons'. In: B. Rolston, and M. Tomlinson (ed's). *Civil Rights, Public Opinion and The State. Working Papers in Criminology.* Belfast: The Print Workshop, pp. 70-96.

Wright, Steve. 1991. Mobility and Transport for Elderly and Disabled Persons. In: Claes-Eric Norrbom, and Agneta Ståhl (ed's). *Mobility and Transport for Elderly and Disabled Persons.* Philadelphia, PA: Gordon and Breach Publishing, pp. 850-867.

Wright, Steve. 1991. The New technologies of Political Suppression. In: Gunter Brausch (ed). *Weapons Technology, Disarmament and Verification.* Mosbach: IPRA Defense and Disarmament Study Group Paper 1. Available from: https://catalogue.sipri.org/cgi-bin/koha/opac-detail.pl?biblionumber=1973&query_desc=kw%2Cwrdl%3A%20Weapons%20technology%2C%20Disarmament%20and%20Verification

Wright, S. 1996. Exporting Tools of Repression, Importing Refugees: Links between the Arms Trade & Human Rights Violations. In: Lex P. Schmid (ed). *Whither Refugee? The Refugee Crisis: Problems and Solutions.* Leiden: PIOOM.

Wright, S. 1996. The New Trade in Technologies of Restraint and Electroshock. In: Duncan Forrest (ed). *A Glimpse of Hell: Reports on Torture Worldwide.* New York: Continuum International Publishing Group.

Wright, Steve. 1997. Tracking the Trade in Light Weapons and Related Technologies: The Omega Database Project. In: Hendrik Bullens (ed). *Arms Industry at the Crossroads: Conversion, Restructuring and Arms Trade in Europe.* Mosbach: IPRA Security and Disarmament Commission Paper 8. Available from: https://catalogue.sipri.org/cgi-bin/koha/opac-detail.pl?biblionumber=16777

Wright, Steve. 1999. Non-Lethal Weapons – The Revolution in Flexible Tools of Political Control. In: Joseph Rotblat (ed). *Remember Your Humanity - Proceedings of the 47th Pugwash Conference On Science & World Affairs, 1-7th August, Lillehammer (Norway).* Singapore: World Scientific Publishing Company.

Wright, Steve. 2000. Political Control and the Internet. In: Steven Hick, Eddie Halpin, and Eric Hoskins (ed's). *Human Rights and the Internet.* London: Palgrave Macmillan, pp. 200-210.

Wright, Steve. 2007. Preparing for Mass Refugee Flows: The Corporate Military Sector. In: David Cromwell, and Mark Levene (ed's). *Surviving Climate Change: The Struggle to Avert Global Catastrophe.* London: Pluto Press, pp. 82-101.

Wright, Steve. 2010. Paul Smoker – A Life in Peace. In: Nigel J. Young (ed). *The Oxford International Encyclopedia of Peace.* Oxford: Oxford University Press. Available from: https://www.oxfordreference.com/view/10.1093/acref/9780195334685.001.0001/acref-9780195334685-e-660

Wright, Steve. 2011. Policing Borders in a Time of Rapid Climate Change. In: Jürgen Scheffran, Michael Brzoska, Hans Günter Brauch, Peter Michael Link, and Janpeter Schilling (ed's). *Climate Change, Human Security and Violent Conflict.* New York: Springer Link, pp.351-370.

Wright, Steve. 2012. The work of Fethullah Gülen and the Role of Non-Violence in a Time of Terror. In: Paul Well, and Ihsan Yilmaz (ed's). *European Muslims, Civility and Public Life: Perspectives On and From the Gülen Movement.* London: Continuum Publishing, pp.175-188.

Wright, Steve. 2013. The Role of Sub-Lethal Weapons in Human Rights Abuse. In: Nick Lewer (ed). *The Future of Non-Lethal Weapons: Technologies, Operations, Ethics and Law.* Abingdon: Routledge, pp. 75-86.

Wright, Steve. 2014. 'Harmless' Weapons and Crowd Control. In: Rowland Atkinson (ed). *Shades of Deviance: A Primer on Crime, Deviance and Social Harm.* London: Routledge, pp.91-94.

Wright, Steve. 2017. Mythology of Cyber-Crime—Insecurity & Governance in Cyberspace: Some Critical Perspectives. In: J. Martín Ramírez, and Luis A. García-Segura (ed's). *Cyberspace: Risks and Benefits for Society, Security and Development.* New York: Springer, pp. 211-227.

PhD Thesis

Wright, S. 1987. *New Police Technologies and Sub-State Conflict Control.* Unpublished PhD thesis, University of Lancaster.

Blog Posts

Wright, Steve. 2013. Exodus from Damascus – Dr Steve Wright. *Leeds Beckett University.* 9th September. Available from: https://www.leedsbeckett.ac.uk/blogs/expert-opinion/2013/09/exodus-from-damascus-dr-steve-wright/

Wright, Steve. 2016. Going Full Circle… *Leeds Beckett Politics and International Relations* [Blog]. 11th March. Available from: https://leedspage.wordpress.com/2016/03/11/going-full-circle/

Wright Steve. 2016. Civilising the Torture and Execution Trade. *Leeds Beckett University.* 25th October. Available from: https://www.leedsbeckett.ac.uk/blogs/expert-opinion/2016/10/civilising-the-torture-and-execution-trade/

Media

Ballantyne, Robin. 1992. At China's Torture Fair. *The Guardian.* 14th August.

Ballantyne, Robin. 1996. Back on the Torture Trail. *Fortress Europe.* Letter No.46, April-May, pp.5-6.

Jenkins, Jolyon, and Robin Ballantyne. 1992. Tools for Tyrants. *New Statesman and Society.* [Online]. 20th November, pp. 17-18.

Lee, Peter, and Steve Wright. 2017. Should We Fear the Rise of Drone Assassins? Two Experts Debate. *The Conversation.* 28th November. Available from: https://theconversation.com/should-we-fear-the-rise-of-drone-assassins-two-experts-debate-87699

Wright, Steve. 1981. Your Unfriendly Neighbourhood Bobby. *The Guardian.* 16th July.

Wright, Steve. 1984. The Hard Sell. The *Guardian.* 21st June.

Wright, Steve. 1987. Tactical Technology. *Science for People.* 65.

Wright, Steve. 1994. Shoot Not to Kill. *The Guardian.* 19th May.

Wright, Steve, and Rob Evans. 1999. British Police Face a CS Gas Attack. *The Guardian.* [Online]. 8th July. Available from: https://www.theguardian.com/science/1999/jul/08/freedomofinformation.politics

Wright, Steve. 1999. War Without Blood? The Hypocrisy of 'Non-Lethal' Arms. *Le Monde Diplomatique.* [Online]. December. Available from: https://mondediplo.com/1999/12/09wright

Wright, Steve. 1999. This Will Blow Your Mind. *The Guardian.* [Online]. 13th May. Available from: https://www.theguardian.com/technology/1999/may/13/onlinesupplement11

Wright, Steve. 2001. A Legal Trade in Death. *Le Monde Diplomatique.* [Online]. January. Available from: https://mondediplo.com/2001/01/02arms1

Wright, Steve. 2001. A Worse Fate Still to Come. *The Guardian.* [Online]. 1st March. Available from: https://www.theguardian.com/science/2001/mar/01/technology

Wright, Steve. 2001. A Shot in the Dark. *The Guardian.* 28th June. https://www.theguardian.com/science/2001/jun/28/physicalsciences.technology

Wright, Steve. 2001. Killing me softly. *New Scientist.* [Online]. 10th August. Available from: https://www.newscientist.com/article/mg17123031-000-killing-me-softly/

Wright, Steve. 2001. More Efficient Killing Fields. *The Guardian.* [Online]. 8th March. Available from: https://www.theguardian.com/theguardian/2001/mar/08/guardianweekly.guardianweekly1

Wright, Steve. 2003. Civilising the Torture Trade. *The Guardian.* [Online]. 13th March. Available from: https://www.theguardian.com/science/2003/mar/13/research.science1

Wright, Steve, and Charles Arthur. 2006. Targeting the Pain Business. *The Guardian.* [Online]. 5th October. Available from: https://www.theguardian.com/technology/2006/oct/05/guardianweeklytechnologysection

Wright, Steve. 2007. Dangerous Prescriptions. *The New York Times.* [Online]. 29th August. Available from: https://www.nytimes.com/2007/08/29/opinion/29iht-edwright.1.7302878.html

Wright, Steve. 2007. When Drugs Become Weapons. *The Guardian.* [Online]. 24th May. Available from: https://www.theguardian.com/technology/2007/may/24/guardianweeklytechnologysection.weaponstechnology

Wright, Steve. 2007. Sedated into Submission. *Le Monde Diplomatique.* [Online]. August. Available from: https://mondediplo.com/2007/08/13sedated

Wright, Steve. 2007. The Body as Battlefield. *Le Monde Diplomatique.* [Online]. August. Available from: https://mondediplo.com/2007/08/12bioweapons

Talks and Conferences

Wright, Steve. 1998. *The Emergence of New Sub-Lethal Alternatives to Landmines: report to the 3rd NGO Tokyo Conference on Anti-Personnel landmines.* Third NGO Tokyo Conference on Anti-Personnel Landmines, 28-29th November 1998, Tokyo. Available from: https://rjl.home.xs4all.nl/THE_EMERGENCE_OF_NEW_SUB-LETHAL_ALTERNATIVES_TO_LANDMINES.html

Wright, Steve. 2013. *Corporate military management approaches to climate change: from refuge to exclusion.* AntiAtlas Conference, Aix-en-Provence. Available from: https://www.antiatlas.net/corporate-military-management-approaches-to-climate-change-from-refuge-to-exclusion-en/

Abstracts

Wright, Steve. 2009. Emerging Military Responses to Climate Change – The New Technopolitics of Exclusion. *IOP Conference Series: Earth and Environmental Science.* **6** Available from: https://iopscience.iop.org/article/10.1088/1755-1307/6/56/562001/pdf

Book Reviews

Wright, Steve. 2009. Review: *'Non-Lethal' Weapons* by Neil Davison. *New Scientist.* 23rd September. Available from: https://www.newscientist.com/article/mg20327276-300-review-non-lethal-weapons-by-neil-davison/

Wright, Steve. 2010. The Corporate Machinery of Global Violence—A Suitable Case for Treatment? *Peace and Conflict: Journal of Peace Psychology.* **16**(1), pp. 109-111. https://doi.org/10.1080/10781910903272718

Wright, Steve. 2011. Laos: Legacy of a Secret. *Medicine, Conflict and Survival.* **27**, p.131-133. https://doi.org/10.1080/13623699.2011.609759

Wright, Steve. 2012. Cities under siege – the new military urbanism. *Medicine, Conflict and Survival.* **28**(2), pp.188-190. https://doi.org/10.1080/13623699.2012.678756

Wright, Steve. 2012. Review of Ball, Haggerty and Lyon's Handbook of Surveillance Studies. *Surveillance & Society.* **10**(3/4), pp. 362-366. https://doi.org/10.24908/ss.v10i3/4.4520

Wright, Steve. 2015. Whistleblowing: A Practical Guide. *Medicine, Conflict and Survival.* **31**(1), pp.73-76. https://doi.org/10.1080/13623699.2014.961697

Wright, Steve. 2016. Chemical control – regulation of incapacitating chemical agent weapons, riot control agents and their means of delivery. *Medicine, Conflict and Survival.* **32**(1), pp.82-84. https://doi.org/10.1080/13623699.2016.1171024

Wright, Steve. 2016. Tear Gassing by Remote Control. *Medicine, Conflict and Survival.* **32**(1), pp.84-85. https://doi.org/10.1080/13623699.2016.1171032

Wright, Steve. 2018. Dis-eases of secrecy – tracing history, memory and justice, Medicine, Conflict and Survival. *Medicine, Conflict and Survival.* **34**(2), pp. 133-135. https://doi.org/10.1080/13623699.2018.1470775
Also Available from: https://eprints.leedsbeckett.ac.uk/id/eprint/4988/3/Wright%20S%20Rappert%20%20GouldCorrected%20version.pdf

Other

Ballantyne, Robin. 1995. Electro-shock weapons: the 'torture trail'. *Fortress Europe Newsletter.* Circular Letter 31 (February 1995). Available from: https://desexil.com/wp-content/uploads/2021/04/cl31.pdf

Ballantyne, Robin. 2007. "As Used on the Famous Nelson Mandela" – The Use of Mechanical Restraints on Prisoners and Detainees. *Cspri Newsletter.* No. 20. Available from: https://omegaresearchfoundation.org/sites/default/files/uploads/Publications/cspri%20newsletter.pdf

Wright, Steve. 2005. Torture Technology – A Booming Industry? *SGR Newsletter.* December, Issue 31, pp. 9-10. Available from: https://www.sgr.org.uk/sites/default/files/SGR_NL31_TortureTech.pdf

Wright, Steve. 2007. Walking in Minefields. *SGR Newsletter.* Summer, Issue 34, p. 17. Available from: https://www.sgr.org.uk/sites/default/files/SGR_NL34_Minefields.pdf

Wright, Steve. 2017. The Landmine Ban: 20 Years On. *SGR Newsletter.* Winter, Issue 45, p. 13. Available from: https://www.sgr.org.uk/sites/default/files/SGRNL45_Landmineban.pdf

Select Resources with Photographs and contributions by Steve or 'Robin Ballantyne'

Amnesty International. 2001. *Stopping the Torture Trade.* London: Amnesty International. Available from: https://omegaresearchfoundation.org/sites/default/files/uploads/Publications/AI%2C%20Stopping%20the%20torture%20trade%2C%202011.pdf

Amnesty International. 2011. *Arms for Repression: Will they be Covered by an Arms Trade Treaty?* London: Amnesty International. Available from: https://www.amnestyusa.org/files/act-30-120-2011.pdf

Amnesty International. 2015. *The Human Rights Impact of Less Lethal Weapons and Other Law Enforcement Equipment.* London: Amnesty International. Available from: https://www.amnesty.org/en/wp-content/uploads/2021/05/ACT3013052015ENGLISH.pdf

[All photographs by Robin Ballantyne]

Amnesty International, and Omega Research Foundation. 2016. *Why the EU Should Ban the Commercial Marketing and Promotion of Inhuman Policing and Prison Equipment.* London: Amnesty International. Available from: https://omegaresearchfoundation.org/sites/default/files/uploads/Publications/EUR0136362016ENGLISH.pdf

Amnesty International, and Omega Research Foundation. 2018. *Combating Torture: The Need for Comprehensive Regulation of Law Enforcement Equipment.* London: Amnesty International. Available from: https://omegaresearchfoundation.org/sites/default/files/uploads/Publications/Amnesty%20Combatting%20Torture%20WEB%20Version.pdf

Corney, Neil, and Nicholas Marsh. 2013. *Aiming for Control: The Need to Include Ammunition in the Arms Trade Treaty.* Oslo: PRIO Paper. Available from: https://controlarms.org/wp-content/uploads/2018/03/Corney-Marsh-Aiming-for-Control-PRIO-Paper-2013.pdf

Farha, Joe, and Kate Wraith. 2015. *The Deployment of Law Enforcement Equipment in Central Asia and the South Caucasus.* Omega Research Foundation Working Paper. Available from: https://www.sipri.org/sites/default/files/SIPRI-OSFno3WP.pdf

Gregory, Martyn. 1996. *Back on the Torture Trail.* Documentary. Available from: https://www.youtube.com/watch?v=3d2Y1ZSvl6M [Robin Ballantyne listed as a consultant]

International Peace Information Service, and Omega Research Foundation. 2016. *Working Paper 2 on China North Industries Group Corporation.* Belgium: IPIS. Available from: https://ipisresearch.be/wp-content/uploads/2017/04/201703_publicatie-Norinco.pdf

Leff, Jonah, and Emile LeBrun. 2014. *Following the Threat: Arms and Ammunition Tracing in Sudan and South Sudan.* Geneva: Small Arms Survey. http://www.smallarmssurveysudan.org/fileadmin/docs/working-papers/HSBA-WP32-Arms-Tracing.pdf

Omega Research Foundation. 2003. *Baton rounds: A review of the human rights implications of the introduction and use of the L21A1 baton round in Northern Ireland and proposed alternatives to the baton round.* Belfast: Northern Ireland Human Rights Commission. Available from: https://omegaresearchfoundation.org/sites/default/files/uploads/Publications/batonrounds.pdf

Omega Research Foundation, and Amnesty International USA. 2008. *Submission in Response to BIS Request for Public Comments on Crime Control License Requirements in EAR.* Washington, DC: Amnesty International USA. Available from: https://omegaresearchfoundation.org/sites/default/files/uploads/Publications/090000648062f0f5.pdf

Omega Research Foundation, Bradford Non-Lethal Weapons Research Project, and Michael Crowley. 2015. *Tear Gassing by Remote Control.* London: Oxford Research Group. Available from: https://omegaresearchfoundation.org/sites/default/files/uploads/Publications/Tear%20Gassing%20By%20Remote%20Control%20Report.pdf

Omega Research Foundation. 2019. *Submission by the Omega Research Foundation on the impact on human rights of the use of less lethal weapons and ammunition technology in the context of assemblies, including peaceful protests.* Contribution to the preparation by the Office of the High Commissioner for Human Rights (OHCHR) of a Report on the promotion and protection of human rights in the context of peaceful protests. Available from: https://www.ohchr.org/Documents/Issues/RuleOfLaw/PeacefulProtest/CSOs/omega-research-foundation.pdf

Omega Research Foundation, and Amnesty International. 2014. *China's Trade in Tools of Torture and Repression.* London: Amnesty International. Available from: https://www.amnesty.org.uk/files/china-tools-of-torture-report.pdf?VersionId=n3ST7Uq6NNSoAougb9MxlBgycJg7yZjX

Oxfam. 1998. Out of Control: The Loopholes in UK Controls on the Arms Trade. Oxford: Oxfam. Available from: https://oxfamilibrary.openrepository.com/bitstream/handle/10546/112381/out-of-control-uk-arms-trade-011298-en.pdf;jsessionid=D0B05586C11F20199CAAE9A99C172BDF?sequence=1

Stone, Mark. 2014. Worst 'Torture Tools' Sold By China Revealed. *Sky News.* [Online]. 23 September. Available from: https://news.sky.com/story/worst-torture-tools-sold-by-china-revealed-10388830

Unpublished Works

Wright, Steve. 1978. *An Empirical Time Series Analysis of some Aspects of the Northern Ireland Conflict 1969-76. The Campaign of the British Army in Northern Ireland. A Case of Self Legitimation?* Unpublished paper.

Index

www.ingramcontent.com/pod-product-compliance
Lightning Source LLC
LaVergne TN
LVHW010652110826
845149LV00014B/3058

* 9 7 8 9 1 8 8 0 6 1 5 5 3 *